Maher Y. Abu-Munshar is Assistant Professor of Islamic History at Qatar University, and was formerly a Lecturer in Islamicjerusalem Studies at the Al-Maktoum Institute for Arabic and Islamic Studies, University of Aberdeen, UK.

'With the indigenous Christian community in the Holy Land dwindling as never before and the relationship between Muslims and Christians in Palestine coming under renewed scrutiny, Maher Abu-Munshar's *Islamic Jerusalem and its Christians* provides an authoritative, reliable and accessible sourcebook with which to understand the complexities of Muslim-Christian relations in the Holy Land. Abu-Munshar's erudition, control of his subject and readable style makes this book an indispensible addition to any bibliography exploring the history of Jerusalem and should be highly recommended to all visitors to Jerusalem of any faith or none. No other book can compete with it in this sphere.'

Martin O'Kane, Professor of Biblical Studies, University of Wales, Trinity Saint David

'Dr. Abu-Munshar provides the reader with a consistent and positive defence of the Muslim position on Jerusalem and Muslim treatment of Christians in the period from the Muslim conquest to the Crusades. The book promises to serve as fascinating fodder for discussion and debate about our modern interpretation of a pivotal period in the relations between Christianity and Islam.'

Paul S. Rowe, Associate Professor of Political and International Studies, Trinity Western University

'This is an important and timely book that should appeal to students and specialists alike. At a time when the clash of civilizations thesis has dominated public as well political discourse, Maher Y. Abu-Munshar has written a much-needed corrective to many misconceptions about Muslim-Christian encounters in Islamic Jerusalem. Based on primary and original sources, this book is an objective investigation of the dynamics and conditions that shaped Muslim-Christian interactions in one of the most significant cities in monotheistic traditions. Focusing on the two most dramatic moments of Islam's presence in Jerusalem, under the leadership of Umar Ibn al-Khattab (d. 644) and Salah al-Din (d. 1193) respectively, Abu-Munshar provides a number of significant insights into the history of religious tolerance and political tension between Muslim and Christian communities in Jerusalem.'

Mazhar Al-Zo'by, Professor of Culture and Politics, Qatar University

'The book brings forward new approaches and horizons as well as new evidence that could stir the academic debate relating to Muslim-Christian relations in general and Muslims' treatment of Christians in Jerusalem in particular... an extremely important piece of research and an invaluable contribution to Middle Eastern, historical and religious studies, as well as international relations.'

Dr. Mahdi Zahraa, Glasgow Caledonian University

Islamic Jerusalem and its Christians

A History of Tolerance and Tensions

Maher Y. Abu-Munshar

Revised paperback edition published in 2013 by I.B.Tauris & Co Ltd
6 Salem Road, London W2 4BU
175 Fifth Avenue, New York NY 10010
www.ibtauris.com

Distributed in the United States and Canada
Exclusively by Palgrave Macmillan
175 Fifth Avenue, New York NY 10010

Copyright © 2013, 2007 Maher Y. Abu-Munshar
First published in hardback by Tauris Academic Studies, an imprint of
I.B.Tauris & Co Ltd, 2007

The right of Maher Y. Abu-Munshar to be identified as the author of this work
has been asserted by the author in accordance with the Copyright, Designs and
Patent Act 1988.

All rights reserved. Except for brief quotations in a review, this book, or any
part thereof, may not be reproduced, stored in or introduced into a retrieval
system, or transmitted, in any form or by any means, electronic, mechanical,
photocopying, recording, or otherwise, without the prior written permission of
the publisher.

ISBN: 978 1 78076 479 5

A full CIP record for this book is available from the British Library
A full CIP record for this book is available from the Library of Congress

Library of Congress catalog card: available

To my beloved wife Alla

CONTENTS

Acknowledgments	ix
Introduction	1
1. Islamic sources and the treatment of non-Muslims	7
2. 'Umar's treatment of Christians	55
3. 'Umar and the Christians of Islamic Jerusalem	81
4. Salah al-Din's treatment of Christians	119
5. Salah al-Din and the Christians of Islamic Jerusalem	143
Conclusion	175
Notes	183
Bibliography	219
Glossary	237
Index	241

LIST OF TABLES

Table 1   Narrator Chains in Ibn 'Asakir's Five Versions   66

LIST OF FIGURES

Figure 1   The Region of Islamicjerusalem   6

ACKNOWLEDGMENTS

Responsibility for this book rests with me, but I wish to express my deep appreciation to those who have helped me along the way. My deepest and sincere gratitude to the Academy for Islamicjerusalem Studies (ISRA) – UK for their support throughout the duration of this research. I owe an immense debt of gratitude to Professor Abd al-Fattah El-Awaisi, founder of the new field of Islamicjerusalem Studies, for inspiring me with his passion for the subject and for his scholarly insight and support. I am also greatly indebted to Dr. Mahdi Zahraa for his invaluable guidance and constructive criticism which made this book possible. I would like to acknowledge the assistance of Dr. Khalid El-Awaisi in helping me to produce a camera-ready version of this book.

Thanks are also due to my students and colleagues at the various places in which I have worked – Al-Maktoum Institute (University of Aberdeen), the University of Malaya and lastly my current position at Qatar University – for their invaluable support and encouragement, and other individuals and libraries too numerous to mention, for their invaluable assistance.

Above all, I am eternally grateful to my father, Younes Abu-Munshar and to the soul of my mother, Khairiyya al-Dwaik (d. 2010), for their unending love, encouragement, patience and prayers during my research, and for the values they instilled in me and the love they gave me. I am also deeply grateful to my brothers, sisters and family-in-law for being a constant source of inspiration, support and encouragement, especially my mother-in-law, Aisha.

Last but not least, I wish to thank my wonderful wife Alla, whose indescribable patience, support and encouragement have helped me at all stages of this project. She spent many evenings with me hovering over the computer screen. Her help has been invaluable. I wish to express my love to my eight-year-old son Salahudin, and to my four-year-old daughter Isra, for making this endeavour a breeze by their smiles and giggles.

Maher Y. Abu-Munshar
Doha, Qatar, August 2012

INTRODUCTION

Islamic Jerusalem (*Bayt al-Maqdis*) is no ordinary place: its significance reaches far beyond its physical stones. During its turbulent history, the followers of all three monotheistic religions made strenuous efforts to conquer the city by any means and at any cost. The era of Muslim rule in Islamic Jerusalem is long compared to some other periods in the city's history. It embraces two distinct phases, the first and principal one being the Muslim conquest under the leadership of Caliph 'Umar Ibn al-Khattab (d. 24 AH[1]/ 644 CE). The second Muslim conquest of Islamic Jerusalem was led by Sultan Salah al-Din (d. 589 AH/ 1193 CE).

These two periods witnessed a history of both tolerance and tension towards non-Muslims, and especially Christians. Caliph 'Umar liberated the Christians from the domination and persecution of Byzantine rule, and allowed Jews to return to the city after being expelled for nearly five hundred years. The second conquest freed Muslims, Eastern Orthodox Christians and Jews from the domination of the Latin Crusaders.

The main aim of this book is to discuss the Muslim treatment of Christians in Islamic Jerusalem and the surrounding Muslim state, focussing on the attitudes and policies of 'Umar and Salah al-Din. These two rulers created a model atmosphere of tolerance and peaceful coexistence among the followers of different religions, and enabled Christians and Jews to live side by side peacefully after centuries of tension. The book's objective has been achieved, first, by identifying the Muslim conquerors' unique vision of Islamic Jerusalem towards non-Muslims, based on information from Islamic primary sources. Second, by a detailed study of the reigns of 'Umar and Salah al-Din, and providing a better understanding of certain historical events in regard to Christians. Third, by conducting a comparative study of these two periods, presenting new data and contributing to the academic debate on the subject. Together these three methods set out principles by which Muslims should deal with Christians.

Those that do take an academic approach discuss only This book comes under the umbrella of Islamicjerusalem studies, a new and intellectually stimulating field of inquiry that attempts to deal with the region of Islamicjerusalem using interdisciplinary and multidisciplinary approaches. Islamicjerusalem is the name given to a region of about fifteen thousand square kilometres that encompassed not only the walled city of Aelia Capitolina (the Roman name for Jerusalem), but also the towns of Jenin in the north, Jericho in the east, Karak (in modern Jordan) and Zoar in the south and Jaffa in the west including the areas in between (see Fig. 1).[2]

This specialized field of study developed when Professor Abd al-Fattah El-Awaisi,[3] from his work in the United Kingdom, became painfully aware of the lack of serious academic research on Jerusalem from an Arab and Muslim point of view, since most research has been undertaken by orientalist, western or Israeli writers. Hence, the history of the region under Muslim rule has been subject to much alteration and distortion.[4]

Although there is a vast literature by Arab and Muslim writers dealing with the issue of Palestine in general and Jerusalem in particular, the majority of these studies are of poor quality, as they address the subject either emotionally or politically. Those that do take an academic approach discuss only contemporary Jerusalem, as a city with east and west parts.[5] As indicated, a central difference between Islamicjerusalem studies and Jerusalem studies is that the former does not confine itself to Jerusalem as a city, but considers it as a region, as El-Awaisi explains:

Islamicjerusalem studies can be fairly eventually characterized and defined as a new branch of human knowledge based on interdisciplinary and multidisciplinary approaches. It aims to investigate all matters related to the Islamicjerusalem region, explore and examine its various aspects, and to provide a critical analytic understanding of the new frame of reference; in order to identify the nature of Islamicjerusalem and to understand the uniqueness of this region and its effects on the rest of the world in both historical and contemporary context.[6]

This new field is developing rapidly. I was one of the first students to complete a Ph.D in Islamicjerusalem studies, and became the first teaching fellow and later lecturer in this subject at the Al-Maktoum Institute for Arabic and Islamic Studies in Dundee, Scotland. The concept of Islamicjerusalem has been further defined by El-Awaisi as:

> A new terminology for a new concept, which may be translated into the Arabic language as *Bayt al-Maqdis*. It can be fairly and eventually characterized and defined as a unique region laden with a rich historical background, religious significances, cultural attachments, competing political and religious claims, international interests and various aspects that affect the rest of the world in both historical and contemporary contexts. It has a central frame of reference and a vital nature with three principal intertwined elements: its geographical location (land and boundaries), its people (population), and its unique and creative inclusive vision, to administrate that land and its people, as a model for multiculturalism.[7]

This vision of Islamicjerusalem is inclusive and accepts diversity. It is therefore of crucial significance to investigate the Muslim treatment of Christians in Islamicjerusalem in previous periods of Muslim rule.

At first the research for this book seemed straightforward, as the sources are abundant and readily available. However, progress was hampered in several ways. The shortcomings of the classical juristic and historical literature are that they tend to report historical events without critical analysis, and do not focus on the Muslim treatment of Christians during and after the first and second Muslim conquests of Islamic Jerusalem. In addition, differing versions of the key document, 'Umar's Assurance of Safety to the People of Aelia, have been reported by early historians, who, like others, have paid little attention to its importance. Early Muslim historians and jurists are also not in agreement about the origins of other significant documents, in particular the Pact of 'Umar and the peace treaty with the Christian Banu Taghlib tribe. Later, at the time of Salah al-Din, Muslim historians once again reported events merely in descriptive form, while in most cases non-Muslim historians have discussed the Crusader period rather than Muslim relations with Christians.

In general, the difficulties of studying the Muslim treatment of Christians are, first, that one has to refer to both juristic and historical literature. Second, most of the literature – especially the juristic books and those covering the first Muslim conquest – is in Arabic, with some sources in Italian and French. Third, the historical information, particularly from the period of 'Umar, was documented long after the actual events. The narratives do not agree, and the different versions of important documents and historical facts add to the problem of assessing their authenticity.

Fourth, the task was made more complex because of diverse opinions between followers of the schools of *fiqh* (Muslim jurisprudence). Among early Muslim jurists and scholars these differences were mainly on issues of how Muslims should treat non-Muslims, on the rights and obligations of *dhimmis* (non-Muslim citizens) and on aspects of the *jizyah* tax paid by *dhimmis* These were a natural consequence of divergent opinions on the interpretation of Qur'anic verses dealing with non-Muslims, which reflected the particular school of thought of the jurist or scholar as well as the method of reasoning used. For example, the Hanafi and Maliki schools were quite lenient in their treatment of non-Muslims, while the Shafi'i and Hanbali schools were more restrictive. For the purposes of this book, I have selected a number of juristic and Qur'anic interpretations and have avoided details of their disagreements except where absolutely necessary.

Among western historians, the history of Islamic Jerusalem during the two periods under discussion has suffered from falsification, and has been strongly attacked by a number of authors who consider that Muslim policies contained much oppression and aggression towards non-Muslims. Some of these writers, for example Abraham and Haddad, went further, asserting that the Muslim system classified non-Muslims as second- or even third-class citizens.[8] However, an analysis of their work shows that their conclusion was based not on scholarly investigation, but on arbitrarily selected information from a wide range of sources.

The best way to deal with such contradictory data is to examine the juristic principles involved, as is done in chapter one. This chapter reviews the evidence of the Qur'an and the Sunnah,[9] a careful reading of which sheds fresh light on the events under discussion. In particular, the tolerance and freedom of religion expressed in the Qur'an are made explicit, as well as the concept of human brotherhood. The purpose and meaning of the *dhimma* pact in Islam, of the *jizyah* tax and the reasons for imposing it, and the obligations and rights of the *dhimmi* are also explained. A brief overview of the concept of *jihad* is given, and its role in relation to non-Muslims.

However, it is not only a question of the framework that Muslim leaders followed, but of their personal attitudes, and a brief study is made of the backgrounds of 'Umar Ibn al-Khattab and Salah al-Din. The second and fourth chapters focus on the treatment of Christians by these two leaders outside Islamic Jerusalem. When events in the years before and after the conquests are examined from the perspective of the two rulers, a clearer picture of their intentions and policies emerges.

The need to examine and re-examine sources also looms large when the treatment of Christians in Islamic Jerusalem is discussed in chapters three and five. Their treatment under the first Muslim conquest is investigated with special reference to 'Umar's Assurance of Safety to the People of Aelia, and under the second conquest it is assessed in light of Salah al-Din's liberation of Islamic Jerusalem. The conclusion summarizes these findings, with some critical remarks and recommendations.

Figure 1: The Region of Islamicjerusalem

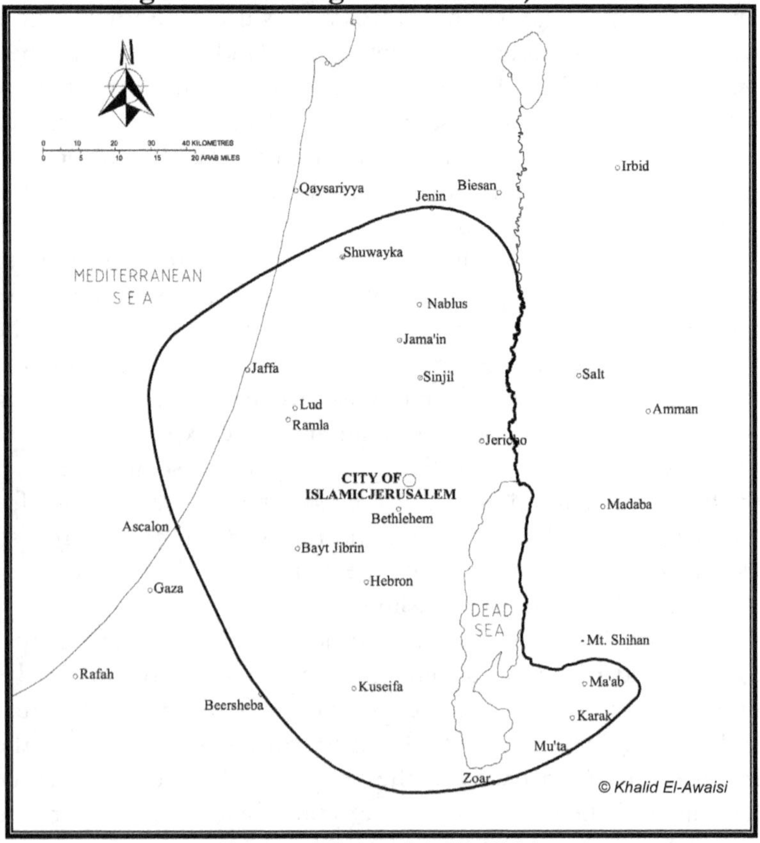

Source: El-Awaisi, K. 2006.

1

ISLAMIC SOURCES AND THE TREATMENT OF NON-MUSLIMS

The attitude of Caliph 'Umar Ibn al-Khattab and Sultan Salah al-Din towards non-Muslims did not arise out of a vacuum, but was inspired by religious injunctions and principles. Unfortunately, because Islam is based on a divine revelation, there is a misconception that it can neither live with, tolerate nor cooperate with the followers of other religions such as Judaism and Christianity. This view has caused prejudice against Islam as a religion that promotes violence, and against Muslims as inherently militant and irrational people. The intention of this chapter is not to tackle differences of belief between Muslims and non-Muslims, or to discuss the history of non-Muslims in Muslim states, except where particularly relevant. Its aim is to explain, from the point of view of the Qur'an and Sunnah point, the behaviour that should characterize Muslim dealings with non-Muslims in daily life and the rules that are applicable to non-Muslims.

There is no doubt that this subject has held a distinctive position in Muslim jurisprudence and historical literature. This can be seen in the Qur'an, in prophetic traditions, in *fatwas* and in the practical applications of caliphs and Muslim jurists.[1] The degree of concern expressed in Muslim law indicates the perceived role of Islam in building solid relations between Muslims and non-Muslims in a Muslim state. Its importance is evident in the debates among Muslim jurists that have taken place in the past, and are taking place in the present.

During Muslim history, certain leaders – particularly the Fatamids[2] – have deviated from Islamic guidelines and committed Islamically unacceptable acts against non-Muslims. This was the result of their perversion and violation of Islamic precepts. In discussing Muslim treatment of non-Muslims, many authors have selected examples that are not derived from Islamic guidelines. In most cases, the conclusions they reached were that Muslims treated non-Muslims badly compared with the teachings of the Qur'an and the Sunnah.

The Muslim view of tolerance and freedom of religion, and the concept of human brotherhood in the Qur'an and in prophetic traditions are discussed below. The *dhimma* pact in Islam and the *jizyah* tax are also examined, along with a brief overview of *jihad* and its relation to non-Muslims.

Muslim Jurisprudence and Non-Muslims

Muslim jurisprudence is based on four sources: first and foremost the Qur'an, followed by the Sunnah.[3] Islamic rules concerning belief, legislation (*shari'ah*) and morality are all based on these two sources. If the Qur'an and Sunnah texts are limited, their general principles can be used as criteria for similar and parallel situations. This helps to provide rules and principles for human behaviour until the Day of Judgement. Generations of learned Muslim scholars have elaborated on both these primary sources. They recognized the general principles and objectives of the rules, and followed the spirit of them in their judgements and *fatwas* for new situations. This led to the establishment of consensus (*ijma'*)[4] and analogy (*qiyas*).[5] The important point to remember is that only the Qur'an and Sunnah are considered as primary sources; the rest are secondary.

When the Prophet Muhammad and his companions migrated from Makkah to Madinah, the first Muslim state was established there under the Prophet's leadership. From the beginning, rules and regulations were required to govern relations between

Muslims and non-Muslims, both those who lived outside the state and those under Muslim rule. No Muslim state has ever been without non-Muslims, so such regulations were essential. Nor was the Muslim state ever perceived as a monopoly of Muslims, and it was intended that members of other religions should enjoy living in it. In some cases, for example after the first Muslim conquest of Islamic Jerusalem, the number of non-Muslims even exceeded that of Muslims.[6] Appropriate rules had to be created to cover their rights and obligations, as they were also citizens, so that they could live in peace and participate in public life. The regulations were intended to bring public prosperity and mutual understanding between the different religions, in place of conflict and hatred.

In general, the basis for the treatment of non-Muslims under Muslim rule was sought in the Qur'an and in the Prophet Muhammad's dealings with certain non-Muslim communities, and in the policies of his immediate successors in light of that guidance.

The Qur'an and the People of the Book

The Qur'an divides non-Muslims into two main categories: the People of the Book and the idolaters. The title People of the Book (*ahl al-kitab*) is given to Jews and Christians. In Arabic, *al-kitab* means the book; and in Islamic terminology 'the Book' refers to Scripture. The People of the Book have a special position in the Qur'an, since their religions were originally based on revealed books such as the Torah and the Bible.[7] Compared to other religions, Jews and Christians are closer to Muslims than those who are unbelievers or atheists.

The beliefs and values that are common to Muslims and the People of the Book can be summarized in four basic principles.[8] First, Judaism, Christianity and Islam all believe in one Creator, who has created the entire universe and is omnipotent. Second, they believe in prophethood, that the Creator has sent messengers or prophets throughout history to guide humanity, to reconcile them to their Creator and to lead them into the path of truth. Third, all three faiths believe in divine revelation, as shown in the Scriptures (holy books) that have been revealed to the prophets in order to guide humanity. There may be strongly felt differences as to which Scriptures are relatively more authentic and have not been changed. But the central concept of belief in Scripture is found in all three religions. Fourth, all of them believe in the law of divine punishment and in the hereafter, and that people in the hereafter will be rewarded or punished according to their beliefs and their compliance with the moral code expounded by the prophets throughout history. In that sense, regardless of the differences, the areas described above provide ground for commonality between Muslims on the one hand and Jews and Christians on the other. As a religion of peace, Islam sets out the following injunctions for Muslims to observe in their treatment of Jews and Christians (*ahl al-kitab*):

> Do not argue with the People of the Book unless in the best manner, save with those of them who do wrong: and say: We believe in what has been sent down to us and in what has been sent down to you.[9]

According to this verse, common ground should be found. Al-Qaradawi, a well-known Egyptian scholar, argues that Muslims are required to deal with *ahl al-Kitab* not only in a good way but in the best way.[10] He believes that the Qur'an granted them a special position by referring to them several times as *ahl al-kitab* rather than as Jews and Christians. The Qur'an signals friendship when it tells Muslims that they are allowed to eat the food of Christians and Jews, while forbidding them to eat the food of other groups such as Magians (*Majus*) and Sabians:

> This day are [all] things good and pure made lawful unto you. The food of the people of the Book is lawful unto you and yours is lawful unto them. [Lawful unto you in marriage] chaste women who are believers, but also chaste women among the People of the Book, revealed before your time.[11]

Consistent with the above, marriage is permitted with the People of the Book on the same terms that a Muslim man would marry a Muslim woman. This is not, however, applicable to others, such as pagans, Hindus, etc. In Islam, marriage is considered as a divine covenant, and mercy, respect and love should be outstanding characteristics of the husband/wife relationship. Even after marriage, the Qur'an permits a non-Muslim woman to observe her faith and celebrate her religious festivals without hindrance from the husband.[12] This shows the level of tolerance in Islam towards a woman from the People of the Book who will be the Muslim's partner throughout life, the mother of his children and the one with whom he shares his inmost thoughts. As the Qur'an says

> They are your garments and ye are their garments.[13]

And:

> Among His Signs is this that He created for you mates from among yourselves, that ye may dwell in tranquillity with them, and He has put love and mercy between your [hearts]. Verily in these are Signs for those who reflect.[14]

The significance of the People of the Book in Islam was clearly portrayed at the beginning of Muslim history when Muslims were a minority in Makkah. At that time there was a prolonged armed conflict between the two powerful northern neighbours of the Arabian peninsula, the Byzantine and Persian empires.[15] In 614 CE Parwez, a Persian leader, occupied Aelia and proclaimed victory over the Roman Empire. Muslims might have been expected to welcome this, as they are nearer geographically to Persia than to Rome. However, Persians were Zoroastrians, while Romans were People of the Book. The Makkans – who were pagan unbelievers – identified themselves with the Persians and were elated by Parwaz's victory, while the Muslims, who numbered only a few hundred at the time, sympathized with the Christians in Aelia. This was because the

Prophet had recognized Jesus as a true Prophet of God, the Bible as originally based on divine revelation and Aelia (Islamic Jerusalem) as a holy city. The Makkans insulted the Muslims because they were on the losing side. The Qur'an reacted to this and prophesied that the Christian defeat at the hands of the Persians and the pagan jubilation at those defeats would both be short-lived:

> The Romans [Byzantines] have been defeated in the land close by: but they, [even] after [this] defeat, will soon be victorious. Within a few years, To God will be the Command in the Past and in the Future: On that day with the help of God, shall the believers rejoice. He gives victory to whom He will, and He is exalted in Might, Most Merciful.[16]

There are a large number of verses in the Qur'an pertaining to Muslim treatment of non-Muslims, whether in or outside the Muslim state. The four main Qur'anic injunctions focus on:

- Human brotherhood
- Religious tolerance
- Justice and fair treatment
- Loyalty and alliance

Human brotherhood
Many verses in the Qur'an refer to humankind being one nation emanating from a single origin. The Qur'an emphasizes that all people were created from one person, Adam,[17] although they differ in size, race, language, nation, tribe, and whether they are believer or atheist, good or bad, constructive or destructive. These differences should not contradict the principle of unity. They are intended, rather, to serve as a medium for people to come together and not to enter into conflict or to despise one another.[18]

Consequently, the protection, rights and security of non-Muslims are derived from the principle of human brotherhood, since all mankind is the creation of God, the only God, without discrimination between Muslims and non-Muslims. Islam enjoins and promotes universal brotherhood, peace and unity. The only difference that the Qur'an recognizes is in piety towards God (*taqwa*):

> O mankind! We created you from a single [pair] of a male and a female, and made you into nations and tribes, that ye may know each other [i.e. not that ye may despise each other]. Verily the most honoured of you in the sight of God is [he who is] the most righteous of you. And God has full Knowledge and is well acquainted [with all things].[19]

As this verse shows, Islam honours mankind, especially believers in God, and mankind should promote peace, unity and universal brotherhood.

Religious tolerance
Religious tolerance is an essential cornerstone for the peaceful coexistence of different religious groups in a community, and is an important right given by Islam to non-Muslims. The Qur'an frequently calls for tolerance and respect towards the People of the Book, who are entitled to freedom of belief, conscience and worship. Neither the Qur'an nor the sayings of the Prophet have ever encouraged the use of force, pressure or manipulation in regard to religious belief. The most obvious verse that emphasises freedom of religion is the following:

> Let there be no compulsion in religion ...[20]

The reason is that faith, to be genuine, needs to be an absolutely free and voluntary act. Indeed, this verse was revealed to condemn the attitude of some Jews and Madinans – those newly converted to Islam in Madinah – who wished to convert their children to their new faith. [21] It is clearly stressed that faith is an individual commitment and even parents must refrain from interfering. The very nature of faith, as emphasized in the basic text of Islam, is that it is a voluntary act born out of conviction and freedom.

Commenting on the above verse, Ibn Kathir[22] (d. 774 AH / 1372 CE) argues that Islam is very clear on this point and that no one must force anyone else to embrace Islam. He states that those who have been guided by God will embrace Islam. However, for those whose hearts God has blinded, it is of no use to accept Islam, because without good will they would not benefit from being forced.[23] Qutb[24] (d. 1386 AH /1966 CE), a well-known Egyptian thinker in the Muslim Brothers and a Qur'anic interpreter, highlights the central concept derived from the verse – freedom of creed and freedom of choice. He believes that this requires the honouring of the human being and respect for his thoughts, will and feelings, and for his choice either to believe, or to reject belief and accept the consequences. Qutb argues that freedom of belief is the most basic right that identifies man as a human being; to deny anyone this right is to deny his or her humanity.[25]

Muhammad Abu Zahra, a contemporary Egyptian jurist, comments that the Islamic rules governing human relations wholly respect freedom of creed and belief.[26] He adds that the Qur'an rejects compulsion to make people embrace a certain religion, and forbids Muslims to compel anyone to adopt a creed or belief. By the same token, 'Abdelati, another Egyptian scholar, says that Islam takes this position because religion depends upon faith, will and commitment.[27] He suggests that these three aspects are worth nothing if they have been induced by force and compulsion.

In addition, al-Mawdudi, a noted Pakistani scholar, say that the term religion in this verse signifies belief in God, and that the entire system of life as it should be led rests upon it. The verse's meaning, he says, is that the system of Islam, embracing moral beliefs and practical conduct, cannot be imposed by force.[28] Wahba al-Zuhaili, a leading contemporary Syrian jurist commenting on this verse, agrees that compulsion in religion is prohibited. The Qur'an does not accept forcing non-Muslims to convert to Islam as a right approach.[29]

Malekian went further, positing a link between the concept of freedom in religion and the words of God, 'For persecution is worse than slaughter'.[30] He claims that this phrase attributes blame to those who persecute others for religious reasons. He emphasizes that interference in the matter of religion is prohibited by Muslim law, and that no one, whether Muslim or non-Muslim, should be forced to accept another religion or be persecuted by others on religious grounds.[31]

An example from the Umayyad period (661–750 CE) demonstrating freedom of religion is when Caliph al-Walid Ibn 'Abd al-Malik forcibly took possession of part of a Christian cathedral in Damascus and incorporated it into a mosque. No redress took place under his successor, Caliph Yazyd Ibn al-Walid Ibn 'Abd al-Malik, but when Caliph 'Umar Ibn 'Abd al-'Aziz succeeded him, the Christians of Damascus reported this injustice. 'Umar wrote to the official in charge to pull down the portion of the mosque that had formerly belonged to the cathedral, and the land was handed back to the Christians.[32]

When 'Ammar Ibn Yasir, one of the Prophet's companions, was forced under torture to say that he was a non-believer and was made to curse God and the Prophet, a Qur'anic verse was revealed to declare that what 'Ammar had uttered was invalid, since he had spoken those words under duress:

> Anyone who, after accepting faith in God, declares himself unbeliever under compulsion is still a believer, his heart remaining firm in faith.[33]

Based on the example of 'Ammar, one can say that the concept of compulsion of anyone is not acceptable in Islam. Indeed, compulsion has never been an appropriate way of converting anyone to a religion. It is therefore logical to say that once the force is removed, the belief that was expressed under force will also go; thus compulsion is useless. Furthermore, if someone is forced to take an action under pressure, he will be pushed into hypocrisy; as a result, the user of force will have to bear responsibility for his own behaviour. The religious freedom of a non-Muslim is to be fully protected, and he/she is to be given total freedom to profess his/her religion.

Justice and fair treatment
The fundamental Qur'anic verses that determine the nature of Muslim treatment of non-Muslims are the following:

> God forbids you not, with regard to those who fight you not for [your] Faith nor drive you out of your homes, from dealing kindly and justly with them: For God loves those who are just. God only forbids you, with regard to those who fight you for [your] faith, and drive you out of your homes, and support [others] in driving you out, from turning to them [for friendship and protection]. It is such as turn to them [in these circumstances] that do wrong.[34]

Set out here are very important injunctions determining the attitude of Muslims to non-Muslims. They are obviously not prevented from establishing good relationships with non-Muslims. On the contrary, the Muslim treatment of non-Muslims should be based on principles of good relationship and justice, especially towards those who have peaceful intentions towards Muslims. More specifically, Muslims are asked to deal with non-Muslims kindly and justly, unless the latter are out to destroy Muslims and their faith.

Al-Tabari[35] (d. 310 AH/922 CE) concludes that the most accurate interpretation of these verses is that Muslims should be just and fair, and have the best relationship with those non-Muslims who are not hostile to Muslims on account of their religion, or drive Muslims from their homes. This includes people of all faiths and sects. Support of this strong opinion comes from the story of Asma' and her mother (see below). Al-Tabari says that God ordered Muslims to treat non-Muslims kindly and justly, and that God loves those who treat people in this way. God's orders are generalized with no exclusion of any particular group or religion. Al-Tabari's view is that God excluded from the above injunction those who caused harm to or waged war against Muslims, and warned Muslims not to be supporters or allies of these groups, or they would be disobeying the command of God.[36]

In like manner, al-Qurtubi[37] (d. 761 AH /1360 CE) comments that this verse represents permission from God to establish good relationships with non-Muslims, especially those who do not treat Muslims as enemies[38] or wage war against them. He agrees with Ibn al-'Arabi[39] (d. 543 AH /1148 CE), who interprets the meaning of 'dealing justly' (Arabic *tuqsitu*) differently from other Qur'anic scholars, when he says that this term does not, in fact, imply 'being just' with non-Muslims, as the translation seems to indicate.[40] According to Ibn al-'Arabi, *tuqsitu* means supporting non-Muslims financially as a demonstration of good relations, because, in light of another verse, Muslim justice is obligatory towards everybody, whether friend or foe.

Moreover, al-Zamakhshari[41] (d.538 AH /1143 CE) says that God gave permission to Muslims to deal justly with non-Muslims who do not wage war against them. However, in his permission God excluded those who cause harm to Muslims and wage war against them. The interpretation of 'dealing justly' means to treat non-Muslims justly and not to oppress them.[42]

Al-Razi[43] (d. 604 AH /1207 CE) agrees with these interpretations and adds that the verse is an authorization of good relations with non-Muslims. In interpreting 'dealing justly', al-Razi quotes Ibn 'Abbas (a well-known companion of the Prophet), who considers that it means having a good relationship. Al-Razi quotes Muqatil when he comments on 'For God loves those who are just', saying that Muslims must adhere to agreements with non-Muslims and treat them justly.[44]

Ibn Kathir in his attempts to interpret this verse, says that it contains the permission to perform good deeds to those who do not fight Muslims in the matter of religion or drive them from their homes. In addition, it enjoins Muslims to deal with non-Muslims kindly, justly and equitably.[45] Qutb discusses the verse and concludes that this good and just relationship should not be disturbed. But, as is the case with other Qur'anic interpretations, Qutb stipulates that this attitude to non-Muslims can change if their aggression has to be dealt with, or if the breaking of a truce is expected, or an obstacle develops to delivering the message of Islam. Apart from that, the behaviour should be based on peace, love and justice for all mankind.[46]

To sum up, the general rule for the treatment of non-Muslims by Muslims is very clearly spelled out and leads to two important observations. First, the basis of this treatment should be justice and kindness, that is, peaceful coexistence. It is also obvious that deviation from the basic rule of friendship and peaceful coexistence can be justified only in certain exceptional situations. These include, for example, when people fight Muslims because of their faith, or try to destroy the Muslim religious identity. This exception is logical, based as it is on the concept of self-preservation. The other exception given in the verse is when Muslims are driven from their homes, when violence and hostility are used against them, or when support is given to others to force Muslims from their homes.

Second, the use of the two keywords 'kindly' and 'justly' is significant. To be 'just', in addition to what has been said, means that Muslims cannot persecute non-Muslims, take away their rights or otherwise damage them simply because they are non-Muslims. To be 'kind' (*tabarruhum*) comes from the Arabic word *birr*, which goes beyond the implication of kindness or justice and has no exact equivalent in English. The Qur'an uses *birr* for the basis of the relationship between Muslims and non-Muslims. The word is normally used to describe the way a Muslim should deal with his or her parents, and encompasses everything that is good in a relationship. Muslim scholars, for example Mawlawi, a contemporary Lebanese jurist, argue that *birr* is the foundation of the relationship between Muslims and non-Muslims. Mawlawi goes further, claiming that *birr* is derived from everything that is good, decent, respectable and compassionate.[47]

In Muslim literature, especially in the prophetic traditions, the Prophet Muhammad uses *birr* for the relationship between a person and his parents. A person needs to *birr* his parents, meaning a treatment that is more than kindness. It is thus obvious that, on the basis of this general rule in the Qur'an, any non-Muslim who accepts the need for peaceful coexistence with Muslims is to be treated with *birr* – justly and kindly. Imam al-Bukhari (d. 256 AH /860 CE) reported that Asma', the daughter of Abu Bakr, the first caliph, said: 'My mother came to me while she was still a polytheist, so I asked God's messenger:

> My mother, who is ill-disposed to Islam, has come to visit me. She wants something from me. Shall I maintain [good] relations with her?' the Prophet replied, 'Yes, maintain [good] relations with your mother.[48]

Interestingly, Imam al-Qarafi (d. 684 AH /1285 CE), a well-known *Maliki* jurist, considered that *birr* or fair treatment to non-Muslims consists of the following:

> Showing kindness to their weak and helping their poor and destitute, and feeding their hungry, clothing their naked, and uttering kind words to them from the position of grace and mercy and not from the position of fear and disgrace and removing their hardship as their neighbours if you [Muslims] have power to remove it, praying for their guidance so that they can become happy and fortunate people, giving them good advice in all their affairs – the affairs of this world and the hereafter and looking after their interest in their absence. If anyone hurts them and deprives them of their property or family, possessions or their rights, you should help them by removing their persecution and make sure to restore all their rights back to them.[49]

On the other hand, it is also reasonable to say that those who incite hostility or hatred against Muslims and try to destroy them cannot expect to have this kind of friendship. This not only applies to non-Muslims; if a Muslim violates the dictates of

Islam, he or she will be punished. Likewise, a non-Muslim who violates the terms of agreement with Muslims and the Muslim state should also be punished. The issue is no more than a requirement to comply with the rules.

As far as the concept of justice is concerned, justice (*'adl*) must be seen to be done towards Muslims and non-Muslims alike. Islam calls for justice not only for Muslims but for all mankind, irrespective of creed, colour, race and nationality. One Qur'anic verse says:

> O ye who believe! Stand out firmly for God, as witnesses to fair dealing, and let not the hatred of others to you make you swerve to wrong and depart from justice. Be just: that is next to Piety: and fear God. For God is well acquainted with all that ye do.[50]

This implies that implementing justice and acting righteously in a favourable or neutral atmosphere is meritorious enough; however, the real test comes when one has to act justly towards people one hates or for whom one has an aversion. This verse was revealed to show the need to deal justly with the Jews in Madinah, whom the Prophet had asked to contribute to the blood money of the two men from Banu 'Amer who had been killed by 'Amir Ibn Umayyah. In the Prophet's presence, the Jews pretended that they had agreed to contribute, but behind his back they were plotting how to kill him. God informed the Prophet of their intention, and the Prophet was very angry about this betrayal. However, God revealed the above verse to ask him not to act unjustly against the Jews over this incident.[51]

Al-Zamakhshari interprets this verse to mean that Muslims should not act unjustly against non-Muslims by killing their women and children or breaking agreements with them simply through hatred. He concludes that Islam has strongly commanded Muslims to be just in their dealings with non-Muslims.[52] Interestingly, al-Qurtubi adds that even if non-Muslims kill Muslim women and children and caused great sadness, Muslims are not allowed to imitate them, as this would prevent justice taking place.[53]

Similarly, Ibn Kathir interprets this verse to mean that a Muslim should not let the hatred of a particular group be a reason for injustice.[54] Justice should be applicable to everybody, both friends and enemies, for God says, 'be just: that is next to piety'. Abu Zahra explains that human relations as regulated by Islam are based on justice, whether the relations are with a loyal or a hostile group.[55] He refers to the above verse, and stresses that justice should be conducive to piety. This and preceding verses define the general principle for Muslim relations and for the treatment of non-Muslims. If some non-Muslims are hostile, cruel, or make trouble, it is not permitted for a Muslim who is in power to deviate even slightly from the path of justice in dealing with them. Finally, the Qur'an urges Muslims to base their relations with non-Muslims on peaceful cooperation, and warns them against placing religious solidarity over covenanted rights and the principles of justice.

Loyalty and alliance
Fair treatment of non-Muslims and cooperation with them are not the same as loyalty (*al-muwalah*). Rather, they are practical ways of promoting good and combating evil. There is a distortion of the word loyalty that expands its meaning to include cooperation. The loyalty that the Qur'an warns about is where a Muslim favours non-Muslims over Muslims when granting love and support. This issue is clarified in several Qur'anic verses, for example:

> Let not the Believers take for allies or helpers Unbelievers rather than Believers.[56]

Also:

> To the hypocrites give the good tidings that there is for them but a grievous penalty. Those who take for Alliance

unbelievers rather than believers: Is it honour they seek among them? Nay, all honour is with God.⁵⁷

In his explanation of these verses, al-Tabari says that they prohibit Muslims, first, from being like non-Muslims in their morals and values, and second, from preferring non-Muslims over Muslims. But he adds that loyalty could even mean supporting non-believers in their efforts against Muslims, such as spying on the Muslim state to the benefit of its rivals and enemies. This type of loyalty is at the expense of Muslims. There is an enormous difference between this and cooperating with Muslim interests for the collective well-being.⁵⁸

The question that arises is how Muslims can fulfil the meaning of *birr*, love, kindness, affection, and good treatment regarding non-Muslims, when the Qur'an itself forbids loyalty to non-Muslims and condemns Muslims who take on non-Muslims as helpers, allies, and supporters, as illustrated in verses like the following:

> O ye who believe! Take not the Jews and the Christians for your allies. They are but allies to each other. And he amongst you that turns to them [for alliance] is of them. Verily God guides not an unjust people.⁵⁹

In an attempt to answer this question, al-Qaradawi points out that these verses are not unconditional, to be applied to every single Jew, Christian, or non-Muslim. Interpreting them in this manner contradicts the injunctions of the Qur'an to show affection and kindness to the benign and peace-loving peoples of every religion.⁶⁰ Most Qur'anic commentators have linked their interpretation to the reason behind the revelation of this verse. For example, al-Zamakhshari and Ibn Kathir⁶¹ say that Muslims should not take on Christians and Jews as supporters, or even support them as if they were Muslims. Al-Zamakhshari explains this by quoting that they are 'allies to each other'.⁶² Both then refer to the reason behind the revelation, which is that 'Ubada Ibn al-Samit abandoned his Jewish allies. However, when the Prophet asked 'Abdullah Ibn Ubay to do the same he refused, saying that he feared the Jews might defeat the Muslims, and should that happen he wanted to be in favour with the Jews and to use that for his own advantage.[63]

Al-Razi agreed with al-Zamakhshari on the reason for the revelation, adding that 'not to take Jews and the Christians for your allies' means not to rely on or ask them for support.[64] Al-Qurtubi states that anyone who takes on Jews and Christians as supporters against Muslims is to be considered as one of the Jews and Christians. He gives a further two reasons for the revelation,[65] with which Ibn Kathir agrees.[66] The first concerns two Muslim men. After observing the defeat of Muslims in the battle of Uhud,[67] one of them decided to become an ally of the Jews, the other an ally of the Christians. The second reason, al-Qurtubi says, is that the verse was revealed after Abu Lubabah's incident, which he does not describe. It seems clear that whatever this incident was, it led to prohibiting Muslims from taking on Jews and Christians as supporters against their own faith.

Other verses in the Qur'an are specific to unbelievers in general rather than to the People of the Book, and prohibit Muslims from taking on unbelievers as allies against Muslims or instead of Muslims.[68] An-Na'im, a contemporary Sudanese scholar, considers that these verses should have been seen as providing the necessary psychological support for the survival and cohesion of a vulnerable community of Muslims in a hostile environment.[69] However, it should be borne in mind that the warning against taking Jewish or Christian allies is not general in application and does not include every individual Christian or Jew. If it were so inclusive, it would contradict other verses and instructions in the Qur'an that permit kindness to those who are decent, have good relations with Muslims and cause them no harm. The following verse in that Qur'anic chapter says:

> Those in whose hearts is a disease. Thou seest how eagerly they run about amongst them [non-Muslims], saying 'We do fear lest a change of fortune bring us disaster'. Ah!

> Perhaps God will give thee [Muslims] victory, or a decision from Him then will make them regret the thoughts, which they secretly harbour in their hearts'.[70]

It is very important to refer to the circumstances in which this verse was revealed. It deals specifically with certain hypocrites who were in the Muslim ranks. On the surface, they claimed to be Muslims. However, they thought it possible that non-Muslims who were in conflict with Muslims at that time might gain the upper hand or even achieve victory. Therefore, they secretly tried to keep up their friendship and alliance with the non-Muslims, even when the latter were actively hostile to Muslims. They did this in the hope that, if the Muslims were victorious, they could support them publicly because they saw themselves as being in the Muslim ranks. On the other hand, if the non-Muslims were the victors, the hypocrites could ask them for protection from the Muslims because they had friendly ties with the non-Muslims. It is clear that the Qur'an is condemning this kind of behaviour from pseudo-believers who called themselves Muslims.

In spite of this, the Qur'an does not dismiss the possibility of future reconciliation. Moreover, Muslims are encouraged to hope for better circumstances and improved relationships. One verse says:

> It may be that God will establish friendship between you and those whom ye [now] hold as enemies.[71]

This shows the attitude of Islam towards those who harm Muslims. As mentioned above, Islam gives a person the right to defend his/her life and his/her rights, but there is still an appeal to repay evil with good if this will result in improved relations. All these verses, both friendly and hostile, are circumstantial, that is, they refer to particular incidents, individuals or groups of people. They did not prevent Muslims from taking on non-Muslims as allies because they were not Muslims, but were associated with particular historical incidents in which a Muslim sought the support of Jews and Christians at the expense of his own people.

The *Dhimma* Pact and the *Jizyah* Tax

To regulate the attitude and the way that Muslims should treat non-Muslims, Islam introduced the *dhimma* pact and the *jizyah* tax. The term *dhimma* literally means pledge and guarantee.[72] It was the contract for protection that was made with Christians, Jews and others (such as Zoroastrians) who were judged to be the People of the Book, as well as any other non-Muslims,[73] when they agreed to live within the Muslim state and to pay *jizyah*. Muhammad al-Buti, a leading contemporary Syrian jurist, argues that the *dhimma* pact was a contract that could be no more than a *bay'ah* (a pledge of allegiance to obey the rules of the state and pursue its public interest), which took place between the head of the state and all citizens.[74] Therefore no one, Muslim or non-Muslim, could be excluded from this *bay'ah* because they were citizens,[75] or, as described by contemporary scholars, they were holders of Muslim state citizenship (*al-jinsiyyah al-Islamiyyah*).[76] The only difference was that Muslims were obliged to obey this *bay'ah* as a religious duty,[77] whereas for non-Muslims it was a fulfilment of their pact or agreement with Muslims that secured their own protection.

The raising of the *jizyah* from non-Muslim citizens within the Muslim state needs some explanation, since it can be misunderstood. The word *jizyah* is derived from the verb *jaza*, meaning 'he renders [something] as satisfaction or compensation [in lieu of something else]', and it represents money collected from the *dhimmi*.[78]

'Abdullah Yusuf 'Ali describes the *jizyah* as 'a poll tax levied from those who did not accept Islam, but were willing to live under the protection of Islam, and were thus tacitly willing to submit to its ideals that were enforced in the Muslim state'.[79] It was a small supplementary tax that was neither heavy nor unjust. Siddiqi, in his translation of *Sahih Muslim*, defines *jizyah* as a sort of compensation paid to the Muslim state by non-Muslims living under its protection, for not participating in military service and yet enjoying the pact of protection (*dhimma*).⁸⁰ Moreover, if a non-Muslim citizen participated in military service during a particular year, he was exempted from the *jizyah* for that year.⁸¹ It can be argued that exempting non-Muslims from military service made sense because it was illogical to ask non-Muslims to fight for the sake of Islam. It would be like enforcing them to practice a system of worship without a basic belief. However, non-Muslims could decide to participate in military service for other reasons, for example, to defend the state they were living in.

Initially, this tax did not exist in the early years of the Muslim state, in Madinah or elsewhere. There is disagreement among scholars as to the actual date that *jizyah* was prescribed. For example, Ibn al-Qayyim (d. 751 AH/1350 CE) states that *jizyah* was not taken from non-Muslims before the revelation of the verse legitimizing it in year 8 AH (629 CE),⁸² whereas Abu 'Ubayd (d. 224 AH/ 839 CE)⁸³ and Ibn Kathir⁸⁴ consider 9 AH to be the year of revelation of this verse and its Qur'anic endorsement:

> Fight those who believe neither in God nor in the Last Day, nor hold that forbidden which hath been forbidden by God and His Messengers, nor acknowledge the Religion of truth, from among the People of the Book, until they pay the *jizyah* with willing submission, and feel themselves subdued.⁸⁵

No fixed rate for *jizyah* was set either by the Qur'an or by the Prophet Muhammad. The jurists, therefore, differ as to the amount of *jizyah* that should be paid.⁸⁶ According to Abu Hanifah, the rate was 48 *dirhams* for rich people, 24 *dirhams* for the middle class and 12 *dirhams* for the poor. He thus specifies the maximum and minimum amounts and disallows any further discussion.⁸⁷ The Hanbali jurists followed the opinion of Caliph 'Umar. They agreed with the Hanafi jurists, but permitted the amount to be increased or decreased in accordance with people's economic situation.⁸⁸ Imam al-Shafi'i does not stipulate the maximum.⁸⁹ Al-Shafi'i suggests one *dinar* per year (about £30 today), which would be the Arabian gold *dinar* of the Muslim states. Imam Malik suggests that, if the *dhimmi* was poor (*ahl al-Wariq*),⁹⁰ the rate would be 40 *dirhams*. However, if he had more money (*ahl al-dhahab*/gold), it would be 4 *dinars*.⁹¹ The difference was between those using silver and those using gold. He also states that it is not permissible to increase this amount. In like manner, Abu Yusuf (d. 183 AH/ 799 CE) wrote that the Muslim state should take from non-Muslims only what was mutually fixed at the time of peacemaking. All terms of the treaty should be strictly adhered to and no addition permitted.⁹²

Generally speaking, the amount specified by jurists is trivial and paid only once a year. In fact, the level of *jizyah* varied and there were exemptions for the poor, females, children, slaves, monks and hermits.⁹³ The different amounts cited by various jurists indicate that there was no fixed rate, and its flexibility depended on time, place and economic situation. The *jizyah* collector had to try to harmonize the different figures given by various jurists and levy an amount in accordance with people's means.

On his attempt to clarify the rationale behind this tax, al-Buti argues that the *jizyah* paid to the Muslim state by non-Muslims was similar to *zakah*,⁹⁴ the obligatory tax paid by Muslims to the Muslim state.⁹⁵ The only difference was that Muslims paid *zakah* as part of their religious duty and as a form of worship, while *dhimmis* paid *jizyah*, a lesser amount, in fulfilment of their social duty to the Muslim state in which they were living, and it was spent in their protection.

Al-Buti also illustrates that choosing the term *jizyah* for this tax or compensation did not derive from a religious decision or Islamic order. There is no evidence in Islam to show that Muslims were worshipping (*ta'abbud*) in naming this tax *jizyah*. They could easily have used another term. Al-Buti clarifies this by giving the example of 'Umar Ibn al-Khattab and the Christians of Banu Taghlib. This group asked 'Umar to take *jizyah* from them in the name of *sadaqa* (a voluntary tax for charity), even if this meant doubling the *jizyah* payment.⁹⁶ Al-

Buti adds that as a result, the majority of scholars, Shafi'is, Hanafis and Hanbalis, agreed that it is acceptable to take *jizyah* from *dhimmis* under the name of *sadaqa*, but the amount is doubled.[97]

The interpretation 'with willing submission' (*'an yadin*), taken from the last part of the verse that legitimizes the *jizyah*, means literally 'from the hand'. It has been variously interpreted. Al-Zamakhshari believes it could have two meanings. First, the hand can be seen as a symbol of power or authority; second, it can be seen as a kind of favour from the Muslims to the *dhimmis* when they were saved from being killed.[98] Al-Razi agrees with al-Zamakhshari.[99] Al-Qurtabi, in his interpretation of the term, discusses several meanings. For example, he quotes Ibn 'Abbas when he says that its meaning is to pay the money personally to the *jizyah* collector and not to send it by anyone else.[100] Similarly, al-Tabari says that *jizyah* is given from the hand of the *dhimmis* to the hand of the collector.[101]

Finally, Ibn al-'Arabi lists fifteen potential meanings, such as giving the money in humility, under a pledge, being rich enough to be able to pay it, coming in person to pay it and not sending someone else, and not thanking the *dhimmi* when he pays, or praying for him, etc.[102] In the latter sense, the hand is the symbol of the ability to pay the *jizyah*, and it is not taken from those who cannot afford it. Children, the elderly, the poor and women are therefore exempted. In fact, a literal interpretation of this verse means that it does not apply to anyone who is not actually fighting against Muslims. The payment here clearly refers to a sign of ending a war and is a token of civil obedience or of regional reconciliation. Agreement to pay *jizyah* signifies the end of fighting.

There are disagreements among Muslim scholars, both Qur'anic interpreters and Muslim jurists, about the meaning of the word 'subdued' (*saghirun*) in the verse. Some Muslim scholars interpret it to mean that *jizyah* will be taken from the *dhimmis* with belittlement and humiliation.[103] However, other Muslim scholars interpret the word to mean submission to the Muslim political authority. Thus, paying *jizyah* shows adherence to the

Muslim state, and in return the state will offer support and protection. For example, al-Shafi'i and Ibn al-Qayyim opine that 'subdued' means accepting the law of Islam with regard to *dhimmis*.[104] Ibn Hazm defines the term by saying that the laws of Islam will apply to them: *dhimmis* should not display their unbelief or do something that Islam does not allow.[105] Al-Nawawi [106] and Ibn al-Qayyim refute the aspect of humiliation and point out that there is no evidence for this sort of behaviour in the Qur'an or the prophetic tradition, or in the practice of the Prophet's companions.[107] Al-Nawawi adds that *jizyah* must be taken kindly, as if removing a debt from someone. Abu Yusuf discusses the kindness of taking the *jizyah* when he states that:

> No one from the *dhimmis* would be beaten in extracting *jizyah* from them; nor would they be made to stand in the sun nor would any persecution be inflicted upon their bodies. Instead kindness will be shown to them. They would be restrained till they paid what was incumbent upon them and they would not be released from this detention till *jizyah* is taken from them in full.[108]

On the same lines, al-Buti adds that non-Muslims are not viewed by Muslim rulers as a burden so long as they remain submissive to the regime in the same way as Muslims.[109] It is unlikely that the Qur'an meant humiliation of the *dhimmis*. If *jizyah* were considered a humiliation, that is, a punishment because they were not Muslims, no one among non-Muslims would be exempted. This is shown in Abu Yusuf's reply about the exemption to *dhimmi* given by the Abbasid Caliph Harun al-Rashid (d.193 AH/809 CE):

> *Jizyah* would not be charged from a destitute to whom charity is given nor from the blind who have no provision or any work nor will it be charged from a *dhimmi* to whom charity is given nor from one who sits [at home due to disability]. But if they are prosperous then it will be charged from them. Similarly would be the case of the blind.

Similarly, *jizyah* would be charged from the monks who live in a monastery but are prosperous. But if they are poor people to whom charity is given by prosperous co-religious people, *jizyah* will not be charged from them. Similarly, *jizyah* is leviable on the people of synagogues if they have declared their whole property as trust for monasteries, the monks and the workers living there, even then *jizyah* will be charged from them and the required amount will be charged from the in charge of the monastery. But if the [person] in charge of the monastery denies having received these donations and he swears by God to this effect and takes an oath in the manner in which his co-religious people take an oath that he has not received anything from the trust, then he will be left alone and *jizyah* will not be levied from him.[110]

Furthermore, immediately after Khalid Ibn al-Walid had conquered al-Hira in southern Iraq, he wrote a letter to Caliph Abu Bakr telling him how he had implemented the *jizyah* tax but had exempted non-Muslims who were poor, old and handicapped:

> I counted the male population, they were seven thousand. On further examination, I found that one thousand of them were permanently sick and unfit. So, I excluded them from the imposition of *jizyah*; and those susceptible to *jizyah* thus remained six thousand people ... I have granted them the right that when a man becomes unfit to work because of old age, or who should otherwise be affected by calamity, or one who was rich but became poor to the extent that he requires the charity of his religion, I shall exempt him from the *jizyah* and he and his family will be supported by the Muslim treasury by means of maintenance allowance as long as he lives in the Muslim territory.[111]

It is beyond doubt that Islam would ever impose *jizyah* as a punishment or compensation from non-Muslims for their lack of belief in God, because it is only required from adult males. If it was a sort of compensation or punishment, then women, children and poor *dhimmis* would have had to pay it too. On the contrary, once a *dhimma* pact is concluded, the *dhimmis* automatically become citizens of the Muslim state and share all the basic rights of Muslims, regardless of which group is the ethnic majority or minority. It should be noted that the terminology of minority has no place in Islamic law.[112] Al-Buti argues that it has no place in the sources of *shari'ah* and that the jurists have never used it. He adds that it is derived from western societies who use it to distinguish between ethnic groups in their midst. This meaning, he says, is alien to the spirit of Islam, because it divides a population into first- and second-class citizens. Everyone who lives in the Muslim state enjoys the same citizenship rights, despite the differences they may have in their religion or population size. Lastly, he states that there are no first -or second- class citizens according to Muslim law.[113]

However, a number of non-Muslim writers assert that non-Muslims living under the Muslim state were treated as second-class citizens.[114] Others go further, claiming that non-Muslims were treated not only as second-class citizens, but as third-class citizens. In the words of Abraham and Haddad:

> In an Islamic State, Islam is the ideology of the State and, therefore, there is no room for those who are outside the State's ideology in the government, they are seen as third-class citizens or aliens and possibly, dangerous creatures whose loyalty is questioned and always suspect ...[115]

These authors establish their view by referring to the status of *dhimmis* recorded in the literature of Islamic law, which says that *dhimmis* were not allowed to be either a head of state (caliph) or a judge.[116] But they contradict themselves. First, they accept that the Muslim state is an ideological state. More specifically, it is a state based on an idea, in this case Islam. According to Muslim belief, the leader of a Muslim state must be a Muslim. Al-Marwadi a Shafi'i jurist, defines leadership in Islam as a position 'prescribed to succeed the Prophethood as a means of protecting the *din* (religion) and of managing the affairs of the world',[117] therefore the position of caliph or judge is a religious office, and one of the conditions that has to be fulfilled is that the person is a Muslim. Hence, in Islam the head of state is the head of the Muslim religion in that state. From this, it can be easily understood why a non-Muslim citizen cannot be elected head of a Muslim state. A caliph or judge must be well-educated and religious; his rank involves giving orders and solving citizens' problems according to Islamic rules with which he should be familiar. Even among Muslims not everyone was entitled to become caliph.[118]

This exception for the head of state does not mean that non-Muslims cannot work with the Muslim ruling elite and hold government positions, or that they are excluded from the political and administrative life of the state. Tritton, in his book *The Caliphs and their Non-Muslim Subjects*, mentions many examples where Muslims employed the People of the Book in governmental positions.[119] Moreover, both al-Mawardi, and al-Farra', a Hanbali jurist, do not hesitate to support the view that the Caliph could appoint non-Muslim citizens as ministers and as members of executive councils.[120] Therefore, excluding non-Muslims from the position of head of state is not discrimination, but a matter of eligibility for the post. It can be said, therefore, that the conclusion reached by some writers to the contrary is incorrect, since non-Muslims have never been classified as second- or third-class citizens. Finally, it should be noted that neither the Qur'an nor the prophetic traditions have ever disallowed Muslims from employing non-Muslims.

The applicability of the *dhimma* system and *jizyah* tax in the contemporary world is an important subject. In my opinion, the *dhimma* pact that was applied in the past is no longer valid in the contemporary world, because, on the one hand, of the huge and complicated changes that have taken place in the rules, regulations and laws governing the relationships between nations and states in the international domain, and on the other hand, the changed relationship between the state and its diverse citizens. If the *dhimma* pact is to be applied in today's world, then we would need to differentiate between two different cases.

First, if the *dhimma* pact is to be utilized in international law as a mechanism to prevent and end conflict, then the traditional *dhimma* pact and *jizyah* tax are inapplicable, as most countries do not recognize this Islamic system. The *dhimma* pact should therefore be developed to suit the requirements of international law and without the stipulation for *jizyah*, an option that is juristically permissible in Islam.[121] Second, on a national level the *dhimma* pact and *jizyah* tax are still applicable, but their names must be changed, for example, to social tax, citizen's contribution, etc. It is well known that non-Muslim citizens in Muslim countries today participate in their nation's military forces; in these circumstances non-Muslims should be particularly exempt from paying this kind of tax.[122] Finally, because a state or country ought to implement equality among its citizens, non-Muslim citizens should be asked to participate in national expenditure in the same way as Muslims did when they paid *zakah*.

Rights and Obligations of *Dhimmis*

Once the leader of a Muslim state agrees with non-Muslims on the *dhimma* pact, non-Muslims become eligible for a number of rights (*huquq*) and benefits. Muslim scholars have discussed the rights of *dhimmis* extensively. For example, Imam al-Mawardi asserted that the leader, being an authority on the Muslim state, must impose *jizyah* on all People of the Book who come under *dhimmi* protection, so that they can be considered residents in Dar al-Islam, the House of Islam The payment of *jizyah* assured them two rights. First, *dhimmis* would be left in peace; second, their domestic security would be assured and their defence from external attack guaranteed.[123] Abu Yusuf advised Caliph Harun al-Rashid on the rights of non-Muslims:

> O Amir of the Faithful, it is necessary that you should show kindness to the *dhimmis* of your Prophet Muhammad and you should keep an eye on them so they are not

oppressed or persecuted, nor is anything imposed upon them beyond their capacity; nor should anything be taken from their properties except with justification which is incumbent upon them. It has been related to the Holy Prophet (peace and blessings be upon him) that he said, 'whoever oppresses one with whom a treaty has been made, or imposes on him a burden beyond his capacity, then he will have to answer me on the Day of Judgment'. Furthermore, the Holy Prophet's talk with 'Umar Ibn al-Khattab at the time of his death, contained 'I commend to the caliph after me that he exercise good treatment on those who are under the Prophet's protection. He should keep to the covenant with them, fight those who are after them, and do not tax them beyond their capacity'.[124]

Ibn Juzay (d. 741 AH/ 1340 CE) states that Muslims should allow *dhimmis* to live in the Muslim state, and assure them of protection regarding their lives and property. Also, Muslims should not interfere with the churches of Christian *dhimmis* or with their lifestyle, such as drinking wine and eating pork, as long as they did not do this in public.[125] Non-Muslims should be left alone to be governed by their own personal laws, and Muslim state should not interfere with these.

There are many verses in the Qur'an, along with prophetic traditions, that prohibit Muslims from showing injustice and from attacking others in general. The first Muslim caliphs used to ask about the situation of non-Muslims whenever non-Muslims from neighbouring provinces came to Madinah. When any complaint came from a non-Muslim, they would give the matter urgent attention in order to ensure that justice was done. For instance, Caliph 'Umar used to question delegates regarding the condition of non-Muslims. He would ask whether any Muslim had hurt the feelings of non-Muslims in their provinces. Once he asked a delegate to tell him about the treatment of non-Muslims at the hands of Muslims in their towns and homes. The delegate replied: 'they fulfil their pledge by exercising only fair treatment'.[126]

Furthermore, al-Qaradawi believes that there is a consensus among scholars of the different juristic schools regarding the obligation of Muslims to protect *dhimmis* and support them, because when Muslims concluded the *dhimma* pact, they undertook to protect non-Muslims from internal oppression, as they had become citizens of the Muslim state. He quotes Ibn 'Abdin a well-known Hanafi jurist, in support of his view that oppressing a *dhimmi* was a greater sin than oppressing a Muslim.[127] Imam al-Qarafi quotes Ibn Hazm from the latter's book, *Maratib al-Ijma'*:

> If enemies at war come to our country aiming at a certain *dhimmi*, it is essential for us that we come out to fight them with all our might and weapons since he is under the protection of God and his messenger. If we did anything less than this, it means we have failed in our agreement for protection.[128]

Ibn Taymiyyah (d. 728 AH/1328 CE), a well-known Syrian jurist uses the example of his request to the leader of the Tartar invasion of Syria, asking him to spare the suffering of his people. The Tartar leader agreed to this in regard to Muslims, but refused to treat non-Muslims (mostly the Christians taken from Islamic Jerusalem) in the same way. Ibn Taymiyyah said that this would not please the Muslims, since the Jewish and Christian families were under their protection. On the insistence of Ibn Taymiyyah, all non-Muslim prisoners of war, including Jews and Christians, were released.[129]

According to Imam al-Mawardi, there are two kinds of conditions in the *dhimma* pact. The first is obligatory and the second is recommended. He divides the obligations (*wajibat*) into six conditions, as follows:[130]

1. Not to disparage or misquote the Book of God.
2. Not to accuse the Prophet of lying or speak of him disparagingly.

3. Not to speak of the religion of Islam with slander or calumny.
4. Not to approach a Muslim woman to commit fornication or with a view to marriage.
5. Not to try and undermine the faith of a Muslim believer in his religion or cause harm to Muslim assets and property or to the religion of Islam.
6. Not to help the enemy or any of their spies.

Ibn Qudama (d. 630 AH /1233 CE), a Hanbali jurist, states in his book *al-Mughni* that the *dhimmi*s' obligations can be summarized in five points:[131]

1. Paying *jizyah* and accepting the laws of Islam with regard to non-Muslims.
2. Not to harm Muslims in their lives and property, that is, not to beat Muslims or steal from them.
3. Not to denigrate or misquote the Book of God. Not to accuse the Prophet of lying or speak of him disparagingly, and not to slander or defame the religion of Islam.
4. To try and avoid those things prohibited by Muslims, such as drinking alcohol in Muslim public places.
5. To be distinct from Muslims by means of an identifying mark, and wearing distinctive clothes.

In discussing the obligations, Imam al-Farra' said they should not hurt Muslims or cause harm to their assets or religion, and summarized them as follows:

1. Not to gather in preparation to fight against Muslims.
2. Not to approach a Muslim woman to commit fornication.
3. Not to marry a Muslim woman.
4. Not to undermine a Muslim's faith in his religion.
5. Not to commit a highway robbery.
6. Not to support a spy.
7. Not to write to the enemy about the situation of the Muslims.
8. Not to kill a Muslim man or woman.[132]

It is obvious that a citizen in any state must have a set of rights and, in return, certain obligations. These rights and obligations keep in society in balance and guide the state in its dealings with individuals and groups. In the case of *dhimmi* citizens, the above rights seem to be fair and to indicate the spirit of tolerance in Islam. They are also clear signs that Islam works to fulfil its commitment to all citizens regardless. Muslims have obligations towards the Muslim state, such as obedience and military service, and it is logical that *dhimmis* should have obligations as well. For example, because Muslims follow the instruction of a divine book, the Qur'an, one of the obligations of *dhimmis* is that they are not allowed to speak badly of the Qur'an. This seems to be a reasonable requirement.

Guidelines from the Sunnah

As a result of his leadership role, the Prophet, as well as being a messenger and legislator, put the theoretical concepts of the Qur'anic verses into practice in his speech and daily life. He began to apply the 'Dos and Don'ts' of the Qur'an in regard to non-Muslims, in accordance with the priority of establishing peace and cooperation between Muslims and others. Obviously, precepts without practice would result in mere idealism that would cease to influence people's lives.[133] Five main cases illustrate the attitude of the Prophet Muhammad towards non-Muslims:

- The migration to Abyssinia
- The constitution of Madinah
- The Prophet's letters to non-Muslim leaders
- Treaties with the People of the Book
- The practices of the Prophet

The migration to Abyssinia

When the Prophet Muhammad began his prophetic mission to call others to Islam, he and his followers faced immense opposition. This turned into a persecution so great that the

Prophet advised his followers to migrate to Abyssinia and seek the protection of the Christian king Negus (Najashi). The situation became extremely grave, and by the middle of the fifth year of the prophethood it was no longer tolerable.[134] Umm Salamah, who was among the group who migrated to Abyssinia, reported that:

> When the Prophet Muhammad saw the affliction of his companions, though he escaped it because of his standing with God and his uncle Abu Talib, he could not protect them. The Prophet said to his companions: 'I propose that you migrate to Abyssinia, where there is a Christian king, well known for his justice. He is said to have not wronged any one in his kingdom and it is a friendly country, until such time as God shall relieve you from your distress'. Therefore his companions went to Abyssinia, being afraid of apostasy, and fled to God with their religion.[135]

The Muslims who migrated (including 83 adult males) were hospitably treated by the Christian king and allowed to practice their religion, as Prophet Muhammad had expected. They encountered gracious hospitality from the Christians in Abyssinia. This was the first migration of Islam.[136] Its significance lay in that it was to a country ruled by a just Christian king. This highlights some of the most profound principles of Islam. First, at that time Muslims and Christians were not in a state of conflict or hatred; and second, even though Muslims had differences with Christians, the latter were viewed as being allies with them against the injustice of the Makkan unbelievers. In fact, the Qur'an[137] and the Prophet had highlighted these facts on several occasions, as explained below.

It is important to emphasize that the principled behaviour shown by Muslims to the People of the Book was the reason why they were so favoured by the Christian king and welcomed in a Christian land. This Muslim migration to Abyssinia opened the first chapter in Christian-Muslim relations.

The constitution of Madinah

On his arrival in Madinah from Makkah, the Prophet Muhammad started to build the basis for relations between the first Muslim state and its non-Muslim inhabitants. He began by applying the principles of good relations and cooperation. There was a substantial Jewish community in Madinah, and the Prophet wrote a document about the immigrants (*al-muhajirun*) and the helpers (*al-ansar*), in which he proposed an agreement between them and the Jews. This agreement spelled out the Jews' rights as non-Muslim citizens in the Muslim state. As a result, the Prophet managed to establish in Madinah a multi-faith political community, based on a set of universal principles that formed the Constitution of Madinah (*sahifat al-Madinah*).

Developing a constitution to regulate the internal and external affairs of the city was one of the major contributions of the Prophet and his companions in Madinah, and can be considered a turning point for its inhabitants. This remarkable work was developed and administrated by the Prophet during the first year of his arrival. The task, with its many civil, judicial and political articles, including defence and alliance, had to be coordinated and approved by the leaders of eleven Jewish tribes, by leaders of the Arab tribes in and around the city and by the Muslims themselves. The constitution was based on cooperation, maintaining virtue and preventing evil. Regarded as the first-ever written constitution, the document stated reciprocal obligations as follows:

> In the name of God the Compassionate, the Merciful; this is a document from Muhammad the Prophet [governing the relations] between the believers and the Muslims of Quraysh and Yathrib and those who are to follow and join them ... The Jews shall contribute to the cost of war so long as they are fighting alongside the believers. The Jews of the Banu 'Awf are one community with the believers (the Jews have their religion and the Muslims have theirs), their freemen and their persons except those who behave unjustly and sinfully, for they hurt only themselves and

their families. The same applies to the Jews of the Banu al-Najjar, Banu al-Harith, Banu Sa'ida, Banu Jusham, Banu al-Aws, Banu Tha'labah, and the Jafna, a clan of the Tha'labah and the Banu al-Shutayba. Loyalty is a protection against treachery. The freemen of Tha'labah are as themselves. The close friends of the Jews are as themselves. None of them shall go out to war save with the permission of Muhammad, but anyone shall not be prevented from taking revenge for a wound. He who slays a man without warning slays himself and his household, unless it be one who has wronged him, for God will accept that. The Jews must bear their expenses and the Muslims their expenses. Each must help the other against anyone who attacks the people of this document. They must seek mutual advice and consultation, and loyalty is a protection against treachery. A man is not liable for his ally's misdeeds. The wronged must be helped. The Jews must pay with the believers so long as war lasts. Yathrib shall be a sanctuary for the people of his document. A stranger under protection shall be as his host doing no harm and committing no crime. A woman shall only be given protection with the consent of her family. If any dispute or controversy likely to cause trouble should arise it must be referred to God and to Muhammad the apostle of God. God accepts what is nearest to piety and goodness in this document. Quraysh and their helpers shall not be given protection. The contracting parties are bound to help one another against any attack on Yathrib. If they are called to make peace and maintain it they must do so; and if they make a similar demand on the Muslims it must be carried out except in the case of a holy war. Every one shall have his portion from the side to which he belongs; the Jews of al-Aws, their freemen and themselves have the same standing with the people of this document in pure loyalty from the people of this document. Loyalty is a protection against treachery: He who acquires aught acquires it for himself. God approves of this document. This deed will not protect the unjust and the sinner. The man who goes forth to fight and the man who stays at home in the city is safe unless he has been unjust and sinned. God is the protector of the good and God-fearing man and Muhammad is the apostle of God.[138]

The rules enunciated in the constitution were aimed at maintaining peace and cooperation, protecting the life and property of the inhabitants of Madinah, fighting aggression and injustice regardless of tribal or religious affiliation, and ensuring freedom of religion and movement. It supported community defence against enemies and promoted justice, goodness and resistance to evil. Jews and Muslims lived side by side in peace for many years. In discussing this treaty, al-Mubarakpuri noted that it came within the context of a larger framework of Muslim relationships. He summarized the most important provisions of the treaty in twelve points:[139]

1. The Jews of Banu 'Awf are one community with the believers. The Jews will profess their religion and the Muslim theirs.
2. The Jews shall be responsible for their expenditure, and the Muslims for theirs.
3. If attacked by a third party, each shall come to the assistance of the other.
4. Each party shall hold counsel with the other. Mutual relations shall be founded on righteousness; sin is totally excluded.
5. Neither shall commit sins to the prejudice of the other.
6. The wronged party shall be assisted.
7. The Jews shall contribute to the cost of war so long as they are fighting alongside the believers.
8. Madinah shall remain sacred and inviolable for all that join this treaty.
9. Should any disagreement arise between the signatories to this treaty, then God, the all-High, and His Messenger shall settle the dispute.

10. The signatories to this treaty shall boycott the Quraish commercially; they shall also abstain from extending any support to them.
11. Each shall contribute to defending Madinah, in case of a foreign attack, in its respective area.
12. This treaty shall not hinder either party from seeking lawful revenge.

Al-Buti attempted to explain the significance of this constitution by referring to a major clause: 'The Jews of the Banu 'Awf are one community with the believers (the Jews have their religion and the Muslims have theirs), their freemen and themselves except those who behave unjustly and sinfully, for they hurt but themselves.' He comments that this is a clear and straightforward text showing that the Muslim state – Madinah – is a partnership between two different groups, Muslims and Jews.[140] No one would be excluded from this partnership except those who behaved unjustly. The appeal of this is that 'except those' does not apply only to Jews, but to everyone resident in Madinah. He argues that when the constitution of Madinah states: 'The Jews, of the Banu 'Awf are one community with the believers', it did not mean that they were part of the Muslim community. If this was the case, it would be a clear statement that their identity was merged into the Muslim state. However, the constitution gave them the right to be an independent community inside the Muslim state. Furthermore, al-Buti adds that other clauses in this constitution assign equality of duties and rights to all the inhabitants of the Muslim state, and none of the clauses is derived from religious differences.

Hamidullah goes further, saying that with this constitution the autonomous Jewish villages acceded of their free will to the confederal state, and as a result recognised Prophet Muhammad as their supreme political head. He says this implies that non-Muslim citizens possessed voting rights in electing the head of the Muslim state.[141]

It is remarkable that the Madinah constitution placed rules of justice over and above religious solidarity, and affirmed the right to justice of the victims of aggression irrespective of tribal or religious affiliation. Of course, any newly established state must work hard to integrate all inhabitants regardless of religion, race or colour, in order to ensure the state's continuation and stability. El-Awaisi argues that core Muslim teachings reject the philosophy of a conflict based on eliminating the other party so that the victor could have the stage to himself.[142] He adds that:

> As confirmation of that idea, Islam favoured another method, namely *tadafu'* or counterbalance, as a means of adjusting positions using movement instead of conflict...This conflict-free method is what Islamic teachings see as a means of preserving a non-Muslim presence in this life. *Tadafu'* is not only to preserve Muslim's sacred places, but to preserve the sacred places of others. The Qur'an says: 'And if God had not counterbalanced (*duf'u*) some people's deeds by others, there surely would have been pulled down monasteries, churches, synagogues, and mosques, in which the name of God is commemorated in abundant measure.' This means that, from a Muslim point of view, *tadafu'* is the means of preserving a plurality of sacred places or the plurality of religions.[143]

Moreover, one of the aims of Islam is to provide a peaceful life based on mutual respect. At the time there were no Christians in Madinah, but the Prophet would have established with them an agreement similar to the Madinah constitution, with the same conditions, had they been living in the city. The Prophet's blueprint for a plural society carries the same moral authority as any other of his practices. The principles of Islam were intended to apply in all places where Muslims lived alongside the followers of other religions.

To conclude, the Prophet's treatment of the People of the Book, in this case Jews, showed religious tolerance as well as prudence. The constitution established the pattern for future relations in the Muslim state between Muslims and non-

Muslims. The basic principle was religious tolerance and non-interference in the religious affairs of the non-Muslim group. The constitution recognized freedom of religion for all citizens. It made non-Muslim citizens equal partners with the Muslim inhabitants of Madinah in the material wealth and progress of the Muslim state. It gave rights of protection, security, peace and justice not only to Muslims, but also to Jews who lived in Madinah, as well as to allies of the Jews who were non-Muslims. It allowed Jews to practice their religion freely.

The Prophet's letters to non-Muslim leaders
According to Muslim belief, the call of Islam must reach everybody.[144] Therefore, Muslim conquests and the spread of Islam outside Arabia were merely a fulfilment of divine command. During the sixth year of *hijrah* (the migration of the Prophet and other Muslims to Madinah) the Prophet sent letters to several kings and rulers beyond Arabia (including the two superpowers, the Byzantines and the Persians), calling on them to accept Islam. He wrote to Negus, King of Abyssinia (Ethiopia); the Viceregent of Egypt; Chosroes, Emperor of Persia; Caesar, Emperor of Rome; Mundhir Ibn Sawa, Governor of Bahrain; Haudha Ibn 'Ali, Governor of Yamamah; Harith Ibn Shammer al-Ghassani, King of Damascus; Jaifer, King of Oman and his brother 'Abd al-Jalandi.[145] The style of these letters is almost the same, with slight variations. In his letter to Heraclius, king of Byzantium, the Prophet states:

> In the name of God, the Most Beneficent, the Most Merciful. From Muhammad, the servant of God and his Messenger, to Heraclius, king of Byzantines. Blessed are those who follow true guidance. I invite you to embrace Islam so that you may live in security. If you come within the fold of Islam, God will give you double reward, but in the case where you turn your back upon it, then the burden of the sins of all your people shall fall on your shoulders. [The message then quotes the following Qur'anic verse] 'Say O People of the Book! Come to common terms as

between us and you: that we worship none but God; that we associate no partners with Him; and that none of us shall take others as lords besides God.' If then they turn back, say ye: 'bear witness that we (at last) are Muslims (bowing to God's will).¹⁴⁶

In the letter to the King of Abyssinia, he wrote:

> This letter is sent from Muhammad, the Prophet to Negus al-Ashama, King of Abyssinia. Peace be upon him who follows true guidance and believes in God and His Messenger. I bear witness that there is no god but God Alone with no associate. He has taken neither a wife nor a son, and that Muhammad is His slave and Messenger. I call you unto the fold of Islam; if you embrace Islam, you will find safety, O People of the Book! Come to common terms as between us and you: that we worship none but God; that we associate no partners with Him; and that none of us shall take others as lords besides God. If then they turn back, say ye: 'bear witness that we are Muslims' [bowing to God's Will]. Should you reject this invitation, then you will be held responsible for all the sins of the Christians of your people. ¹⁴⁷

King Negus of Abyssinia and the Vicegerent of Egypt welcomed the invitation;¹⁴⁸ Negus and the ruler of Bahrain accepted Islam, and Emperor Heraclius acknowledged Muhammad's prophethood, but replied that his nation would not be adopting Islam, and the Emperor of Persia tore the letter into shreds.¹⁴⁹

These letters to leaders and kings show the Prophet's respect for their rank. On the other hand, he called himself the servant of and the messenger of God. The Prophet also emphasized the common areas of belief, rather than any differences. Lastly, he managed to communicate the message of Islam to most kings and leaders of that time. While some accepted the message and others did not, the idea of embracing Islam and the arrival of a new prophet preoccupied all of them.

Treaties with the People of the Book

In addition to sending letters, Prophet Muhammad continued to build new relations by concluding a number of treaties with the People of the Book. He entered into many alliances with non-Muslims, securing peace and tranquillity for Muslim and non-Muslim alike. Muslim historians noted these treaties. For example, Imam Abu Yusuf and al-Baladhuri reported several pacts made by the Prophet Muhammad with the People of the Book living in Najran, Tabalah, Jarash, Ayla, Adhruh, Maqna,[150] al-Jarbah, Yemen and Oman, in which they were promised protection of their lives, rights, property and beliefs in return for paying *jizyah*. The text of the pact with the Christians of Najran, who lived in southern Arabia north-east of Yemen in the midst of an idolatrous tribe, is typical:

> In the name of God, the Compassionate and Merciful, this is what Muhammad the Prophet of God wrote to the people of Najran, when they were under his command ... And for the people of Najran and its bordering country, there is the protection of God and the compact of Muhammad the Prophet (regarding their property, their lives, their land and their people, whether present or absent, in their families and their trade, whether great or small. No Bishop will be forced to renounce his bishopric nor any monk will be asked to forsake his monastery nor any diviner abandon his profession.
> None of them will be subjected to humiliation. There will be no retaliation for the bloodshed committed in pre-Islamic times. They will not be made to suffer any loss; they will not be reduced to destitution. No troops will trample upon their land. If any of them claims his right, justice will be done to him: neither will he be wronged, nor will he be allowed to do any wrong to others. I will not be responsible if any of the governors devours usury and no man will be taken to task on account of wrong done by others. Whatever this document contains has the protection of

God and the protection of the Prophet till God issues some other command so long as people discharge their duties rightly and do not attempt to flee away after doing wrong. Abu Sufyan Ibn Harb, Ghailan Ibn 'Amr Malik Ibn 'Awf from Banu Nasr, Aqra' Ibn Habis Al-Hanzali and Mughira Ibn Shu'bah witnessed the document. This document was written for them by 'Abdallah Ibn Abu Bakr.[151]

Prophet Muhammad signed a similar pact with the Christians of Ayla (al-'Aqabah, in southern Jordan). He first sent a letter to Yuhanna, the Christian chief of Ayla, inviting him to come to terms with Islam and offering conditions for peace:

> To Yuhanna Ibn Ru'ba and the chiefs of the people of Ayla. Peace be upon you. Praise be to God, besides whom there is no god. I shall not fight you until I have written to you. Accept Islam or pay the *jizyah*, and obey God and His Prophet and the messengers of the Prophet ...[152]

Yuhanna accepted the conditions and hastened to the Prophet Muhammad's camp. A treaty was concluded between them, as follows:

> In the name of God, the Compassionate, the Merciful; This is a guarantee from God and from the Prophet Muhammad, the messenger of God, to Yuhanna Ibn Ru'ba and the People of Ayla; for their vessels and their travellers is the security of God and Muhammad, the messenger of God, and for who are with them, whether from al-Sham [Syria] or Yemen or from the sea-coast; those who breach this pact by causing a grave event (*hadath*), their wealth will not save them; they will be the fair price of whosoever captures them; it will be unlawful to prevent them [the people of Ayla] from going to the springs of water, or to stop them from the road they follow, by land or by sea.[153]

This demonstrates the practical application of the Prophet Muhammad's pacts or treaties with the People of the Book. First, once they had accepted the agreements, they became part of the Muslim state and benefited from its protection. It should be noted that new terms appeared in these pacts – the *jizyah* tax and the concept of the *dhimma* pact and *dhimmis*. Non-Muslims agreed to pay *jizyah*, and in return the Prophet granted them freedom to practice their religion and live a peaceful life under the protection of the Muslim state.

In addition, it can be seen from his actions that the Prophet Muhammad provided excellent facilities for non-Muslims. He highlighted the duties of Muslims towards non-Muslims, warned Muslims against mistreating *dhimmis* and threatened them that if they did so, God would punish them. For example, he said:

> He who hurts a *dhimmi* hurts me, and he who hurts me hurts Allah.[154]

Moreover, the Prophet asserted the significance of the pledge with non-Muslims:

> Whoever kills a person having a treaty with the Muslims, shall not smell the fragrance of paradise though its fragrance is perceived from a distance of forty years.[155]

Muslims were ordered to treat conquered people with warmth and love, and to be compassionate and understanding. The Prophet said:

> Do not kill an old man, a small child, or a woman. Do not commit acts of treachery nor make profits of the spoils of war.[156]

> Release the captured, support whoever asks for help, feed the hungry, and visit the sick.[157]

Let it be known, if any one including Muslims commits injustice, or insults, aggravates, mistreats or abuses a person of the People of the Book [protected by the state or by an agreement], he will have to answer me [or his immoral action] on the Day of Judgment.[158]

Years before the conquest of Egypt by the Muslims, the Prophet did not forget to instruct and advise Muslims on how they should treat non-Muslims, particularly the Copts. Ibn 'Abd al-Hakam (d. 256 AH /817 CE) a Muslim historian, outlined ten traditions dealing with the Prophet's advice. For example, one Hadith of the Prophet is:

When you conquer Egypt, take good care of the Copts, and treat them well as they have a pledge (*dhimmtan*) and kinship (*rahman*).[159]

These sayings and practices of the Prophet Muhammad illustrate the commendable principles in the Muslim treatment of non-Muslims.

An Overview of *Jihad*

Although *jihad* holds an important position in Islam, it is not my intention to discuss its legislation or literature. My focus is on the important role of *jihad* in governing the relationship between Muslims and non-Muslims. This is a very large subject, and I refer interested readers to the literature of *fiqh* to learn more about it.[160]

The word *jihad* is derived from Arabic *j-h-d*, which means to struggle, strive, attempt, endeavour or make an effort. *Jihad* is also constructed from the Arabic word *juhd*, which means exerting one's capacity and power in repelling the enemy to the best of one's ability, whether by word or deed.[161] The Qur'an says:

O ye who believe! Shall I lead you to a bargain that will save you from a grievous Chastisement? That ye believe in

God and his Messenger, and that ye strive [your utmost] in the cause of God, with your wealth and your persons: that will be best for you, if ye but knew![162]

Jihad has played a major role in Muslim treatment of non-Muslims. It is obvious from the above verse that Muslims are allowed to fight non-Muslims if the latter take up arms against them. A review of the prophetic traditions shows that the Prophet fought in only two situations. First, when Muslims were being attacked or when they expected an attack, such as knowing that an enemy was making preparations for attacking the Muslim community. The Prophet in his wisdom could not have waited until his people had been attacked. The Qur'an says:

> If then any one transgresses the prohibition against you, transgress ye likewise against him. But fear God, and know that God is with those who restrain themselves.[163]

Second, if the king or leader of a country set up a religious barrier between his people and Muslims, and then persecuted the Muslims among his own people to make them give up their faith. In other words, fighting can be to safeguard the Muslim call to embrace Islam, by making sure that people are free to follow Islam if they wish and to protect them from persecution. If a battle is unavoidable, non-Muslims should be given three choices. These are illustrated in the Hadith narrated by Sulaiman Ibn Buraid:

> Whenever the Prophet appointed any one as a leader of any army or detachment, he exhorted him to fear God and to be good to the Muslims who were with him. He would say: When you meet your enemies who are non-Muslim invite them to three courses of action, if they respond to any one of them you also accept it and withhold yourself from doing them any harm: invite them to accept Islam ... if they refuse to accept Islam, demand *jizyah* from them. If they agree to pay, accept it from them and hold off your hands.

> If they refuse to pay the tax, seek God's help and fight them ...[164]

The three choices are, first, ask them to embrace Islam; second, if they refuse, then conclude a *dhimmi* pact with them; and third, if they do not agree, the final option is to fight them. *Jihad* is thus the last choice and is usually undertaken in specific circumstances when all other options fail. Even during *jihad*, the Prophet continued to advise his army and Muslims in general against any transgression against non-Muslims, and to avoid acting unjustly. As we have seen, this attitude is derived from the Qur'an:

> Fight in the cause of God those who fight you but do not transgress limits; For God loves not the transgressor.[165]

The real purpose of *jihad* is not to convert people to Islam – there should be 'no compulsion in religion', according to the Qur'an – but to remove injustice and aggression. Muslims are allowed to continue good relations with non-Muslims. Islam teaches that conflict and warfare are to be used only against those who fight Muslims. *Jihad* is also permissible in self-defence, but Muslims are not allowed to use this to act wrongly or to exceed limits. For example, the Prophet ordered his army to show mercy even on the battlefield. 'Abduallah Ibn 'Umar narrated:

> During some of the *ghazawat* [expeditions] of the Prophet, a woman was found killed. The Prophet disapproved the killing of women and children.[166]

The Prophet's companions followed in his footsteps when advising Muslims what to do in the event of *jihad*. Abu Bakr's orders to one of the armies departing to al-Sham are a good example:

I recommend you to fear God and obey Him. When you engage with the enemies and win over them do not loot, do not mutilate the dead, do not commit treachery, do not behave cowardly, do not kill children and elderly or women, do not burn trees or damage crops, do not kill animals unless lawfully acquired for food. You will come across men confined to hermitages in which they claim to have dedicated their lives to worshipping God, leave them alone. When you engage with the non-Muslims invite them to embrace Islam. If they do not wish to do so invite them to pay *jizyah*. If they accept either, accept from them and stop fighting. But if they reject both, then fight them.[167]

This was the usual practice of the Prophets and his companions in a time of war. To sum up, war is not an objective of Islam, nor of Muslims. It is the last choice, to be used only when all other measures fail. The verses on the Qur'an containing words such as 'war', 'fight', and 'attack' must first of all be interpreted within their historical context.

Conclusion

Guidelines for the Muslim treatment of non-Muslims are clearly spelled out in the Qur'an. The Qur'anic injunctions have been discussed under headings of human brotherhood, religious tolerance, justice and fair treatment, and loyalty and alliance. Most of the fundamental human rights, such as the right to life, the right to personal freedom, the right to justice and the right to equality are guaranteed, and should be implemented without regard to religion, creed, colour or sex. Muslims who follow these guidelines will be adhering to Islam. Any deviation from them does not represent the original principles about relations with non-Muslims. If these Qur'anic teachings were accepted, there would be mutual understanding and tolerance leading to the spirit of coexistence that is essential for peace and prosperity.

When the Prophet sought to regulate a Muslim society where *dhimmis* had to pay *jizyah*, he was keen that these taxes would not constitute indirect pressure on non-Muslims. *Jizyah* was not enforced as a kind of punishment because *dhimmis* refused to convert to Islam, or to humiliate them. On the contrary, it was meant to enhance their feelings of citizenship, since it was clear that it covered the expense of protecting non-Muslims from outside attack.

In the Qur'an, the terms of the relationship between Muslims and non-Muslims were chosen wisely and deliberately, and their meaning and connotations have not been subject to disagreement among scholars. Fortunately, the various injunctions are not confined to a specific time or place, but have general application. This negates the allegation that they are a set of theories, and history has proven that when they were put into practice, non-Muslims were treated kindly and justly. It is evident that a high level of organization was initiated by the Prophet, and that he guaranteed non-Muslims full rights as citizens of the Muslim state. His practices guided later caliphs and Muslim leaders in their dealings with non-Muslims for centuries to come.

2

'UMAR'S TREATMENT OF CHRISTIANS

It was common practice for Muslim conquerors to negotiate pacts with conquered peoples. These treaties were quite similar in structure and content and reflected a spirit of tolerance towards non-Muslims. They consisted of three main elements: safety for their persons, property and churches, and an assurance of freedom of religion. These guarantees made it clear that the lives, property and religion of non-Muslims would be protected from any kind of interference; that churches would not be demolished and there would be no encroachment on areas near churches. Freedom of religion was guaranteed in the stipulation of no compulsion in respect of religion.

The simplicity of these agreements changed dramatically with the promulgation of a long and controversial treaty called the Pact of 'Umar (*al-Shurut al 'Umariyyah*) and another agreement known as the Banu Taghlib peace treaty. The various documents recording these are completely different from the others in content and length. Moreover, they contained a large number of conditions, rules and penalties that were unfamiliar to the teaching of Islam and did not conform to the sort of treaties that Muslims used to issue to non-Muslims. This chapter will attempt to evaluate their accuracy of these two documents and the degree of tolerance attributed to Caliph 'Umar.

The Background and Character of 'Umar

When studying the relationship of a ruler with a group of people, it is instructive to examine the ruler's background and discover the basis of his interaction with others. 'Umar Ibn al-Khattab (d. 24 AH/ 644 CE) was born in Makkah and belonged to the Banu 'Adi, one of the main sub-tribes of the Quraysh.[1] He was literate – uncommon at those days – and was one of the Prophet Muhammad's close companions. When he converted to Islam, he was as determined and impetuous in defending the religion as he had been in persecuting it. Immediately after the Prophet's death, Abu Bakr, supported by 'Umar, took power. During his caliphate 'Umar was one of his chief advisers, and before his death in 634 CE Abu Bakr nominated 'Umar as his successor.[2] 'Umar was confirmed in office and became the second caliph of Islam (634–44 CE).[3]

During 'Umar's reign the Muslim state grew at an unprecedented rate, taking over Mesopotamia and parts of Persia from the Sassanids, and Egypt, Palestine, Islamic Jerusalem, al-Sham (greater Syria, including Lebanon, Palestine and Jordan), North Africa and Armenia from the Byzantines. Many of these conquests followed watershed battles on both the western and eastern fronts. 'Umar undertook wide-ranging administrative reforms and closely oversaw public policy, establishing an advanced administration for newly conquered lands, including several new ministries and bureaucracies, as well as ordering a census of all the Muslim territories. [4]He also began the process of codifying Islamic law. He took pains to provide effective and speedy justice for the people, and set up an effective system of judicial administration according to Islamic principles.[5]

'Umar was known for his simple, austere lifestyle. He continued to live much as he had when the Muslims were poor and persecuted. In 16 AH (637 CE), he decreed that the years of the Islamic era should be counted from the year of the *hijra* in 622 CE.[6] He was notable for his ability to separate truth from falsehood, and the Prophet Muhammad conferred on him the title of *al-faruq* (the separator between what is true and what is false).⁷

'Umar was a ruler of great justice and peace. Because of his noble qualities he was given the title Commander of the Faithful.⁸ Non-Muslim scholars generally treat him as a pivotal figure in the history of Islam, since it was under his aegis that the Muslim domain expanded and conquered the great powers of the day, the Sassanid and Byzantine empires. They analyse his decisions primarily in military and political terms, and are less concerned with the religious or character judgements that are of interest to Muslims.⁹

The Treaty with the Banu Taghlib Tribe

The peace treaty with the Christian tribe of Banu Taghlib is one of the important events that highlight the treatment of non-Muslims during Caliph 'Umar's reign. It has been referred to by a number of jurists, historians and orientalists, who have concluded that the document issued to the Banu Taghlib was the work of 'Umar.¹⁰

A discussion of it requires answers to the following questions. Is it true that 'Umar instigated those conditions? Were the Banu Taghlib really exempted from paying the *jizyah*? Were they prohibited from baptising their children? It should be borne in mind that the attribution of the treaty to 'Umar was derived from different texts, such as those of Abu 'Ubayd, Abu Yusuf, al-Baladhuri, Yahya Ibn Adam and others. Their narratives were in the form of a discussion between 'Umar and his companions about the Banu Taghlib, in particular their geographical location, as they were a powerful tribe, and what Muslims could offer to avoid antagonising them.¹¹

It is also important to explain the circumstances of this peace treaty and the need to impose such conditions. Al-Tabari reports that in the year 17 AH/ 638 an expedition under the leadership of al-Walid Ibn 'Uqbah set forth from Madinah to continue the conquest of the Arab peninsula. The expedition passed through several regions until it reached the lands of the Banu Taghlib, where it found that many of the tribe had already left and sought refuge within the Byzantine empire. When 'Umar was informed of this he wrote to the emperor demanding their extradition, otherwise he would expel all Arab Christians into the Byzantine empire. In response to this threat, the emperor sent them back.[12] Al-Tabari says that 4000 people returned. Al-Walid Ibn 'Uqbah then refused to accept anything from them except their conversion to Islam. When they refused, al-Walid wrote to 'Umar.[13] He replied:

> That rule [that you want to impose upon them] is only applicable to the Arabian Peninsula; nothing but strict surrender to Islam is acceptable for those living in the Arabian Peninsula. But leave the people of Banu Taghlib as they are, on the condition that they do not bring up their [newborn] children in Christian fashion, and accept [it] if any member of Banu Taghlib embraces Islam.[14]

Al-Walid acted on this letter and negotiated with the Banu Taghlib that they would not christen their newborn babies or prevent anyone from embracing Islam. In addition, he asked them to pay the *jizyah* tax. The Banu Taghlib agreed to the first two conditions, but refused to pay money on *jizyah* terms. As a result, according to al-Tabari, al-Walid sent the leaders of the Christian tribe to 'Umar. On their arrival, 'Umar asked them to pay the *jizyah*. They told him that they would talk about this if he granted them safety. 'Umar agreed, and they explained that they considered paying *jizyah* to be beneath their dignity as Arabs,[15] and a humiliation to their pride if it were to be levied in return for protection of life and property. They threatened to leave the area and go back to the Byzantine empire if the Muslims insisted on collecting the money as *jizyah*.[16] 'Umar discussed the matter with his companions and, according to Yahya Ibn Adam, in his book *Kitab al-Kharaj*:

> 'Ubada Ibn al-Nu'man said to 'Umar Ibn al-Khattab: O Commander of the Faithful! You know the might of Banu Taghlib, that they are living close to the enemy, and should

they assist the enemy against you, it would be a burdensome affair. Therefore, if you decide to give them something, do so. Thereupon he made a treaty with them, making a condition that they should not baptize any of their children as Christians and that for them the *sadaqa* [a voluntary donation for charity] should be doubled. 'Ubada used to say: they had a treaty but they did not act accordingly.[17]

Caliph 'Umar granted their wish, saying:

Do not humble Arabs; take the *sadaqa* from Banu Taghlib[18]

It can be seen that under the peace terms with the Banu Taghlib, the Christians must not baptize their children and their *sadaqa* should be double what the Muslims paid. Furthermore, none of them should be forced to change his or her religion.[19] From the above references, the only conclusion can be that 'Umar was the first to establish these conditions with the Banu Taghlib. However, after examining many Muslim historical sources, I am confident that 'Umar himself did not lay down such conditions – they were first promulgated by the Prophet Muḥammad himself. Ibn Sa'd narrates:

Muhammad Ibn 'Umar al-Aslami informed us: he said: Abu Bakr Ibn 'Abd Allah Ibn Abi Sarah related to me on the authority of Ya'qub Ibn Zayd Ibn Talhah he said: a deputation of Banu Taghlib, consisting of sixteen believers [Muslims], and Christians with golden crosses waited on the Apostle of God. They stayed in the house of Ramlah Bint al-Harith. The apostle of God made peace with the Christians on the condition that they would not baptize their children into Christianity. He gave generous rewards to the faithful among them.[20]

This narration was given by Ibn Sa'd in the section of his book about the different delegations who came to the Prophet asking for safe conduct in the year 9 AH (630 CE).[21] Ibn Sa'd was one of the scholars who examined in great depth all the reports about the delegations. Al-Tabari refers to a narration that contains some conditions similar to those cited by Ibn Sa'd, but adds that these conditions were limited to the Christians in the Banu Taghlib delegation and to those who had delegated the negotiations to them.[22] Therefore, members of this group were the only ones prohibited from baptising their children.

It seems that the narrations of both Ibn Sa'd and al-Tabari have solved a major problem of who was the first to establish these conditions. According to them, it was the Prophet Muhammad. This is the conclusion whether one relies on Ibn Sa'd's narration, which covers the whole of the Banu Taghlib tribe, or al-Tabari's, which covers only some members of the tribe. Both agree that 'Umar was not the originator of such conditions. In fact, according to al-Tabari, the Muslims of the Banu Taghlib themselves requested Prophet Muhammad to establish these conditions,[23] in order to protect their children in the future, especially during times of war. That is to say, the Muslims of Banu Taghlib were trying to protect their children from being baptized after their (Muslim) parents' death, which seems logical.

It is known that certain groups of people were regularly exempted from paying *jizyah*. They included *dhimmis* who participated in *jihad* with Muslims, and women, children and the elderly, as shown in the previous chapter. In the case of the Banu Taghlib, what took place was not an exemption from *jizyah*, but a form of appeasement by changing its name to *sadaqa*, provided that the amount paid was double. The name *jizyah* was never sacred; it was a term used to define the amount of money taken from *dhimmis*. It can therefore be argued that 'Umar's decision to call this payment *sadaqa* is not objectionable as long as it ended up in the Muslim treasury (*bayt al-mal*).

Now that the originator of the conditions imposed on the Banu Taghlib has been established, the question arises of why Caliph 'Umar reimposed these conditions. To answer it, a closer look at the surrounding circumstances is necessary. Shibli

Nu'mani suggests that a jurisprudential argument took place during 'Umar's term of office about the religion of the young children whose fathers belonged to a Christian tribe, but who had embraced Islam before their death.[24] Would these children be treated as Muslims or Christians? Would their relatives have the right to baptize them and bring them up as Christians? In response, 'Umar decreed that in these particular circumstances their relatives should not be allowed to baptize them or bring them up as Christians.[25] This is in line with *shari'ah* principles, that the children of a Muslim father should inherit Islam from their father and be treated as Muslims. Al-Tabari, discussing this prohibition, quotes from the treaty that was concluded with the Banu Taghlib:

> They shall not Christianize the children of those who have already embraced Islam.[26]

Shibli Nu'mani contends that the condition was not based on a hypothetical situation, because a number of people from the Banu Taghlib did embrace Islam, and it was necessary to insert a provision in the treaty to safeguard their interests and those of their children.[27] However, Caetani, a well-known Italian orientalist, argues that the Christian families of the Banu Taghlib suggested these conditions themselves for economic reasons.[28]

The record shows that 'Umar's treatment of the Banu Taghlib was merciful. Yahya Ibn Adam reported that Ziyad Ibn Hudayr used to tax the Banu Taghlib several times a year. One of the tribe's elders went to 'Umar and told him of this. 'Umar said, 'You will be relieved from that', and wrote to Ziyad ordering him not to tax them more than once a year.[29] Despite this edict, there were some reports that 'Umar used to instruct his workers to deal firmly with the Banu Taghlib. For example, when he dispatched Ziyad Ibn Hudayr to the tribe to collect *'ushr* (one-tenth),[30] 'Umar ordered him to be firm with the Christians of the Banu Taghlib because they were Arabs, and as a result might accept Islam. 'Umar had never considered them and the other Christians in the Arab peninsula as true Christians. He did not agree with marrying their women or eating their slaughtered animals, although Islam allowed this conduct with Christians. 'Umar went further, saying that the Christians of the Banu Taghlib got nothing from Christianity other than drinking alcohol and eating pork. According to al-Shafi'i, 'Ali Ibn Abi Talib held the same point of view.[31]

It seems that despite this prohibition the Christians of Banu Taghlib continued to baptize the children of deceased Muslims. The evidence is in the narration of 'Ubada: 'they had a treaty but they did not act accordingly',[32] as well as in that of 'Ali Ibn Abi Talib:

> If I have an opportunity, I will deal with Banu Taghlib my way, I will execute their warriors, and I will enslave their women because they broke the agreement. Therefore, I am free from any responsibility towards them from the day they baptized the deceased Muslim children.[33]

The case of the Christians of Banu Taghlib demonstrates clearly that Caliph 'Umar in no way undermined the concept of freedom of religion. It is also evident that *jizyah* can be levied under any name, as long as the non-Muslims agree to pay the amount specified.

The Pact of 'Umar

The Pact of 'Umar, or *'ahd 'Umar*,[34] is a key document outlining the obligations of non-Muslims living in the Muslim state and defining the relationship of *dhimmis* with Muslims and with the state.[35] It shows the treatment of Christians by Muslims in the Muslim state in general, and especially when 'Umar Ibn al-Khattab was caliph.

Some scholars consider this pact to be foundational for the treatment of non-Muslims and a reflection of the general teaching of Islam concerning them. This view, however, has been opposed by a number of scholars. The problem is that during some periods of Muslim history, the justification to treat Christians in a biased way was based on the pretext of implementing the negative or discriminatory aspects of the Pact of 'Umar. However, an examination of 'Umar's conduct towards non-Muslims has shown him to be extremely tolerant, and exemplary in his efforts to follow the instructions of the Qur'an and the Sunnah.

Opinions differ concerning the attribution of the pact to 'Umar. Some jurists and historians, such as al-Khallal (d. 311 AH/923 CE),[36] Ibn Hazm (d. 456 AH/1063 CE),[37] al-Tartushi (d. 520 AH/1126 CE),[38] Ibn Qudama (d. 630 AH /1233 CE),[39] Ibn Taymiyyah (d. 728 AH/1328 CE),[40] Ibn 'Asakir (d. 571 AH/1176 CE),[41] Ibn al-Qayyim (d. 751 AH/1350 CE),[42] Ibn Kathir (d. 774 AH/1373 CE),[43] al-Hindi (d. 975 AH/1567 CE)[44] and 'Ali 'Ajin,[45] agreed that the pact could be attributed to 'Umar. Jurists like al-Salih,[46] Hammam Sa'id[47] and Zakariyya al-Quda[48] and orientalists such as Caetani (d. 1935),[49] Tritton[50] and Cohen[51] doubted the authenticity of this attribution. The argument of each group was grounded in textual analysis, as well as consideration of the sociopolitical context and the practical examples of Caliph 'Umar's treatment of Christians living in the Muslim state.

There are several versions of the Pact of 'Umar, with similarities as well as differences in vocabulary or sentence order; some differ in detail, both in their stipulations and literary structure. A number of western orientalists claim that Ibn Hazm documented the first appearance of the Pact of 'Umar in his book, *Mratb al-Ijma' fi al-'Ibadat wa al-Mu'amalat wa al-Mu'taqadat*.[52] This is a serious error, as I have discovered that the first version was documented by al-Khallal.[53] Another version, by Ibn 'Asakir, is among the earliest written records and has attracted most of the scholarly attention. It is the version most often cited in this chapter and describes the pact in the following way:

> 'Abd al-Rahman Ibn Ghanam (d. 78 AH/697 CE) said as follows: When 'Umar Ibn al-Khattab, may God be pleased with him, accorded a peace to the Christians of al-Sham, we wrote to him as follows: In the name of God, the Merciful and Compassionate. This is a letter to the servant of God

'Umar (Ibn al-Khattab), Commander of the Faithful, from the Christians of such-and-such a city. When you marched against us, we asked you for safe-conduct (*aman*), for ourselves, our descendants, our property, and the people of our community, and we undertook the following obligations toward you: We shall not build, in our cities or in their neighbourhood, new monasteries, churches, convents, or monks' cells, nor shall we repair, by day or by night, such of them as fall in ruins or are situated in the quarters of the Muslims. We shall keep our gates wide open for passers-by and travellers. We shall give board and lodging to all Muslims who pass our way for three days. We shall not give shelter in our churches or in our dwellings to any spy nor hide him from the Muslims. We shall not teach the Qur'an to our children. We shall not manifest our religion publicly nor convert anyone to it. We shall not prevent any of our kin from entering Islam if they wish it. We shall show respect toward the Muslims, and we shall rise from our seats when they wish to sit. We shall not seek to resemble the Muslims by imitating any of their garments, the *qalansuwa* (cap), the turban, footwear, or the parting of the hair. We shall not speak as they do, nor shall we adopt their *kunyas* (surnames). We shall not mount on saddles, nor shall we gird swords nor bear any kind of arms nor carry them on our persons. We shall not engrave Arabic inscriptions on our seals. We shall not sell fermented drinks. We shall clip the fronts of our heads. We shall always dress in the same way wherever we may be, and we shall bind the *zunar* (waist belt) round our waists. We shall not display our crosses or our books in the roads or markets of the Muslims. We shall use clappers in our churches only very softly. We shall not raise our voices when following our dead. We shall not show lights on any of the roads of the Muslims or in their markets. We shall not bury our dead near the Muslims. We shall not take slaves who have been allotted to Muslims. We shall not build houses overtopping the houses of the Muslims. When

I brought the letter to 'Umar, May God be pleased with him, he added, 'We shall not strike a Muslim.' We accept these conditions for ourselves and for the people of our community, and in return we receive safe-conduct. If we in any way violate these undertakings for which we ourselves stand surety, we forfeit our covenant (*Dhimma*), and we become liable to the penalties for contumacy and sedition.

'Umar Ibn al-Khattab replied:

Sign what they ask, but add two clauses and impose them in addition to those, which they have undertaken. They are: 'They shall not buy anyone made prisoner by the Muslims,' and 'whoever strikes a Muslim with deliberate intent shall forfeit the protection of this pact.'[54]

The document has six structural characteristics:

1. Restrictions on Christian places of worship such as churches, monasteries and monk's cells.
2. Hospitality to Muslim travellers and serving them food.
3. No harm to Muslims and Islam.
4. Christians should dress in a distinctive way and not imitate Muslims.
5. Christians are prohibited from doing and saying certain things.
6. Restrictions on commercial relations between Christians and Muslims, such as partnerships.

Since 'Umar's Pact has been reported as a narration, the rules of Hadith scholars should be applied when examining the authenticity of Ibn 'Asakir's document. The three main issues are:

- The chain of transmitters of the pact (*isnad*).
- An examination of the text (*matin*).
- The validity of attributing the pact to 'Umar.

Opinions on the chain of narrators

Ibn 'Asakir was unique in reporting five narrations of 'Umar's pact.[55] Four of them, however, have been found to contain some problems in their chains of narrators. The chains of the five versions are shown in Table1.

Table 1
Narrator Chains in Ibn 'Asakir's Five Versions

Version 1	Version 2	Version 3	Version 4	Version 5
Abu Muhammad Sahl Ibn Bisher al-Isfraini	Abu al-Qasim al-Suhami	Abu Muhammad Taher Ibn Sahl	Abu Muhammad Taher Ibn Sahl	Abu al-Hussain al-Khatib
Abu al-Hasan 'Abd al-Da'm Ibn al-Hasan al-Qatan	Abu Bakr al-Bayhaqi	'Abd al-Da'm Ibn al-Hussain	'Abd al-Da'm al-Qatan	Abu 'Abd Allah al-Khatib
'Abd al-Wahab Ibn al-Hussain al-Kulabi	Abu Muhammad 'Abd Allah al-Asbahani	'Abd al-Wahab al-Kulabi	'Abd al-Wahab al-Kulabi	'Ali Ibn al-Hasan al-Raba'i
Abu Muhammad 'Abd Allah Ibn Ahmad Ibn Zubar	Abu Talib 'Ali Ibn 'Abd al-Rahman Ibn Abi 'Aqil	**Abu Muhammad Ibn Zubar**	**Abu Muhammad Ibn Zubar**	Abu al-Faraj al-'Abbas Ibn Muhammad
Muhammad Ibn Ishaq Ibn Rahawih al-Hanzali	'Ali Ibn al-Hasan al-Khul'i al-Shafi'i	Muhammad Ibn Hisham Ibn al-Bukhtari	Muhammad Ibn Maymun al-Sufi	'Abd Allah Ibn 'Atab
Bishr Ibn al-Walid	'Abd al-Rahman Ibn 'Umar Ibn al-Nahas	Al-Rabi' Ibn Tha'lb al-Ghanwi	Isma'il Ibn Mujald Ibn Sa'id	Muhammad Ibn Muhammad Ibn Mus'ab
'Abd al-Hamid Ibn Bihram	Abu Sa'id Ahmad Ibn Muhammad al-A'rabi	Abu al-Qasim al-Suhami	Sufyan al-Thawri	'Abd al-Wahab Ibn Najda al-Hawti

Shahr Ibn Hawshab	Muhammad Ibn Ishaq al-Sufar	Abu Bakr al-Ja'fi	Talha Ibn Musrf	Muhammad Ibn Himyar
'Abd al-Rahman Ibn Ghanam	Al-Rabi' Ibn Tha'lb Abu al-Fadl	Abu Taher al-Faqih	Masruq	'Abd al-Malik Ibn Hamid
	Yahya Ibn 'Uqba Ibn Abi al-'Ayzer	Abu al-Hasan 'Ali Ibn Muhammad Ibn Sahnawih	'Abd al-Rahman Ibn Ghanam	Al-Sari Ibn Mutif
	Sufyan al-Thawri	Abu Bakr Ya'qub Ibn Yusuf al-Mutaw'i		Sufyan al-Thawri
	Al-Walid Ibn Nuh	Al-Rabi' Ibn Tha'lb		Al-Walid Ibn Nuh
	Al-Sari Ibn Mutrf	**Yahya Ibn 'Uqba Ibn Abi al-'Ayzer**		Talha Ibn Musrf
	Talha Ibn Musrf	Sufyan al-Thawri		Masruq Ibn al-Ajda'
	Masruq	Al-Walid Ibn Nuh		'Abd al-Rahman Ibn Ghanam
	'Abd al-Rahman Ibn Ghanam	Al-Sari Ibn Mutrf		
		Talha Ibn Musrf		
		Masruq		
		'Abd al-Rahman Ibn Ghanam		

Table 1: The chains are shown in chronological order based on Ibn 'Asakir.[56] The names in bold are the untrustworthy narrators.

According to Al-Khatib Al-Baghdadi (d. 463 AH /1071 CE)[57] and Al-Dhahabi (d.748 AH /1347 CE),[58] the untrustworthy narrators are Abu Muhammad 'Abdullah Ibn Ahmad Ibn Zubar (whose name appears in two of the Ibn 'Asakir versions) and Yahya Ibn 'Uqba (whose name appears in the other two versions), both of whom are notorious for fabricating the Hadith. I am therefore inclined to believe that the first four narrations are invalid. It is self-evident to Muslim scholars – indeed, to scholars in general – that a narration is more likely to be guaranteed if all the narrators in its chain are trustworthy. The fifth narration, according to 'Ajin, appears to have a full chain of trustworthy narrators.'[59] He examined the different chains listed by Ibn 'Asakir and concluded that the fifth narration is the most authentic one.[60]

Ibn Qayyim al-Jawziyya referred to three versions and commented on their narrator chains, but failed to demonstrate that he had conducted a thorough verification process.[61] In fact, although he seems to have had doubts about the validity of the chains, he tries to avoid discussing this by claiming that the fame of a narration rules out the need to investigate its narrator chains.[62] That is to say, Ibn al-Qayyim diverged from his own methodology of verification, despite being aware that fame is no proof of authenticity, especially when an important subject is at stake. Furthermore, the fame of this pact developed a long time after its assumed date of issue. Ibn al-Qayyim's texts of the pact were subject to other problems as well (see below).

'Ajin agrees with Sa'id's classification of Ibn al-Qayyim's versions as very weak and containing unknown narrators.[63] In the end, Sa'id refused to accept the Pact of 'Umar as a document issued by the caliph himself.[64] 'Ajin, however, seems to reject this conclusion.

The text of the pact
The fifth version of Ibn 'Asakir is similar to other versions documented by different scholars. It is narrated without specifying the name of the city – it refers 'to such and such a city', or to one that is nameless. Yet, how could such an

important document omit the name of the city that it addresses? How could Caliph 'Umar not even ask the city's name after modifying the document? And why did the Christians of that city not insist on having the name of their city included? 'Ajin argues that this happened unintentionally, that 'Abd al-Rahman Ibn Ghanam might have forgotten to state the name of the city because he had to issue pacts to numerous cities at that time.[65] But did this actually happen? It seems unlikely. Early sources fail to offer either confirmation or denial. In addition, 'Ajin says elsewhere in his article that the pact was written after a long negotiation between Muslims and Christians.[66]

If this is the case, then the name of the city about which they were negotiating should have appeared in the document. One wonders also why later scholars, for example Ibn al-Qayyim, who wrote almost 150 years after Ibn 'Asakir, was confused about the city's name. In the three versions he mentions, the first shows that the people of al-Jazira[67] wrote to 'Abd al-Rahman Ibn Ghanam, who then communicated with Caliph 'Umar. In the second version, 'Abd Al-Rahman wrote directly to the caliph when he concluded a peace treaty with the Christians of al-Sham. The third version says that 'Abd al Rahman, in a letter to Caliph 'Umar, described the stipulations made by the Christians of al-Sham themselves.[68]

Tritton argues that in a normal case, conquered people would not decide the terms on which they would enter into an alliance with their victors. He criticizes the assertion that conquered Christians forbade themselves all knowledge of the Qur'an, yet refer to it in their letter to the caliph, 'until they pay the *jizyah* with willing submission, and feel themselves subdued'.[69]

'Ajin argues that the reason for not allowing the Christians to teach their children the Qur'an is because if they did, they would not teach them the real meaning and would fabricate Qur'anic verses.[70] The text of the pact also contains some vocabulary that was uncommon in 'Umar's period. As an example, al-Salih explains that *zunar*, a Greek word meaning waist belt, was not well-known in the Arabian peninsula at the time.[71] Tritton finds it hard to believe that discriminatory laws in the pact would have been thought up by the Christians themselves. He also addresses some inconsistencies between different versions of the pact relating to the people with whom it was concluded, the place where it was signed and whether the ruler issuing the pact was 'Umar or one of his commanders.[72]

In regard to the identity of the ruler, it is worth noting that Ibn 'Asakir reported the same text of the pact in another of his 70 volumes, in the form of a letter from the Christians of al-Sham that was handed to Abu 'Ubaydah, the chief commander in Syria (al-Sham), instead of to 'Abd al-Rahman Ibn Ghanam:[73]

> When thou camest into our land we asked of thee safety for our lives and the people of our religion, and we imposed these terms on ourselves; not to build in Damascus and its environs church, convent, chapel, monk's hermitage, not to repair what is dilapidated of our churches nor any of them that are in Muslim quarters; not to withhold our churches from Muslims stopping there by night or day…not to teach our children the Qur'an…we will not abuse a Muslim, and he who strikes a Muslim has forfeited his rights …[74]

According to this narration, there is no mention at all of 'Abd al Rahman, and a new name appears – Abu 'Ubaydah. Why did Ibn 'Asakir name two different people in the same document with different narrations? It seems that Ibn 'Asakir himself was unsure about the authenticity of this narration.

Validity of the attribution to 'Umar
Did the Pact of 'Umar originate with this caliph? 'Ajin was not the first to argue in favour of this. He was preceded by Ibn Taymiyyah, who asserted that the pact's conditions had been laid down by 'Umar Ibn al-Khattab.[75] According to Ibn Taymiyyah, the terms of the pact were constantly renewed and imposed on Christians by certain Muslim rulers, such as 'Umar Ibn 'Abdul 'Aziz, who followed the example of 'Umar Ibn al-Khattab very strictly. Ibn Taymiyyah said that Harun al-Rashid, Ja'far al-Mutawakkil and others had revived the terms of 'Umar's pact

and ordered the destruction of churches, such as those in all Egyptian lands.[76] In addition, Ibn Taymiyyah asserted that the chief scholars from the well-known schools of jurisprudence discussed these terms and alluded to the need for the Imam to constrain the People of the Book and subjugate them to these terms.[77] Ibn Taymiyyah even claimed that this pact was the most famous subject in the books of *fiqh* and Islamic literature, and the one that was generally accepted and agreed on by the great Muslim scholars and their companions, and indeed by the whole Muslim *ummah* (nation).[78]

Ibn Kathir commented on the Qur'anic verse, 'and feel themselves subdued (*saghirun*)',[79] by saying that the term means disgraced, humiliated and belittled. Therefore, Muslims are not allowed to honour the people of *dhimma* or to elevate them above Muslims, as they are miserable, disgraced and humiliated. He added that this was why 'Umar Ibn al-Khattab demanded that his conditions be met by the Christians.[80]

'Ajin says that this pact reflects the Islamic way of treating non-Muslims, as derived from the Qur'an and the Sunnah.[81] It seems he was trying to defend the opinions of Ibn Taymiyyah and Ibn al-Qayyim, who represent the trend of inflexibility against non-Muslims. He quoted all Ibn Taymiyyah's comments on the Pact of 'Umar, and regarded Ibn Kathir's citation of the pact as validation of its attribution to 'Umar. On the other hand, al-Albani, a modern Hadith scholar (and a follower of Ibn Taymiyyah's school), has doubted the pact's chain of narrators.[82]

Caetani doubts that this pact belongs to the Caliph 'Umar and believes that its text was written later.[83] Tritton likewise questions the attribution to 'Umar.[84] He points out that the pact 'presupposes closer intercourse between Christians and Muslims than was possible in the early days of conquest.'[85] He adds that a search of historical sources shows that references to the pact became common only at the beginning of the ninth century. Tritton supports his argument by referring to the sample statement, preserved in al-Shafi'i's famous book *Kitab al-Umm*, that was issued to Christians whenever a Muslim leader had to conclude a peace treaty with them:

If a Muslim leader wants to conclude a peace treaty with Christians in return for their paying *jizyah*, he should start it with in the name of God, the most compassionate, the most merciful. This is a pact written by so and so the servant of God, the commander of the faithful in year so and so to the Christians so and so who live in the city so, and the Christians of the city so, I, and all Muslims, promise you and your fellow Christians security as long as you and they keep the conditions we impose upon you. Which are: you shall be under Muslim laws and no other, and shall not refuse to do anything we demand of you. If any of you says of the Prophet, of God's book or His religion what is unfitting, he is debarred from the protection of God, the Commander of the Faithful, and all Muslims; the conditions on which security was given are annulled; and the Commander of the Faithful has put his property and life outside the pale of the law, like the property and lives of enemies. If one of you commits fornication with or marries a Muslim woman, or robs a Muslim on the highway, or turns a Muslim from his religion, or helps their enemies as a soldier or guide to Muslim weakness, or shelters their spies, he has broken his agreement, and his life and property are without [the protection of the] law. He who does less harm than this to the goods or honour of a Muslim shall be punished.

We shall scrutinize your dealings with Muslims, and if you have done anything unlawful to a Muslim we shall undo it and punish you; e.g. if you have sold to a Muslim any forbidden thing, [such] as wine, pigs, blood, or an [unclean] carcass, we shall annul the sale, take the price from you [if you have received it] or withhold it from you [if it has not been paid]; we shall pour out the wine or blood and burn the carcase. If he [the Muslim] wishes it to be destroyed we shall do nothing to him, but we shall punish you. You shall not give him any forbidden thing to eat or drink, and shall not give him a wife in the presence of your witness nor in an illegal marriage. We shall not scrutinize nor enquire into a contract between you and any other unbeliever. If either party wishes to annul the contract, and brings a request to us, if we think that it should be annulled we shall annul it, if it is legal we shall allow it. But if the object has been taken and lost we shall not restore it, for a sale between unbelievers has been finished. If you or any other unbeliever asks for judgment we shall give it according to Muslim law; if we are not approached we shall not interfere between you. If you kill accidentally a Muslim or an ally, Christian or not, then the relatives [of the killer] shall pay blood money, as among Muslims. For you, relatives are on the father's side. If a homicide [killer] has no relatives then his estate must pay. A murderer shall be killed unless the heirs wish to take blood money, which shall be paid at once. A thief, if his victim complains, shall pay a fine. The slanderer shall be punished if the punishment is fixed; if not, he shall be punished according to Muslim law.

You shall not display in any Muslim town the cross nor parade your idolatry, nor build a church nor place of assembly for your prayers, nor beat the nakus [ring the church bell], nor use your idolatrous language about Jesus, the son of Mary, to any Muslim. You shall wear the *zunnar* above all your clothes, cloaks and others, so that it is not hidden; you shall use peculiar saddles and manner of riding, and make your *kalansuwas* [a type of hat] different from those of the Muslims by a mark you put on them. You shall not take the crest of the road nor the chief seats in assemblies, when Muslims are present. Every free adult male of sound mind shall pay poll tax, one *dinar* of full weight, at New Year. He shall not leave his town till he has paid and shall not appoint a substitute to pay it, the *jizyah* amount to be paid at the end of the year; poverty does not cancel any of your obligations nor abrogate the protection given you. If you have anything we shall take it. The *jizyah* is the only burden on your property as long as you stay in your town or travel in Muslim land, except as merchants. You may not enter Makkah under any conditions. If you travel with merchandise you must pay one-tenth to the Muslims, you may go where you like in Muslim land, except Makkah, and may stay in any Muslim land you like except the *hijaz*, where you may stay three days only till you depart. These terms are binding on him who has hair under his clothes, is adult, or has completed fifteen years before this date, if he agrees to them; if not, there is no treaty with him. Your little boys, immature lads, lunatics, and slaves do not pay *jizyah*. If a lunatic becomes sane, a boy grows up, a slave is set free and follows your religion, he pays *jizyah*. The terms are binding on you and those who accept them; we have no treaty with those who refuse them. We will protect you and your lawful [according to our law] property against any one, Muslim or not, who tries to wrong you, as we protect our own property; our decisions about it will be the same as those about our own property, and ourselves. Our protection does not extend to forbidden things, like blood, carcasses, wine and pigs, but we will not interfere with them; only you must not obtrude them on Muslims towns. If a Muslim or other buys them we will not force him to pay, for they are forbidden and have no price; but we will not let him annoy you about them, and will not force him to pay. You must fulfil all the conditions we imposed on you. You must not attack a Muslim nor help their enemies by word or deed.

This is the treaty of God and His promises and the most complete fulfilment of promise He has imposed on any His creatures; you have the treaty of God and His promise and the protection of N.N.['no name'] the Commander of the Faithful, and of the Muslims to fulfil their obligations towards you. Your sons, when they grow up, have the same obligations as you. If you alter or change them then the protection of God, of N.N. the Commander of the Faithful, and of the Muslims is taken from you. He, who is at a distance, yet receives this document and approves it, these are the terms that are binding on him and on us, if he approves them; if he does not approve, we have no treaty with him.[86]

With al-Shafi'i's statement in mind, Tritton argues that the Pact of 'Umar originated as 'an exercise in the schools of law on drawing up pattern treaties'.[87] He concludes that no one knew about the Pact of 'Umar, although it is known that documents carrying 'Umar's name enjoyed much fame. There is no doubt that there are a lot of similarities between the Pact of 'Umar and the al-Shafi'i version, but does this mean that Tritton is right? If the Pact of 'Umar was an exercise in schools of law, then the jurists would have adopted it. However, this was not the case. Imam al-Shafi'i cites another statement in his same book (*al-Umm*), which is completely different from the above version in regard to how Muslims should treat Christians in religious matters:

> The government must not interfere with any practice of the *dhimmis*, although contrary to Muslim law as long as it is not done in public notice. So, in a town where there are no Muslims living, Christians may build churches and tall houses, and no one may interfere with their pigs and festivals. A *dhimmi* may lend money at interest to another or contract a marriage not recognized by Muslim law, and no one can interfere ...[88]

In Muslim literature, none of the early historians, such as al-Baladhuri, al-Waqidi, al-Ya'qubi, al-Tabari, al-Azdi, Ibn al-A'them, Ibn al-Athir and many others mentions anything about the Pact of 'Umar in their well-known books, even though they discuss the conquest of al-Sham and other places. For example, Ibn al-Athir (a late historian, compared to the others), in *al-Kamil fi al-Tarikh*, refers to the peace treaty concluded by Abu 'Ubaydah with the Christians of Hims (modern Homs) in return for their agreement to pay *jizyah*. He also addresses the conquest of Halab (Aleppo) and how Muslims concluded a peace treaty with its inhabitants. He says nothing about the Pact of 'Umar.[89]

Contemporary scholars writing about the Muslim treatment of non-Muslims have not discussed the Pact of 'Umar nor paid any attention to it. For example, Hamidullah, in his book *Majmu'at al-Watha'iq al-Siyasiyya Lil'ahd al-Nabawi wa al-Khilafa al-Rashida*, describes in great detail a large number of political documents pertaining to treaties, as well as letters, official and otherwise, issued by the Prophet and his successors. 'Umar's Pact, despite its importance, is referred to only briefly in the final two pages of this book. Hamidullah quotes the text from the *Tafsir of Ibn Kathir*, with the observation that Ibn Kathir's text is without reference (*isnad*).[90]

Since Hamiduallah paid considerable attention to the peace treaties concluded during 'Umar's reign, it seems he was not convinced that this pact could be attributed to 'Umar, or he would have included it in his book along with the other treaties from 'Umar's era. In fact, Hamidullah expressed his doubts by inserting question marks after some sentences he quoted from the text, for example:

We will not teach our children the Qur'an?
We will not speak their language?
... And that which has been reported by the scholars?[91]

Zaydan, in his famous book, *Ahkam al-Dhimmiyyn wa al-Musta'minyn fi Dar al-Islam*, discusses in great detail the situation of non-Muslims in the Muslim state. He completely ignores the Pact of 'Umar, which suggests he concluded that it does not belong to 'Umar, especially as he provides many illustrations of 'Umar's benign attitude towards non-Muslims – examples that clearly contradict the terms of the so-called Pact of 'Umar.[92]

'Umar issued peace treaties to conquered peoples, the normal procedure when Muslims conquered any land. This is clearly shown in Muslim literature. However, it seems evident that 'Umar himself did not issue the document in question. The so-called Pact of 'Umar was developed by unknown people during Muslim history to include conditions that have no relevance or link to the period of the early Muslim conquests. These conditions can be associated with situations of the *dhimma*, beginning at the time of 'Umar Ibn 'Abdul 'Aziz, Harun al Rashid, through to the decrees of al-Mutawakkil (d. 232 AH/786 CE).[93]

In his attempt to identify the factors behind the Pact of 'Umar, Safi explains that *shari'ah* rules underwent drastic revision, beginning in the eighth century of Islam. This was a time of great political turmoil throughout the Muslim world. The Mongols had invaded Central and West Asia, inflicting tremendous losses on various dynasties and kingdoms and destroying the seat of the Abbasid caliphate in Baghdad. This coincided with the Crusaders gaining control of Palestine and the coast of Syria. In the west, Muslim power in Spain was being gradually eroded. Safi concludes that it was in this atmosphere of mistrust and suspicion that a set of provisions, attributed to an agreement between Caliph 'Umar and the Syrian Christians, appeared in treaties written by Ibn al-Qayyim. The origin of these provisions is therefore suspect, says Safi, although their intention is clearly to humiliate Christian *dhimmis* and to set them apart in dress code and appearance.[94]

A deteriorating sociopolitical and economic situation, resulting from the conflict in Egypt between the Baghdad-based Abbasids and the Tolonis (the ruling group of Muslims in Egypt and Syria, led by Ahmad Ibn Tolon), was prevalent especially at the time of the Abbasid caliphate. In addition, the *dhimmis* in the state had achieved very high status and also controlled large economic and political segments of the country.[95] All these factors created an opportunity for the so-called Pact of 'Umar to be created as a real document attributed to 'Umar. Its aim seems to have been to curb the enormous power of the *dhimmis*.

'Umar's Conduct towards the *Dhimmis*

The Qur'anic verse, 'let there be no compulsion in religion',[96] was the cornerstone of Muslim relations with Christians in religious matters during the time of the second caliph, 'Umar Ibn al-Khattab. It should be clearly stated that neither Muslim jurists, Muslim chronicles, nor orientalists past or present have provided any example of an incident in which a Christian was forced to embrace Islam. In fact, Muslim history and literature cite a large number of examples confirming freedom of religion at that time.

For example, Abu 'Ubayd, in his book *al-Amwal*, cites the story of Caliph 'Umar and his personal servant Astiq, a Christian.[97] 'Umar frequently tried to convince Astiq to embrace Islam, but when he refused, 'Umar did nothing except recite the words of the Holy Qur'an, 'let there be no compulsion in religion'.[98] Astiq says that when 'Umar was about to die, he freed Astiq from slavery and told him he could go wherever he wanted. This bears witness to 'Umar's spirit of tolerance: in spite of his immense power as leader of the Muslim nation, he propagated Islam only in the form of exhortation and persuasion. Beyond that, he made it clear that nobody should be compelled to change his or her religion. This tolerance is evident in the pacts and treaties that 'Umar concluded with conquered peoples.[99]

A large number of incidents reported in the Muslim juristic and historical literature illustrate 'Umar's favourable conduct towards *dhimmis*. He was well-known for instructing his army commanders to deal justly with non-Muslims. For example, it was reported that 'Umar (after he was stabbed by a *dhimmi*) told his would-be successor: 'I commend to the Caliph after me that he conduct good treatment to those who are under the Prophet's protection. He should keep the covenant with them, fight those who are after them, and not tax them beyond their capacity.'[100] 'Umar's concern for the well-being of *dhimmis* was thus shown even on his deathbed.

The manner of 'Umar's treatment of *dhimmis* was supported by his interpretation of the Qur'anic verse: 'Alms are for the poor and the needy'.[101] According to 'Umar, the poor (*al-fuqara'*) were the Muslims and the needy (*al-masakin*) were the *dhimmis*, including Christians and Jews. 'Umar's interpretation was promulgated after the following incident reported by Abu Yusuf:

> 'Umar passed by the door of people at which there was a beggar who was an old blind man. 'Umar struck his arm

from behind and asked, to which People of the Book do you belong? He said, I am a Jew. 'Umar said: what has compelled you to begging? The Jewish man replied, I am begging in order to get money to pay for *jizyah* and my need, as I am old. Then 'Umar held his hand, and took him to his house and gave him something and some money. 'Umar then sent him to the Muslim treasurer (*bayt al-mal*). 'Umar instructed the treasurer to take care of this man and whoever was like him. 'Umar added that with this man we have not done justice to him as we took *jizyah* from him when he was young but we forsook him when he was old. Verily, the *sadaqa* is for the poor and destitute. And this one is a destitute from the People of the Book. So 'Umar exempted taking the *jizyah* from him.[102]

Finally, 'Umar combined words with deeds when he sanctioned blood retaliation (*qisas*) in favour of an Egyptian Coptic man against Muhammad, the son of 'Amr Ibn al-'As, ruler of Egypt. 'Umar uttered these historic words to 'Amr: 'O, 'Amr, how could you have enslaved the people, when their mothers have born them free'.[103] This incident occurred when the son of 'Amr hit the Coptic man, saying: 'I am the son of the honoured people'. The Copt reported this to 'Umar, who did not hesitate to recall 'Amr and his son from Egypt, and told the Copt to hit 'Amr's son back.[104]

The humiliating conditions enumerated in the so-called Pact of 'Umar are utterly foreign to the mentality, thoughts and practice of this caliph. It seems certain that the chain of narrators supporting this attribution includes untrustworthy individuals. The text's main defects are that it contains a nameless city; it uses words alien to those prevailing at the time of 'Umar, such as *zunnar*; it prohibits teaching the Qur'an; and it is not clear with whom the treaty was concluded. These deficiencies support the contention that 'Umar was not the originator of this document. In addition, the remarkable care and concern displayed in 'Umar's attitude to *dhimmis* confirms the rejection of the so-called Pact of 'Umar as attributable to Caliph 'Umar Ibn al-Khattab.

Conclusion

The Pact of 'Umar was not the work of Caliph 'Umar Ibn al-Khattab, and the conditions of the treaty issued to the Banu Taghlib tribe did not originate with him. During his reign 'Umar issued several pacts and treaties, none of which was in the same style as the documents under discussion, nor did they contain similar conditions. In the pact with the Banu Taghlib he implemented the conditions that the Prophet Muhammad had issued to this tribe, which were not applicable to all its members. It has also been shown that the Muslim members of the Banu Taghlib were the ones who requested the conditions. Throughout his rule, 'Umar adhered to Islamic principles in his treatment of non-Muslims, in this case Christians, and his relationship with non-Muslims was governed by clear legal rules and regulations.

3

'UMAR AND THE CHRISTIANS OF ISLAMIC JERUSALEM

Wars and battles usually bring destruction and bloodshed to both sides. However, this was not the case in 16 AH/637 CE in the conquest of Aelia (Islamic Jerusalem). This chapter addresses the Muslim treatment of Christians in Aelia after the first Muslim conquest. The basis of their treatment was laid down when Patriarch Sophronious agreed to hand over the keys of Aelia peacefully to Caliph 'Umar Ibn al-Khattab, the leader of the victorious Muslim army, and in return the caliph issued his Assurance of Safety to the People of Aelia (al-'Uhda al-'Umariyyah).

It is important to return to the pre-conquest period and briefly examine the religious status of the Christians in Aelia and the circumstances in which the Muslim army was able to conquer the city. A comparative study of the main versions of 'Umar's Assurance is then made, and the role of this famous document in portraying the Muslim treatment of Christians and creating a positive atmosphere for relations between the two religions in Islamic Jerusalem is discussed.

Before the first Muslim conquest of Aelia, the Arabs who had emigrated from the Arab peninsula and Yemen were living in al-Sham (Syria, Lebanon, Jordan and Palestine) and were well-established on both sides of the River Jordan. They formed the majority of the local population.[1] Some Arab tribes had lived in Palestine since before 2000 BC.[2] Shahid points out that the

Judham, 'Amilah and Lakhm tribes comprised most of the Arab population in Palestine before and after the Muslim conquest.[3] The geographical distribution of the Arab tribes in al-Sham has been shown by 'Athaminah.[4]

Prior to the first Muslim conquest, Aelia was a largely Christian region ruled by the Byzantines. Most of its inhabitants had converted to Christianity after the Emperor Constantine professed his Christian faith in 312 CE. Constantine fostered Christianity throughout the empire and it became the official religion in 324 CE.[5]

As time passed, the Christian population in Aelia increased dramatically. The Christians consisted of both Arabs and non-Arabs from various places who differed in language, culture and civilization. Although they shared the same religion, they were divided into many sects and groups.[6] This caused instability in Aelia's Christian community, and in the fifth century serious disagreements erupted between the Monophysites and the Byzantine emperor about the coexistence of the divine and human natures of Christ.[7] In the seventh century, the Emperor Heraclius (610–41 CE) attempted to resolve the schism created by the Monophysites and Chalcedonians in 451 CE and suggested the compromise of Monoenergism. This combined the Chalcedonian belief that Christ had two natures with the Monophysite view that He had one 'will.' The definition of the term 'will' was left deliberately vague. Monoenergism was accepted by the Patriarchs of Constantinople, Antioch and Alexandria as well as by the Armenians, although not by the Patriarch of Aelia or by Pope Honorius I in Rome.[8]

As a result, the Christians in Aelia, who were mainly Monophysite, suffered religious persecution when the Emperor Heraclius tried to force his interpretation of Christianity on them.[9] He also directed that the central government adopt these beliefs, but his attempts at reconciliation only increased dissension. The Christians who opposed the emperor's views suffered persecution and violence.[10] Runciman observes that the Christian emperors were not very tolerant. They also wished to use Christianity politically, as a unifying force to bind their subjects to the government.[11]

Thus, at the time of the Muslim conquest, the lives of the Christians of Aelia were rent by conflict, dispute and disagreement, accompanied by persecution for those who did not conform to the particular beliefs of the imperial regime at that time.

Towards the Conquest of Islamic Jerusalem

Muslims had been interested in Islamic Jerusalem (*Bayt al-Maqdis*) since the time of the Prophet Muhammad. The Prophet himself had issued a number of traditions *(ahadith)*, in which he told his followers about the future conquest of Bayt al-Maqdis (Islamic Jerusalem). For instance, in a statement to Shaddad Ibn Awss, one of his companions, he said:

> Al-Sham will be conquered, and Bayt al-Maqdis will be conquered, and your sons will be the Imam*s* there, if God wills.[12]

And to another of his companions, 'Awf Ibn Malik, he predicted six incidents that would occur before the last day:

> O 'Awf, Count six things between now and judgment day. The first is my death ... and the second is the conquest of Bayt al-Maqdis ...[13]

Both in the Qur'an and in several prophetic traditions, the Prophet emphasized the importance of Islamic Jerusalem and particularly of its al-Aqsa mosque. The city was perceived as holy to Islam long before Muslims set foot in the region. For instance, Abu Hurairah narrated:

> The Prophet said: set out intentionally on a journey only to three mosques i.e. al-Masjid al-Haram (in Makkah), Masjid Ar-Rasul (in Al-Madinah) and al-Masjid al-Aqsa, (in Islamic Jerusalem).[14]

The prophet asserted the significance of Islamic Jerusalem to the Muslims, despite the fact that the whole area including Aelia was ruled by the Byzantines at that time. The Muslim state in Madinah was in its early stages, and Muslims were still relatively weak. But the significance of Islamic Jerusalem was such that Muslims made it their sacred duty to bring holiness back to the region.

The Prophet Muhammad began his mission in the early years of the seventh century CE, when Aelia had been under Byzantine control for more than six centuries. This prophetic mission had a profound influence on the history of Islamic Jerusalem. The preparations for the campaign to conquer Aelia, to safeguard the borders of the Arabian peninsula from the Byzantine threat and to destroy the prestige of the Byzantine empire were reflected in three major events during the Prophet's life. These were the battle of Mu'ta in 8 AH (629 CE),[15] the raid of Tabuk in 9AH (630 CE)[16] and Osama Ibn Zayd's mission in 11 AH (631 CE).[17] El-Awaisi recounts how these events had a synergistic effect. First of all, they showed Muslims how they could spread the message of Islam beyond the Arabian peninsula. Second, they began the destruction of Byzantine power. Third, they were preliminary steps on the way to the great campaign directed at al-Sham and the conquest of Aelia.[18]

After the death of the Prophet, the first caliph, Abu Bakr, completed Osama Ibn Zayd's mission and led the Muslim armies in victory over al-Sham. Abu Bakr's exhortation in his letter to Khalid Ibn al-Walid was reported by Ibn al-Murajja:

> Hurry to your brothers in al-Sham. By God's name, if a village from the villages of Bayt al-Maqdis (Islamic Jerusalem) has been conquered this is better to me than conquering Iraq.[19]

El-Awaisi argues that Abu Bakr, who at that time was 'the highest political and religious authority', always understood the Prophet's vision for Islamic Jerusalem, and that the conquest of the city was a central strategic aim for him.[20] After Abu Bakr's death, his successor, 'Umar Ibn al-Khattab, continued the project. This culminated in the conquest of Aelia, which as Islamic Jerusalem became part of the Muslim state.

There is disagreement among historians regarding the reason for the arrival of 'Umar Ibn al-Khattab in al-Sham. Some historians believe it was in response to the request of the Christians of Aelia, who had agreed with Abu 'Ubaydah to surrender Aelia only to Caliph 'Umar personally.[21] Other historians argue that it was in response to the request of 'Amr Ibn al-'As, who wrote to 'Umar after he understood from the Christians of Aelia that the person to whom Jerusalem would be surrendered had the name of 'Umar.[22] Still others suggest that 'Umar came to al-Sham to sort out a number of matters, such as dividing the booty, supervising the judicious distribution of properties taken over by the Muslims, organizing the military command in al-Sham, making arrangements for the stipends paid to troops and for their rations and setting the inheritance of those martyred in battles. Whatever the reason, during 'Umar's stay at al-Jabiyah (the Golan Heights), Aelia was conquered and he went there to witness the surrender and receive the keys.[23]

The majority of Muslim and non-Muslim historians agree that the conquest of Aelia took place after the decisive battle of al-Yarmuk in 15 AH (636 CE). This defeat of the Byzantine army was a major turning point on the way to Aelia, and was considered by Gabrieli to be one of the most important battles in history.[24]

Sophronious, the patriarch of Aelia, insisted on the presence of Caliph 'Umar when he surrendered the city. Searching through the narrations, it is clear that the patriarch rejected negotiations with 'Umar's commanders during the Muslim siege of the city. As life in Aelia became more difficult, Sophronious informed his people that he would surrender the walled city to the Muslims if the caliph had the name 'Umar and fitted a certain description. His reason was that he had read this in Christian holy books.[25] When the Muslims heard of the patriarch's terms – which included paying *jizyah* after surrender to 'Umar – some of them tried to trick him.[26] Sharhabil, one of the Muslim commanders, suggested that instead of waiting for 'Umar to come all the way from Madinah, Khalid Ibn al-Walid should be sent forward as the Caliph 'Umar. Khalid and 'Umar and were very similar in appearance, and since the people of Aelia knew 'Umar only by report, they would not see through the subterfuge.

The following morning the Patriarch was informed of the caliph's presence, and Khalid, dressed in simple clothes of the poorest material, as was 'Umar's custom, rode up to the fort for talks with the patriarch. But it did not work. Khalid was too well-known, and there were Christian Arabs in Jerusalem who had visited Madinah and seen both 'Umar and Khalid and were able to spot the differences. Moreover, the patriarch must have wondered how the caliph happened to be there just when he was needed! The trick was soon discovered and the patriarch refused to talk with Khalid. Abu 'Ubaydah wrote to 'Umar about the failed mission and invited him to come to Aelia.[27]

It is doubtful that a Christian prophecy with 'Umar's description existed in Christian holy books because of the following unanswerable questions. First, why did the patriarch not mention anything about Caliph 'Umar before, during the siege? Aelia was under siege for four months. If the patriarch knew of this prophecy, why did he not offer to surrender the city earlier? Furthermore, I could not find any reports by priests or monks in al-Sham or Aelia that refer to a prophecy describing 'Umar. This is especially significant because of Aelia's importance to Christians all over al-Sham, a region that had now fallen into Muslim hands. Also, several peace pacts had already been concluded with Muslims. Why had Muslim leaders not been told about the prophecy describing 'Umar, especially when they were preparing to march on Aelia?

It appears that the patriarch had several valid reasons for wanted Caliph 'Umar to come personally and receive the keys of Aelia. First, because of the sanctity of Aelia for Christians, the patriarch preferred the surrender to take place in the presence of the head of the Muslim state rather than a local commander. Second, he wanted a guarantee from the head of state preserving

Christian places of worship as well as Christian lives. Third, he may have had other issues that he wanted to negotiate with 'Umar as head of state, in order to ensure their implementation.

Finally, it could be argued that the patriarch was certain Aelia would eventually fall into Muslim hands, especially after the long siege. The Muslim armies were able to tolerate the very bad weather conditions, despite being unfamiliar with them.[28] The people of Aelia had suffered much hardship, and realized they did not stand a chance against the Muslim armies. They had also not forgotten the massacres, pillage and destruction of holy places carried out by the Persians when they stormed the city two decades earlier, and feared that the Muslims would do the same if they took it by force.[29] However, sensing that the Muslims were keen to avoid bloodshed, the city's Christian defenders tried to extract maximum guarantees for their security. An assurance of safety signed by the head of state rather than the local commander was far more reliable.

Further evidence that there was no prophecy about 'Umar in the Christian holy books is that the historian Theophanes does not refer to it.[30] On the contrary, according to Theophanes, when the patriarch saw Caliph 'Umar with his old garment walking into the walled city of Aelia he quoted an ominous prophecy from the Bible: 'When ye therefore shall see the abomination of desolation, spoken of by Daniel the prophet, stand in the holy place (whoso readeth, let him understand), then let them flee ...'[31] Why should the patriarch insist that Caliph 'Umar should come in person and then regard his arrival as polluting the holy city? It is obvious that the patriarch's request was some sort of subterfuge, especially because it was extremely traumatic for Christians to have to surrender their holy city. I am also inclined to believe that the religious dispute between the patriarch and the Byzantine emperor, outlined above, was among the reasons[32] for surrendering to Muslims, as it enabled the patriarch to remove Byzantine supremacy.

'Umar Ibn al-Khattab, for his part, would have wanted to visit Islamic Jerusalem sooner or later. It was, after all, connected with many of the prophets, including David, Solomon and Jesus, and with the Night Journey (*isra'*) and the Ascent (*mi'raj*) of Prophet Muhammad, as well as being the place to which Muslims directed prayer (*qiblah*) while in Makkah and for the first 17 months they were in Madinah. 'Umar agreed to the Christian request, and combined a visit to the holy city with gaining the goodwill and trust of its people.

Caliph 'Umar arrived in Aelia, with the simplicity and humility of appearance and manner that was characteristic of early Muslims, to receive in person the submission of the holy city. He was advised that his demeanour would not impress locals who were used to seeing kings and emperors richly dressed and well-guarded.[33] He answered:

> We are a people whom God has empowered with Islam. We do not seek pleasure other than God.[34]

Sophronious must have been delighted that the caliph had accepted his offer to come to Aelia for the city's surrender. He invited 'Umar to pray in the church at the hour of prayer. Sahas argues that Sophronious considered the Muslims and the caliph to be protectors of Aelia and its holy places from the domination of the Jews, who were the enemies of the Christians.[35] He maintains that the conquest of Aelia led to an opportunity for the Christians to contain the Jews, with the help of the Muslims, through the concessions granted to them in 'Umar's Assurance of Safety.[36] However, this claim has been flatly rejected in the latest study of 'Umar's Assurance, by El-Awaisi.[37]

'Umar's Assurance of Safety to the People of Aelia

Soon after he arrived, 'Umar gave an Assurance to the inhabitants of Aelia that guaranteed their security and religious freedom. This document, *Al-'Uhda al-'Umariyyah'*, is of great importance, since it defines the status of Christian communities under the new Muslim rule and establishes the foundation of how Muslims should treat Christians in Muslim territories (and especially in Islamic Jerusalem). Nevertheless, opinions differ concerning its authenticity. It is therefore important to describe the various versions of the Assurance and to examine two of them more closely. These are al-Tabari's version, written almost three centuries after the event but regarded as the most famous and longest version of the Assurance, and the version of the Orthodox patriarchate of Jerusalem.

It is obvious from searching the literature that not all historians have reported the text of 'Umar's Assurance. The early historians, such as al-Waqidi (d. 207 AH/822 CE), al-Baladhuri (d. 279 AH/ 892 CE), Ibn al-Athir (d. 630 AH /1233 CE), and Abu al-Fida' (d. 732 AH /1332 CE), confined themselves to discussing the significance of the Assurance rather than the text itself. Other historians, such as al-Ya'qubi (d. 284 AH /897 CE), the patriarch of Alexandria, Eutychius (Ibn al-Batiiq) (d. 328 AH /940 CE), al-Tabari (d. 310 AH /922 CE), al-Himyari (d. 727AH/ 1327CE), Mujir al-Din al-Hanbali (d. 928 AH 1521 CE) and Ibn al-Jawzi (d. 597 AH /1200 CE), reported the text of this document in their books, either in an abridged version or as a long text.

Al-Waqidi is among the earliest historians to report (twice) the content of 'Umar's Assurance, without the text, in his book *Futuh al-Sham* (The Conquest of Syria). In the first narration he says that when 'Umar came to Islamic Jerusalem and was identified by its inhabitants, they opened the gates of the walled city and went out to ask for the pact and for a *dhimmi* contract. They accepted that they would have to pay the *jizyah*. 'Umar agreed, and told them to go back to their homes. Having been granted what they asked for, they returned to their homes and left the gates of the city wide open.[38] In his second narration, al-Waqidi reports that 'Umar went to Aelia and stayed there ten days after he had written the Assurance for its Christian inhabitants, and that he allowed them to stay in Aelia in return for paying *jizyah*.[39]

Al-Baladhuri mentions three narrations about the conquest of Islamic Jerusalem and the significance of 'Umar's Assurance. According to the first one, when Abu 'Ubaydah was besieging the city of Aelia, the Christians besought him to grant peace and safety to them like the Christians of the cities of al-Sham, on terms of payment of *jizyah* and *al-kharaj* (land tax). They were willing to conclude a peace treaty on one condition, that 'Umar would come from Madinah in person to conclude it. Abu 'Ubaydah wrote to 'Umar, with the result that 'Umar came to al-Jabiyah, then travelled to Aelia where he wrote the Assurance.[40]

In the second narration transmitted by al-Baladhuri, in the name of Yazid Ibn Abu Habib, 'Umar dispatched Khalid Ibn al-Thabit al-Fahmi with troops from al-Jabiyah to Aelia. After a brief battle the city was handed over to Khalid, who concluded a peace treaty according to which the area inside the city walls was to remain in possession of the Christians, while the area outside it became the property of the Muslims. The treaty was agreed on condition that 'Umar would ratify it in person. Khalid informed 'Umar of the inhabitants' readiness to surrender, whereupon the latter travelled from al-Jabiyah to Aelia and took possession of the city on these conditions. 'Umar then returned to Madinah.[41]

In the third narration, al-Baladhuri reported that Abu 'Ubaydah went to Palestine after the conquest of Qansarin in the year 16 AH/637 CE and led the siege on Aelia, whose the inhabitants asked him for a peace treaty. He accepted their request in 17 AH/638 CE, on condition that 'Umar himself would come to ratify it and would write to them accordingly.[42]

Ibn al-Athir wrote a note about the significance of the Assurance to the People of Aelia. He reported that the Christians of Aelia sent a delegation to 'Umar Ibn al-Khattab while he was staying at al-Jabiyah. When the Muslims saw a detachment of horsemen with drawn swords glittering in the sun coming towards their camp, they took up arms in order to beat back what appeared to be an enemy attack (of Christians). However, 'Umar realized at once that it was a delegation from Aelia coming to offer surrender. The caliph then wrote an Assurance of Safety for the Christians of Aelia in return for their payment of *jizyah,* and they opened the gates of the walled city to him.[43]

These narrations agree that the Christians of Aelia were granted an Assurance in return for the payment of *jizyah*. On the

'UMAR AND THE CHRISTIANS OF ISLAMIC JERUSALEM 91

other hand, al-Ya'qubi was among the first historians to give an abbreviated narration of this document, as follows:

> You are given safety of your persons, properties and churches that will not be inhabited (taken over) or destroyed unless you cause some public harm.[44]

Eutychius gave a similar text:

> This is a document from 'Umar Ibn al-Khattab to the people of Aelia. They are given safety of persons, children [sons and daughters], and churches that will not be destroyed or inhibited [by Muslims].[45]

These two versions differ little and appear to have been taken from the same source. Mujir al-Din al-Hanbali (d. 928 AH /1521 CE) provided a text similar to al-Tabari's version (see below) and quoted from Sayf Ibn Abi Hazem, via 'Uthman, via Khalid and 'Ubada. There is no difference between al-Tabari's and al-Hanbali's versions, except in some vocabulary which does not necessarily change the meaning. Ibn al-Jawzi (d. 597 AH /1200 CE) gave nearly the same text, which was reported by Sayf via al-Tabari. The only difference is that Ibn al-Jawzi's version comes as a summary to al-Tabari's.[46] It runs as follows:

> 'Umar wrote to the inhabitants of Bayt al-Maqdis (Islamic Jerusalem): I guarantee for you the safety of your persons, properties, families, your crosses and your churches. You will not be taxed beyond your means, and whosoever decides to follow his people then he will be guaranteed safety (*aman*) and you pay the *kharaj* like the other cities of Palestine.[47]

It should be added that Ibn al-Jawzi, when naming the witness to 'Umar's Assurance, substituted 'Ali Ibn Abi Talib for 'Amr Ibn al-'As, who was named in al-Tabari's version. Nevertheless, history shows that 'Ali Ibn Abi Talib was in Madinah at that time.[48]

Al-Tabari's Version of 'Umar's Assurance

Al-Tabari was born at the end of 224 AH /839 CE and wrote his history between 290 AH /902CE and 303 AH/915 CE.[49] His version of 'Umar's Assurance is quoted from Saif Ibn 'Umar (d. 170 AH /786 CE):

> In the name of God, the most Merciful, the most Compassionate. This is the assurance of safety (*aman*) which the worshipper of God [the second caliph] 'Umar (Ibn al-Khattab), the Commander of the Faithful, has granted to the people of Aelia. He has granted them an assurance of safety (*aman*) for their lives and possessions, their churches and crosses; the sick and the healthy [to everyone without exception]; and for the rest of its religious communities. Their churches will not be inhabited [taken over] nor destroyed [by Muslims]. Neither they, nor the land on which they stand, nor their cross, nor their possessions will be encroached upon or partly seized. The people will not be compelled (*yukrahuna*) in religion, nor any one of them be maltreated (*yadarruna*). No Jews should reside with them in Aelia. The people of Aelia must pay the *jizyah* tax like *ahl al-Mada'in* the people of the [other] region/cities, they must expel the Byzantines and the robbers. As for those [the first Byzantine group] who will leave [Aelia], their lives and possessions shall be safeguarded until they reach their place of safety, and as for those [the second Byzantine group] who [choose to] remain, they will be safe. They will have to pay tax like the people of Aelia. Those people of Aelia who would like to leave with the Byzantines, take their possessions, and abandon their churches and crosses will be safe until they reach their place of safety.
> Whosoever was in Aelia from the people of the land (*ahl al-ard*) [e.g., refugees from the villages who sought refuge in

Aelia] before the murder of *fulan* [name of a person] may remain in Aelia if they wish, but they must pay tax like the people of Aelia. Those who wish may go with the Byzantines, and those who wish may return to their families. Nothing will be taken from them until their harvest has been reaped.

The contents of this assurance of safety are under the covenant of God, are the responsibilities of His Prophet, of the Caliphs, and of the Faithful if [the people of Aelia] pay the tax according to their obligations. The persons who attest to it are: Khalid Ibn al-Walid, 'Amr Ibn al-'As, 'Abd al-Rahman Ibn 'Awf, and Mu'awiyah Ibn Abi Sufyan. This assurance of safety was written and prepared in the year 15 [AH].[50]

Until 1953 CE this was regarded as the longest and most explicit text, and it certainly contains the most details and restrictions. In that year, however, the Orthodox patriarchate in Jerusalem published a new version of 'Umar's Assurance (see below), presenting it as a close translation of the original Greek text kept in Istanbul.

Al-Tabari was among the few Muslim historians who supported their narrations by naming the chain of narrators (*isnad*). In spite of this, 'Ajin, on examining al-Tabari's version, commented that its chain of narrators was broken and its content could not be attributed to Caliph 'Umar Ibn al-Khattab. He therefore refuted the authenticity of al-Tabari's version, claiming it was produced and had become popular in circumstances when Muslims were weak, and was intended to show non-Muslims that Islam was tolerant of other religions. [51] At the same time he asserted that the Pact of 'Umar should be the basis of the way in which Muslims should treat Christians.

El-Awaisi, on the contrary, argues that Sayf Ibn Umar's chain of narrators quoted in al-Tabari is strong and valid. He bases his argument on the fact that two narrators, Khalid Ibn Mi'dan al-Shami (d.108 AH/726 CE)[52] and 'Ubadah Ibn Nusai (d. 118

AH/736 CE),⁵³ were trustworthy followers (*tabi'is*) of the first generation after the companions of the Prophet.⁵⁴

I agree with El-Awaisi on the strength of the chain of narrators in al-Tabari's version, for three reasons. First, the opening paragraph of this Assurance is in line with the treaties issued to other cities in the al-Sham region. Second, the versions narrated by historians before al-Tabari did not differ much from the essence of his version; and third, 'Umar's conduct towards the Christians of Islamic Jerusalem after the conquest, described below, reflects a clear implementation of the conditions stated in al-Tabari's version. Nevertheless, it is necessary to discuss the text in order to determine the extent to which this document can be accepted as a blueprint for the way Muslims should treat Christians in Islamic Jerusalem.

The document's core statements
The statement that 'Umar granted the people of Aelia safety for 'their persons, their possessions and churches' represented the normal terms of the assurances granted by Muslims to all conquered peoples at that time. With the exception of the condition relating to the Jews, the first paragraph of al-Tabari's version is similar to these treaties. Such guarantees reflected the spirit of tolerance shown by the conquering Muslims⁵⁵ towards non-Muslim peoples. It is clearly stated that the lives, properties and religion of Christian subjects would be safe from any kind of interference or molestation, that their churches would not be damaged or demolished and no encroachment would be made on areas near churches. Freedom of religion was assured in the stipulation of no compulsion in respect of religion. Because these commitments conformed to the regular practice of a Muslim conqueror, the essentials of the document can be treated as authentic.

El-Awaisi argues that 'Umar did not sign a treaty between two parties, but gave the people of Aelia an assurance of safety.⁵⁶ I agree with this, and would like to emphasize the importance of distinguishing between giving an assurance and asking for one. In normal circumstances, a peace treaty emerges as a result of negotiations between two parties. In this case, only one party – the Muslims – signed 'Umar's Assurance. The Christians, led by Sophronious, do not seem to have signed this document. This indicates that the Assurance was given to them as a pledge rather than as a treaty.

Exclusion of the Jews
The weaknesses in al-Tabari's version start with the statement that the Jews should be banned from living with the Christians in Aelia. This restriction was not supported, or even mentioned, in any narrations before al-Tabari's. It does not seem to be have been implemented, especially as there is no mention in the Muslim record that 'Umar expelled Jews from Aelia or prevented them from staying there. Al-Quda argues that it is strange to have a condition in the Assurance that was not implemented. He comments that it was well-known that Muslims in general respected pacts and followed them accordingly.[57]

Al-Duri refutes the condition of excluding Jews from living in Aelia in this version of 'Umar's Assurance. He asserts that details prohibiting a certain population from living in a conquered city were unusual and never appear in the texts of similar pacts made in al-Sham. The reference to Jews in the Assurance is apparently absent from all Muslim literature. Al-Duri adds that it is believed this information first appeared in the chronicle of Michael of Syria.[58] Another historian, al-Himyari, attributes it to a specific demand made by the Christians of Aelia.[59] Ibn al-Jawzi does not even refer to the Jews when discussing 'Umar's Assurance in his book, *Fada'il al-Quds* (The Merits of Jerusalem).[60]

El-Awaisi argues that the exclusion of Jews from residing in Aelia (during the first Muslim conquest) is not confirmed historically. He says that this condition is unacceptable under Muslim law, as it contradicts the basic teaching of Islam,[61] and supports his argument by citing verses 60: 8–9 from the Qur'an.[62] Moreover, Karen Armstrong states that:

When Caliph 'Umar conquered Jerusalem from the
Byzantines, he was faithful to the Islamic inclusive vision.
Unlike Jews and Christians, Muslims did not attempt to
exclude others from Jerusalem's holiness. Muslims were
being taught to venerate them.[63]

It was not the policy of Muslims to prevent *dhimmis* from living
in the Muslim state, as all had equal right of residency in Islamic
Jerusalem. This leads me to argue that the reason behind this
condition was the conflict between Christians and Jews.

The conflict between Christians and Jews
The recurrent conflict between Christians and Jews in Aelia
began when the region was under Roman rule in the first
century CE and continued after the Jewish revolts against the
Roman empire in 66 CE and especially 132 CE,[64] when the
Romans expelled the Jews from the region of Aelia and forbade
them to enter the city.[65] This was almost five hundred years
before the Muslim conquest. The situation did not improve
when Christianity became the official religion of the Roman
empire in 312 CE. On the contrary, the regime followed the
policy of its predecessors and continued the expulsion of Jews
from Aelia. Nevertheless, there were short periods when Jews
were allowed to stay in Aelia, such as during the Persian
occupation of 614–28 CE.[66]

This conflict was apparent during the Muslim conquest of al-
Sham. The Jews were very keen to go back to Aelia, and hoped
that the Muslims would conquer Aelia and allow them to do
so.[67] Sarkis (d. 1915) provides examples of the 'cruel aggression
and oppressions of the Byzantines', to which the Jews had been
subjected for a long time. For instance, he states that the
Emperor Constantine oppressed the Jews and forced them to
convert to Christianity. Some Jews did convert, others pretended
to be Christians and those who refused were killed.[68] In
addition, El-Awaisi quotes a Jewish historian stating that the
Jewish response to the first Muslim conquest was positive, in
that it brought an end to Byzantine rule.[69]

In a recent publication, 'Athaminah asserts that on the eve of the Muslim conquest the Jews were among a large minority who hated and resented Byzantine rule.[70] He adds that the Byzantine empire had placed the Jews at the top of its list of enemies.[71] It seems that at the time of the conquest of Aelia the Jews were no threat to the Christians as they were not living in the city, but were a minority scattered across al-Sham. El-Awaisi argues that the condition of excluding the Jews in al-Tabari's version of the Assurance is an infringement, addition or interpretation invented by some Muslim jurist, and he suggests it was produced:

> [to] please the rulers or match the general circumstances and socio-political developments that affected the position of the People of the Book during certain periods of history especially in the Abbasid State.[72]

It is possible that some time later, when the Christians accepted the reality of Muslim rule in Islamic Jerusalem and that Jews were no longer prevented from living in the region, the Christians felt threatened by this situation and inserted this condition into the Assurance recorded in al-Tabari's version.

The expulsion of the Byzantines
Al-Tabari's version also stated that the Christians of Aelia must expel the Byzantines and thieves from living with them. It was quite natural that 'Umar should think of expelling them from Aelia. However, there was an apparent problem in the condition that allowed the Byzantines the option of staying in Aelia and paying *jizyah*, or leaving the city altogether. El-Awaisi maintains that 'Umar put Byzantines and robbers in the same category because both were, indeed, thieves. He argues that the Byzantines had occupied and stolen the land and its resources, while robbers had stolen the people's possessions.[73] However, this condition appears to contain a contradiction. The beginning of the sentence says that the Byzantines must be expelled, while towards the end they are given the choice of leaving, or of staying and paying the *jizyah*. El-Awaisi suggests that a deeper

understanding of this sentence reveals no contradiction, as it distinguishes between two groups of Byzantines. The first reference is to the Byzantine armed forces and robbers who must be expelled, and the second reference is to Byzantine visitors to the holy places.[74]

Al-'Affani argues similarly that the text, or this condition, might have been inserted to distinguish between two groups. First, the Byzantine armies or soldiers, who should leave; second, those who visited the city as pilgrims or stayed for worship around the Christian holy sites.[75]

The question of Fulan

The inhabitants of Aelia were given the opportunity to stay if they paid *jizyah*, or leave with the Byzantines and thieves. However, the statement also specifies 'whosoever was in Aelia from the people of the land (*ahl al-ard*) before the murder of Fulan'.[76] Al-Quda points out that this unknown name, Fulan, is mentioned in the document without the date of his murder. This makes it difficult to identify the person, so that it is impossible to implement the condition and to regard this as the text of a binding treaty.[77] El-Awaisi argues that the phrase, 'before the murder of Fulan', may refer to a person who was well-known at the time of the Muslim conquest. He suggests that the name might have been mistranscribed from al-Tabari's original manuscript, and could be '*falak*', '*falaj*', '*falah*' or '*fulan*'.[78]

I agree that Fulan may refer to a well-known person, but not with El-Awaisi's interpretation. A search of narrations about the circumstances surrounding the conquest of Aelia reveals that the name Fulan[79] appears in more than one of them. For example, al-Tabari, in his chapter entitled 'fath Bisan wa Ajnadin', records that when 'Amr Ibn al-'As was fighting the Byzantine commander Artabun in Palestine, 'Amr was joined by 'Alqamah Ibn Hakim and Masruq Ibn Fulan al-'Akki in his battle with the Christians of Aelia.[80] From this, it seems that Fulan was known as the father of one of the Muslim leaders. If this is correct, then he was neither an inhabitant of Aelia, nor a Byzantine, nor a thief.[81]

Al-Tabari's version of 'Umar's Assurance, written nearly 300 years later, invites some observations. The first is about the date of 15 AH (636 CE) at the end of the document. There is no doubt that that this was not in the original, but was added later. If it was correct, it would have led to differing opinions about the date of the conquest of Aelia,[82] which was not the case – the consensus is that it was 16 AH.

Further, it was not until the 16th year after the *hijrah* that 'Umar inaugurated the *hijri* calendar,[83] and it is very doubtful that al-Tabari's document would share the same date as the *hijri*, especially since Sayf refers to a false date used by al-Tabari. Besides, al-Baladhuri reports that 'Amr Ibn al-'As began the siege of Aelia after the victory of al-Yarmuk in 15 AH and that Abu 'Ubaydah came to help him in 16 AH. It is therefore inconceivable that any document before the 16th year of the *hijrah* could be dated using the *hijri* calendar.[84] This means that the date in al-Tabari's version was added later.

Another issue concerns the witnesses used in this document. It is very surprising that Abu 'Ubaydah is not one of them, as he was chief commander of the Muslim armies. Abu 'Ubaydah might also have been expected to be a witness: it was he who asked 'Umar to come to the city to complete its surrender, and who communicated between 'Umar and the Christians of Aelia.

The Orthodox Patriarchate and 'Umar's Assurance

On the 1 January 1953 the Orthodox patriarchate of Jerusalem published a new version of 'Umar's Assurance. They stated that it was a literal translation of the original Greek text kept in the Greek Orthodox library in the Phanar quarter of Istanbul.[85] There is clearly a need to examine the authenticity of this document and to determine the extent to which it can be attributed to Caliph 'Umar Ibn al-Khattab. Published in English for the first time, it reads as follows:

In the name of God, the most Merciful the most Compassionate. Praise to God who gave us glory through Islam, and honoured us with Iman, and showed mercy on us with his Prophet Muḥammad, peace be upon him, and guided us from darkness and brought us together after being many groups, and joined our hearts and made us victorious over the enemies, and established us in the land, and made us beloved brothers.

Praise God O servant of God for his grace. This document of 'Umar Ibn Al-Khattab giving assurance to the respected, honoured and revered patriarch, namely Sophronious, patriarch of the Royal sect on the Mount of Olives, *tur al-Zaitun,* in holy Jerusalem, *al-Quds al-Sharif,* which includes the general public, the priest monks, nuns wherever they are. They are protected. If a *dhimmi* guard the rules of religion, then it is incumbent on us the believers and our successors, to protect *dhimmis* and help them gain their need as long as they go by our rules. This assurance (*aman*) covers them, their churches, monastery and all other holy places which are in their hands inner and outer: the Church of the Holy Sepulchre; Bethlehem, the place of Prophet Issa (Jesus); the big church; the cave of three entrances, east, north and west; and the remaining different sects of Christians present there and they are: the *Karj,* the *Habshi* and those who come to visit from the Franks, the Copts, the east Syrians, the Armenians, the Nestorians, the Jacobites, and the Maronites, who fall under the leadership of the above mentioned patriarch. The patriarch will be their representative, because they were given from the dear, venerable, and noble Prophet who was sent by God, and they were honoured with the seal of his blessed hand. He ordered to look after them and to protect them. Also we as Muslims [believers] show benevolence today towards those whose Prophet was good to them. They will be exempted from paying *jizyah* and any other tax. They will be protected whether they are on sea or land, or visiting the

Church of the Holy Sepulchre or any other Christian worship places, and nothing will be taken from them. As for those who come to visit the Church of the Holy Sepulchre, the Christians will pay the patriarch *dirham* and a third of silver. Every believing man or woman will protect them whether they are sultan or ruler or governor ruling the country, whether he is rich or poor from the believing men and women. This assurance was given in the presence of huge number of noble companions: 'Abdullah, Othman Ibn 'Afan, Sa'id Ibn Zayd and 'Abd Al-Rahman Ibn 'Awf and the remaining noble companions' brothers. Therefore, what has been written on this assurance must be relied upon and followed. Hope will stay with them, Salutation of God the high on our master Muhammad, peace be upon him, his family and his companions. All praise to God lord of the world. God is sufficient for us and the best guardian. Written on the 20th of the month *Rabi' al-Awal*, the 15th year of the Prophet *Hijra*. Whosoever reads this assurance from the believers, and opposes it from now and till the Day of Judgment, he is breaking the covenant of God and deserving the disapproval of his noble messenger. [86]

Jasir came to the conclusion that this version was forged, although he did not analyse its content. He argues that by closely scrutinising the text, one can easily recognize forgeries in it.[87] However, he gives no examples of these. Sahas devotes most of an article to discussing other writers, such as the Israeli historian S. D. Goitein, on the authenticity of 'Umar's Assurance. He concludes that the Orthodox patriarchate's version is the most authentic one.[88] Recently, in my communication with Sahas, I found that he had begun to doubt this conclusion, saying that he had found other such covenants attributed to 'Umar and to subsequent caliphs and, much later, to the Turkish authorities. He added that the question of rights over certain sacred sites seemed to have been a passionate concern of the Christians; hence the existence of several documents, authentic or otherwise. He is at present working on these texts and questions.⁸⁹

Al-'Arif, a Palestinian historian, doubts the Greek Orthodox version for several reasons. First, it differs widely from those adopted by Muslim historians. Second, the Arabic style of the document is quite different from that prevailing at the time of 'Umar.⁹⁰ He demonstrates this in a number of examples, with which El-Awaisi agrees – he says that the author of the document did not adhere to the Arabic language and used foreign expressions. In El-Awaisi's opinion, the document is written in poor Arabic. Arabs in the first centuries of Islam did not use the word *al-milat* with *taa maftuha* (ت) at the end of (الملت). They knew it as *al-milah* with *taa marbuta* (ة) at the end of (الملة). Also, *al-jizyat* (الجزيت) is used in an unfamiliar way and written as *al-jizyah* (الجزية).⁹¹ Al-'Arif argues that such usages indicate a text written during the late Ottoman era. El-Awaisi agrees that using *taa maftuha* instead of *taa marbuta* was common during the Ottoman era. Al-'Arif also says that some lines were illustrated with various types of flower, but such artistic decoration was unknown in the early centuries of Islam, especially in the first century after the *hijra*.

Third, al-'Arif argues that at the time of the Muslim conquest, Islamic Jerusalem was not known by any name except Aelia.⁹² However, in the Orthodox version it is called al-Quds al-Sharif. El-Awaisi argues that, logically, 'Umar would address the inhabitants of the city using the name that they were familiar with, rather than a different one.⁹³ Fourth, this version gives the names of various Christian sects, such as the Franks, Copts, Armenians, Nestorians, Jacobites and Maronites. El-Awaisi points out that the mention of the Franks in this document raises more doubts about its authenticity, because this term was not known until the time of the Crusaders.⁹⁴

The assumptions that al-'Arif and El-Awaisi reached were that this document was probably fabricated in the early years of Turkish Ottoman rule, is proved by my own research on the document. It should be noted that under the Ottoman caliphate the Christians were not classified as a single community, because they belonged to various denominations and nationalities such as Latins, Copts, Greek Orthodox, etc. The majority in the al-Sham region were Greek Orthodox Arabs; their patriarch had a seat in Istanbul, where, as Asali says, he made his voice heard.[95] The other denominations and sects were small minorities in the Ottoman caliphate, particularly in Islamic Jerusalem, but the Roman Catholic Church had the support of the Catholic powers in Europe. The situation of the Christian communities in Islamic Jerusalem was always closely affected by the vicissitudes of relations between the Ottomans and the European powers.[96]

The evidence supporting an Ottoman period forgery is found in an incident mentioned by the Italian historian G. Golubovich[97] in the seventeenth century about the struggle between Greeks and Catholics for control of the holy places. It presents a typical case of manipulation of the Assurance of 'Umar. Golubovich notes that the Greek Patriarch Theophanius (1608–44 CE) was assisted by his nephew Gregory, who spent three years in Istanbul forging assurances and pacts attributed to 'Umar, Mu'awiyah, Sultan Muhammad II and Sultan Salim. With the help of a substantial bribe of 40,000 *écus*, Sultan Murad IV (1623–40 CE) issued three decrees in 1634 CE that gave the Greek Orthodox Church precedence over the Latin (Roman Catholic) Church in religious festivals in the Holy Sepulchre basilica. In other words, the Greek Orthodox had won control of the sanctuaries of Islamic Jerusalem.[98] However, in the following year Theophanius and Gregory fell out, and Gregory revealed the forgeries to ambassadors from Istanbul, who were able to get the proclamation revoked and the sanctuaries restored to Roman Catholic control in 1636 CE.[99]

In his forgery, Gregory was also mistaken in assigning the Assurance of 'Umar to the 15th year of the *hijra*, and in saying that Jerusalem surrendered unconditionally and was exempted from paying the *jizyah*, as this would have been unthinkable to 'Umar. The Ottoman authorities rejected this version in 1636, 1690, and 1852 CE.[100]

Why did the Orthodox patriarchate suddenly publish this document in 1953, long after it had been written? I suggest that their motives were the same as those behind its fabrication in the first place. Al-Quda states that the Greek Orthodox Church was trying to gain ascendancy over other Christian churches, in order to put an end to its conflict with the Roman Catholics as to which of the two major denominations should have control over the Holy Sepulchre.[101] El-Awaisi argues that:

> The Greek Orthodox Church in Jerusalem which represented the majority of the Christians in the City, felt in 1953 that it was the right time to issue a new version of 'Umar's Assurance which gave them the upper hand over the other Christian communities in Jerusalem. As Jordan was the first Arab Muslim political regime after four centuries of non-Arab rule, the Orthodox Arabs expected the ruling Hashemite family of Jordan to show sympathy with their position in Jerusalem.[102]

To sum up, the essential authenticity of 'Umar's Assurance of Safety is beyond doubt, and it should be accepted as historically factual. Its key statements are guarantees of security to the Christians of Aelia about their churches and goods, a commitment to exclude Byzantines and thieves, and the imposition of the *jizyah* tax. However, the later date of its appearance, the evident elaborations in the text, the inaccuracy of its dates, and its confusion and repetitions do not allow me to state with certainty that it is the original unembellished text of the Assurance given by 'Umar in 16 AH to the Christians of Aelia. It has become evident that some conditions, in particular the exclusion of Jews from the city, were fabricated later and attributed to 'Umar.

It is likely that the conflict between Christians and Jews was a factor behind the additions to 'Umar's Assurance in al-Tabari's version. Its intention was to establish the superiority of the Christians. The Orthodox patriarchate's version was the outcome of conflict between various Christian denominations over leadership of the churches in Jerusalem, and an attempt to ensure the superiority of the Greek Orthodox Church.

Reaction of the Christians of Aelia to the Conquest

A central question is the attitude of the Christians of Aelia towards the Muslims and the conquest. Did they welcome their new rulers? Jasir concludes that they did not. He doubts the historians who claim that the Christians welcomed the Muslim conqueror, and cites examples of Christians fiercely resisting the Muslim army prior to the conquest of al-Sham, such as at the battle of Mu'ta.[103] I would argue that if they did fight fiercely, this may have been demanded of them by the situation. They were also part of the Byzantine army and were compelled to become involved in military operations. Nevertheless, Jasir goes further, asserting that the Christians of Aelia changed their attitude towards the Muslims when they realized the extent of Muslim power, and that their defeat was inevitable after the battle of al-Yarmuk.[104]

In contrast, Runciman maintains that the Christians in Aelia greatly welcomed the Muslim conqueror, as the Muslims had saved them from the persecution they had endured under the Byzantines.[105] He quotes from the Jacobite patriarch of Antioch, Michael the Syrian, in the days of the Latin kingdoms, who reflected on the situation of his people at the time of the first Muslim conquest:

> The God of vengeance, who alone is the Almighty ... raised from the south the children of Ishmael [the Muslims] to deliver us from the hands of the Romans.[106]

Runciman adds that the Greek Orthodox community:

> Finding themselves spared the persecution that they have feared and paying taxes that, in spite of the *jizyah* demanded from the Christians, were far lower than in the Byzantine times, showed small inclination to question their destiny.[107]

Al-Azdi says that one of the signs of welcome from the Christians was when the Muslim army reached the Jordan valley and Abu 'Ubaydah pitched camp at Fahl, whereupon the Christian inhabitants of the area wrote to the Muslims, saying:

> O Muslims, we prefer you to the Byzantines, though they are of our own faith, because you keep faith with us and are more merciful to us and refrain from doing us injustice and your rule over us is better than theirs, for they have robbed us of our goods and our homes.[108]

Caetani took the view that the fear of religious compulsion by the Emperor Herculius, coupled with a strong aversion to Byzantium, made the promise of Muslim tolerance appear more attractive than the connection with the Byzantine empire and a Christian government. He went further, saying that after the initial terror caused by the arrival of an invading army, a profound turnaround took place in favour of the Muslim conquerors.[109] Runciman comments on the lack of tolerance of the Byzantine Christian emperors, who wanted to impose their own doctrine on other Christians and use religion as a unifying factor to extend government control.[110] Armstrong agrees, concluding that it was not surprising that the Nestorian and Monophysite Christians welcomed the Muslims and found Islam preferable to Byzantine rule.[111]

Sahas maintains that the theological stance of the patriarch, who believed in the Chalcedonian principle of the dual nature of Christ (both God and man), versus the Byzantine emperor who believed in the unity of Christ, was the explanation for the surrender of Aelia to the Muslims.[112] Hitti takes a different approach, claiming that the Christians of al-Sham in general, and Aelia in particular, saw Islam as a new Christian sect and not as a religion. The controversy among Christians towards Islam was therefore based on rivalry rather than on a clash of fundamental principles.[113] For this reason, Butler quoted Ibn al-'Ibri when he was describing the extent of intra-Christian disagreement and the ensuing Christian optimism towards the Muslim armies:

When our people complained to Heraclius, he gave no answers. Therefore the God of vengeance delivered us out of the hands of the Romans by means of the Arabs. Then although our churches were not restored to us, since under Arab rule each Christian community retained its actual possessions, still it profited us not a little to be saved from the cruelty of the Romans and their bitter hatred against us.[114]

Butler comments how melancholy it was to read that the welcome by Christians of Muslim rule was seen as providential and a deliverance from the rule of fellow Christians. He adds that this in itself shows how impossible the emperor's scheme was for church union, and that it contributed to his downfall.[115]

Runciman discusses how, after the first Muslim conquest, Christians, Zoroastrians and Jews all became *dhimmis* under Muslim rule. They were allowed freedom of religion and worship in return for paying *jizyah*. He adds that each denomination or sect was treated as a 'semi-autonomous community' in Islamic Jerusalem, with the religious leader of each being responsible for the group's good behaviour under the caliphate.[116] Armstrong goes further, contending that the Muslims established a system that enabled Jews, Christians and Muslims to live together in the city for the first time.[117] She says this was a result of the inclusive vision developed by the Muslim rulers of [Islamic] Jerusalem, a vision that did not deny the presence and devotion of other religions, but respected their rights and celebrated plurality and coexistence.[118] On the same lines, El-Awaisi argues that:

The Muslims liberated the Christians from the Byzantine occupiers of the city, rid the Jews from oppression at the hand of the Byzantines and restored their presence in the city.[119]

In the words of Azzam Tamimi, the Muslim conquest of Aelia

put an end to centuries of instability, religious persecution and colonial rule once by the Egyptians, another time by the Greeks, a third by the Persians, and a fourth by the Romans.[120]

Among other commentators, Karlson agrees that the Christians welcomed the Muslims. He says that the Christians favoured living under the rule of their 'cousins', with whom they shared the same language, customs, etc., rather than living under the authority of the Greek, Romans or Persians.[121] Al-Hamarnah argues that the Christians, especially the Arab Christians, aided the Muslims in the war, seeing them as rescuers from Byzantine oppression. He claims that the Jocobite movement, which had been very active against the injustices of Byzantine rule, suddenly became quiescent. Al-Hamarnah attributes this to the Muslim conquest, and says that Muslim rule brought peace and tranquillity to the eastern Christians, who for a long time had been under persecution from the state and a high tax burden.[122]

Hourani agrees that the Christians welcomed the Muslim conquerors, but for different reasons. He claims that for most of the Christian population it did not matter much whether they were ruled by Persians, Greeks or Muslims, provided that they were secure, lived peacefully and were taxed at a reasonable level. He goes on to say that for some, the replacement of Greeks and Persians by Muslims even offered advantages. This was because those who opposed Byzantine rule for theological reasons might find it easier to live under the Muslims, who were mostly Arabs like them.[123] Shams al-Din and Fletcher believe that the Muslims could be seen as saviours to the persecuted Monophysite Christians of al-Sham.[124] Tibawi agrees, and adds that the Christians who benefited from Islamic tolerance welcomed the Muslims as heaven-sent.[125]

I am inclined to believe that the Christians in al-Sham in general, and Aelia in particular, welcomed the Muslims, especially when they experienced favourable treatment from them. Al-Baladhuri reported that the Christians preferred the Muslims to the Byzantines because of their tolerant attitude, and that they were prepared to help them against the Byzantines.[126] Furthermore, al-Baladhuri says that the Muslim armies were unable to provide full protection to some cities in al-Sham and had to withdraw after realizing that the Byzantines were preparing to attack. Because of their inability to provide protection, the Muslims returned the *jizyah* they had collected to the *dhimmis*. I would argue that historical, cultural and ethnic affiliations played a substantial role in the Christian acceptance of their Muslim conquerors, since all were Arabs.

In 'Umar's Assurance of Safety the Muslim treatment of Christians was based on respect and security, and laid the foundation for future policy. Any other behaviour would violate the fundamental understanding between the two faiths. The Assurance's main points are: personal and financial security, freedom of belief and worship, the right to be protected and defended by the Muslim state, and freedom of movement.[127] Indeed, 'Umar's Assurance is a reference text for relations between Islam and Christianity, and shows how positively 'Umar viewed this.

As El-Awaisi says, 'Umar's Assurance significantly contrasts with the destruction, killing, and displacement that had characterized the region's history until then.[128] He describes the Assurance as the jewel of the first Muslim conquest of Islamic Jerusalem, and the beacon for developing Islamic Jerusalem's unique and creative vision.[129] The Assurance is regarded as a major turning point in historical and juristic terms. According to Hamami, it defined the relationship between Islam and Christianity and laid the foundations of respect not only in the era of Muslim expansion, but for later centuries and, by inference, for the future.[130]

'Umar and the church of the Holy Sepulchre

One of the guarantees in 'Umar's Assurance was that Christian churches would not be converted into dwellings or destroyed, and that there would be no compulsion in regard to religious rights. Among the events that demonstrated his respect for places of worship belonging to other religions was his refusal to pray in the church of the Holy Sepulchre.

According to Eutychius, an early historian who recorded the event, as soon as the gate of Aelia was opened, 'Umar entered with his companions and was escorted around the city by the Greek Orthodox patriarch. They then went and sat in the atrium of the church of the Holy Sepulchre. When the time for Muslim prayer came, 'Umar told Patriarch Sophronious, 'I wish to pray'. The patriarch replied, 'Amir of the faithful, pray in the place where you are'. 'Umar replied: 'I shall not pray here'. Therefore the patriarch led him to the church. But 'Umar told him, 'I shall not pray here either', and he went out onto the stairway before the door of the church of St Constantine, in the east. He prayed alone on the stairway. Then, having sat down, he told Patriarch Sophronious, 'Do you know, O Patriarch, why I did not pray inside the church?' 'Prince of the faithful,' said the patriarch. 'I do not know why.' 'Umar replied, 'If I had prayed inside the church, it would have been lost by you and would have slipped from your power; for after my death the Muslims would take it away from you, together saying, "Umar prayed here'. But give me a sheet of paper so that I may write you a decree. And 'Umar made a decree in these terms: 'The Muslims shall not pray on the stairs, unless it be one person at a time. But they shall not meet there for the public prayer announced by the prayer call.'[131] Having written this decree, he gave it to the patriarch.

Clearly, if 'Umar had prayed in the church, the Muslims might later have used that as an excuse to build a mosque there to commemorate the first Muslim prayer in Islamic Jerusalem. Sahas commented that Sophronious, himself a devout man, understood the need for 'Umar to pray, and also knew that a Muslim could pray anywhere and it did not have to be in a mosque.[132] Therefore he offered 'Umar the opportunity of praying inside the church.

This event indicates the extent of understanding and tolerance that 'Umar possessed. He had a firm grasp of the Qur'anic injunction, 'there is no compulsion in religion', and of the rights of Christians to their places of worship. It is important to note that although this event is not documented in early Muslim historical or juristic literature, it is mentioned in some later Muslim historical texts, such as al-'Arif.[133] Its authenticity cannot be disregarded altogether because 'Umar was known for such actions. Al-Kilani, a Jordanian scholar, quoting Balmer and Bezanit on 'Umar's refusal to pray in the church, says:

> This noble action by 'Umar to prevent this church being taken by Muslim calls forth our admirations for this man. Despite the civilization we have reached in the 19th century, we will never imagine the nobility and the wonderful behaviour Muslims had when they ruled [Islamic] Jerusalem.[134]

However, there are some, for example Runciman, who point out that 'Umar's reason for not praying inside the church became a reality when Muslims built a mosque, called 'Umar's mosque', on the outer steps of the church.[135] But it seems he did not visit the location, because the mosque is several metres away from the church and a public path separates the two. According to Yusuf, the mosque is southwest of the church at approximately 150 metres distance.[136] It was therefore not built on the church steps as Runciman claimed.

Another event that shaped relations between Muslims and Christians in Islamic Jerusalem was the handing over of the keys of the Holy Sepulchre church by Patriarch Sophronious to Caliph 'Umar. This is said to have taken place when 'Umar visited the church and refused to pray inside it. Father Armando Pierucci states that the reason the Muslims were entrusted with the keys of the Holy Sepulchre was because of the animosity among the different Christian denominations. The various Christian groups who used the church did not trust one another enough to let them in when it was their turn.[137] By handing over the keys, it seems that Sophronious had guaranteed the safety of the Holy Sepulchre church and protected it from future dispute among the Christians about the right to control it. The history of Aelia had been notoriously bloody and destructive; the city had experienced many occupations and invasions, and each time the invaders had brought destruction and war rather than prosperity and peace. The situation was now different, because the Muslims had conquered the city without shedding blood.

As soon as 'Umar received the keys, he passed them to one of his companions, 'Abd Allah Ibn Nusaibah, who had accompanied him in the city's surrender. As al-'Arif says, the Nusaibah family, who inherited the keys, are one of the best-known Arab families in Jerusalem to this day.[138] The keys remained in their trust, except during the Crusader period of approximately 90 years. The keys were returned to the Nusaibah family immediately after Salah al-Din's liberation of the city.[139]

This incident illustrates a very important point: the Christians put their trust in the Muslim caliph concerning the holiest place in Christianity. It seems that the reason for this was their understanding that the Muslims respected all places of worship. I am inclined to support the authenticity of this narration on the basis that the Nusaibah family has kept the keys,[140] with no objection from the Christians in Islamic Jerusalem or elsewhere, throughout this long period of time.

The market and Abu 'Ubayd's peace treaty
In his book *al-Amwal*, Abu 'Ubayd reported an agreement between 'Umar and the Christians of Aelia that took place after negotiations between the city's residents and one of 'Umar's commanders, Khalid Ibn Thabit al-Fahmi. One of its terms was that everything within the city walls should remain in the hands of the Christians as long as they paid the *jizyah*, but that the area outside the walls would be taken over by the Muslims.[141] This account has not been supported by any of the early Muslim historians, including al-Waqidi, al-Ya'qubi, al-Tabari, al-Murajja, al-Azdi, Ibn al-A'them and others, and I doubt its authenticity for several reasons.

First, the name Khalid Ibn Thabit al-Fahmi was not known before this narration and did not appear in any other early Muslim historical literature. Second, why did 'Umar send an unknown man to negotiate with the people of Aelia when the city had been under Muslim siege for some time, and other well-known associates of his were there? Third, according to Ibn al-Murajja, after 'Umar entered Aelia he went to view the marketplace. He saw two markets, one in the north and the other in the south. When he enquired to whom they belonged, the answer was the Christians. He then said: 'If the market in the north and south belongs to Christians, then the middle [one] belongs to us [Muslims]'.[142]

The fundamental terms of 'Umar's Assurance prevented Muslims from interfering in the Christian way of life or with their property in the city, so why would he want to establish a market in the middle of the city, especially within a few days of concluding a peace agreement? Normally a city market is located inside the city, at its centre, and the Assurance had clearly stated that what was 'inside the walls was to be for Christians'. If the market were outside the walls, then 'Umar had no need to ask about its owners, as it would have no longer belonged to the Christians. The area around the city was so large that 'Umar could have established a Muslim market anywhere. It seems that Abu 'Ubayd's account is invalid.

Appointing a New Patriarch

The freedom of religion that was clearly spelled out in 'Umar's Assurance is an essential pillar in the treatment of non-Muslims. Goitein points out that the patriarchal seat in Aelia was vacant for some time after the death of Sophronious in 638 CE. He claims that the Muslim conquest threw the Christian community of Aelia into complete disarray and it remained a flock without a shepherd.[143] He notes that after Sophronius's death no new patriarch was appointed until 706 CE,[144] and appears to suggest that the reason was Muslim interference in Christian religious matters. I disagree, on grounds that it could indicate the opposite – that the Muslim government could well have been complying with the freedom of religion guarantee, and also because other reasons have been suggested for the vacancy.

Jasir, whose book contains a list of the names and duration of every patriarch in Aelia from 451–1106 CE, confirms the vacancy of the patriarchal seat in Islamic Jerusalem for almost seventy years, until John V was enthroned in 706 CE.[145] Why was a new patriarch not appointed for such a long period? Under 'Umar's Assurance, the Muslims were forbidden to interfere in the religious affairs of Christians in the city. The right to appoint patriarchs belonged only to the Christians. Did the Muslims breach the terms of the Assurance? I suggest that the long vacancy could be evidence not of Muslim interference, but of non-interference, even though the post was politically important to the Muslim state. It is also certain that any interference by Muslims forcing the Christians to appoint a new patriarch would have been recorded, and this is not the case.

'Athaminah argues that the reason for this long vacancy was the ongoing religious dispute between the Christians of Islamic Jerusalem, the majority of whom were Monophysites, and the Byzantine emperor in Constantinople (outlined above).[146] After the Muslim conquest, the Christians tried to eliminate the influence of the Byzantines after expelling them from the city. It seems that each group firmly stood its ground. 'Athaminah says that when this theological problem was resolved, a new patriarch was appointed. He concluded that the Muslims did not hinder the filling of this post.[147]

Hamilton attributes the long vacancy in the patriarchate to another conflict – the ongoing war between the Muslims and the Byzantine empire.[148] This so preoccupied Byzantium's religious and political leaders that local matters were overlooked, even in [Islamic] Jerusalem. During this period the church of the Holy Sepulchre was supervised by a number of priests whose authority was limited, since they represented the patriarchate and not the patriarch himself.[149]

Contrary to Goitein, I would like to argue that when 'Umar conquered Aelia, the status of the Christians underwent an immediate change, and rights were granted in their favour. One consequence of the Muslim conquest was that the non-Chalcedonian churches (those who did not accept Christ's dual nature and were therefore opposed to the Orthodox and Roman Catholic beliefs) were able to establish themselves in Islamic

Jerusalem on terms of parity with the Orthodox Church. The Armenians appointed a bishop there in 650 CE, and the presence of a Jacobite (Syrian Monophysite) bishop was attested from 793 CE.[150]

Karlson argues that despite the fact that Islam arose at a time marked by mercilessness and intolerance, the Muslims did not try to wipe out the followers of other religions, as the Crusaders did later. He concludes that the presence of Christians in the area up to this day is evidence of Islamic tolerance.[151]

Finally, Christian pilgrimage to the holy places in Islamic Jerusalem was not interrupted as a result of the conquest. Tibawi says that the flow of Christian pilgrims from the days of St Helena (250–330 CE) continued when Aelia fell under Muslim rule[152] 'Athaminah agrees, adding that the pilgrims were not hindered. Nevertheless, their number decreased as a result of hostile relations between the Muslims and the Byzantine empire.[153] Such a drop in number would be normal, as pilgrims would be nervous of travelling in an atmosphere of war. Jasir quotes Niqula Ziyadah, a Christian historian, as saying:

> The liberation of Jerusalem by the Muslims did not stop the Christian pilgrims from visiting the Holy places in Jerusalem. They encouraged them to come and visit.[154]

'Athaminah goes further, asserting that the building and renovating of churches and the monasteries did not cease under Muslim rule.[155] Jasir quotes Father Yusuf al-Shammas al-Mukhallisi, a Lebanese Christian, who commented on the Muslim treatment of Christians at the time of the first Muslim conquest:

> Except in paying the *jizyah*, the Muslim conquerors have not interfered with anything; they kept everything as it was before. The new situation was that the Muslims gave Christian sects independence with great privileges to their heads and religious leaders. Therefore, it was natural that the Jacobites were closer to the Caliphs than the Malikanis,

as the Jacobites were far from any reminder of the Byzantines. This tolerance continued until the end of the seventh century.[156]

Some historians, such as Ibn al-Murajja, report that when 'Umar gave his Assurance to the Christians of Islamic Jerusalem, he took in return the Pact of 'Umar,[157] an agreement in which the Christians agreed to a number of restrictions. As discussed in chapter 2, these undertakings related to religious practices (not displaying Christian crosses, not ringing church bells loudly), public behaviour (not showing lights on the roads, not wearing Muslim-style clothing) and showing generally subservient behaviour to Muslims (such as giving up seats to them).

Al-'Arif, in his book *al-Mufassal fi Tarikh al-Quds* (A Detailed History of al-Quds), refers to Mujir al-Din al-Hanbali's confirmation of this report. However, a close reading of al-Hanbali's text reveals no such mention at all, and al-'Arif gives no reference or page number when he quotes al-Hanbali.[158] The document that al-'Arif cites begins as follows:

> In the name of God, the merciful Benefactor! This is a letter addressed by the Christians of Aelia, to the servant of God 'Umar Ibn al-Khattab, Commander of the Faithful. When you came to this country, we asked you for safekeeping for us, our offspring, our goods and our companions in religion. And we made in your presence the following pledge ...[159]

The claim that 'Umar took a pact from the Christians of Islamic Jerusalem is very worrying, especially when neither early Muslim and non-Muslim historians, nor Muslim jurists, say anything about it, even though they discuss 'Umar's Assurance of Safety extensively. Although there are different versions of 'Umar's Assurance, the immense difference between its overall tolerance and the harsh stipulations of the so-called Pact of 'Umar is very clear. In fact, the two documents contradict each other. It seems likely that those who allege that 'Umar took a pact from the

Christians of Aelia in return for his Assurance built their assumption on the importance of Islamic Jerusalem to the Muslims, and the need to control the Christians through harsh regulations in order to limit their authority in their holy places and thus in the city.

Conclusion

When 'Umar Ibn Khattab conquered the region, Islamic Jerusalem held great significance for the Muslims, not only as the site of the Night Journey and Ascent of the Prophet Muhammad, but as the city of earlier prophets from David *(Dawud)* to Jesus *(Issa)*. Yet 'Umar allowed the existing Christian population to remain, to keep their churches and to worship freely despite his disagreement with their religion. He valued observance of the Islamic requirement of just treatment of the People of the Book more highly than establishing 'Islamization' in the newly conquered territory.

Considering the holy nature of Islamic Jerusalem, the Muslims were especially keen to avoid a battle, and the city's Christian defenders soon realized that they did not stand a chance against the Muslim armies. This resulted in a peaceful transfer of the city to the Muslims. 'Umar set out his historic Assurance of Safety, which was, in effect, the first international guarantee of the protection of religious freedom. It was an outstanding example of the tolerance of Muslims in administering the countries in which they lived alongside the followers of other religions.

'Umar was a magnanimous leader. He ensured that the church of the Holy Sepulchre was safeguarded for Christian worship, and despite the subsequent influx of Muslims from Madinah, the city retained a largely Christian character. Finally, the assurance issued by 'Umar provided a lasting framework for dignified coexistence between Christians and Muslims.

4

SALAH AL-DIN'S TREATMENT OF CHRISTIANS

As we have seen, the first Muslim conquest of Islamic Jerusalem in 16AH/ 637 CE was a landmark that shaped relations between the people of diverse faiths who lived in the region.[1] However, just over 450 years later Islamic Jerusalem fell to the Crusader army, followed by great slaughter and the banishment of much of the surviving population. Within a few decades, Salah al-Din had risen to power in Egypt and began preparations to reconquer the holy city. This chapter discusses Salah al-Din's background and political emergence; his treatment of the Christians under his rule in Egypt and whether this was connected to the occupation of Islamic Jerusalem by Christian Crusaders; his attempts to unite Egypt and al-Sham and his perception of Islamic Jerusalem.

Some historians maintain that the reason for the launching of the first Crusade and a war against Muslims was to rescue Christians in the holy city from Muslim persecution. This should be subject to a critical analysis of the situation in Islamic Jerusalem immediately before the Crusades, as well as a consideration of other possible reasons.

Reasons for the Crusades

Pope Urban II (d. 1099 CE) repeatedly issued calls to the Christians in Western Europe to go to Jerusalem and rescue the Christian holy places and the tomb of Jesus from the hands of the Muslims. His efforts bore fruit on 27 *Dhu al-Qi'dah*, 488 AH/ 27 November 1095 CE,[2] when he spoke to a massive crowd near Clermont in France. The pope's sermon, as Housley says, was one of the most important ever preached, because the first Crusade would not have occurred without it.[3] This speech has been reported in six different versions.[4] Despite clear differences in the text, all agree that he called for the liberation of Jerusalem from the Muslims and for the recovery of former Byzantine territories.

The speech also contained a large number of accusations against Muslims and Islam. For example, that Muslims had circumcised the Christians,[5] destroyed churches, appropriated church buildings for Muslim rites, or turned them into sheepfolds and cattle stalls.[6] In addition, it was alleged that priests (Christian) and Levites (Jewish priests) had been slain in the sanctuaries, and Christian virgins had been forced to choose between prostitution and death by torture.[7] These accusations have little basis in fact and are not confirmed either in Muslim or non-Muslim histories. The actual situation of the Christians in Islamic Jerusalem before the Crusades (discussed below) refutes the pope's allegations.

As a result of the pope's clarion call, thousands of European Christians raised the banner of the Crusades and headed east, the cross sewn on their garments as a symbol of their religious campaign. As they crossed Europe and northern al-Sham, they killed many Muslims and Jews. They were forced to rest at some stations, and established a few local enclaves such as al-Ruha (Urfa) and Antakya (Antioch). This large Crusader army reached the walls of Islamic Jerusalem in 492 AH/7 June 1099 CE, and laid siege to the city for nearly forty days. The siege was tightened until the city finally fell into their hands, whereupon they massacred most of its Muslims and Jews.

There is disagreement between Muslim and non-Muslim historians as to the number of Muslims massacred by the Crusaders. Ibn al-Athir, for example, states that it was nearly seventy thousand.[8] Crusader chroniclers consider this figure too high and estimate it to be no more than twenty thousand.[9] There are a number of Christian chronicles and eyewitness accounts to these massacres, in addition to some Muslim testimonies of the savagery perpetrated by the Crusaders. However, in establishing the context for these events, it is important to return to the speech delivered by Pope Urban II, its motives and consequences.

William of Tyre, an early historian, recounts that a hermit by the name of Peter had visited Islamic Jerusalem a few years before the Crusades and met Simeon, the patriarch of Jerusalem.[10] The patriarch told the hermit that the Christians in the city were being persecuted and prevented from freely practising their religion. He asked him to convey this message to Europe. Peter promised to pass it on to the pope and the kings of Europe and to request that they send troops to liberate Jerusalem from Muslim rule. Peter fulfilled his promise, taking the message to Urban II, who immediately commenced a journey around Europe calling for a crusade to liberate Jerusalem and return it to Christian hands. The pontiff's efforts bore fruit at Clermont, where his long and impassioned speech expressed considerable malevolence towards Muslims. He called on the Christians of the west to take up arms, and promised complete forgiveness of sins to whoever would do so.[11]

In this speech the pope managed to unite the hearts of Europeans, who at that time were engaged in numerous internal conflicts, and inspired many of them to march shoulder to shoulder to the Holy Land. Excerpts of his address are reported by William of Tyre:

> The cradle of our faith, the native land of our Lord, and the mother of salvation, is now forcibly held by a people without God, the son of the Egyptian handmaiden. Upon the captive sons of the free woman he imposes desperate conditions under which he himself, the relations being reversed, should by right have served ... For many years past, the wicked race of Saracens, followers of unclean superstitions have oppressed with tyrannical violence the holy places where the feet of our Lord rested. The faithful

are made subject and condemned to bondage. Dogs have entered into the holy places, the sanctuary has been profaned, the people, worshippers of God, have been humbled. The chosen race is now enduring undeserved tribulations, the royal priesthood slaves in mud and bricks. The city of God, the chief over provinces, has been rendered tributary. Whose soul is not softened, whose heart does not melt, as these indignities recur to his mind? Who, dearest brethren, can listen to this with dry eyes?

The city of the King of all Kings, which transmitted to others the precepts of an inviolable faith, is forced against her will to be subject to the superstitions of the Gentiles. The church of the Holy Resurrection, the last resting place of the sleeping Lord, endures their rule and is desecrated by the filth of those who have no part in the resurrection, but are destined to burn forever, as straw for everlasting flames. The revered places, consecrated to divine mysteries, places which received the Lord in the flesh as a guest, which saw His signs and felt His benefits, and, in full faith, showed forth in themselves the proofs of all this, have been made sheepfolds and stables for cattle. That most excellent people whom the Lord of Hosts blessed, groans aloud, exhausted beneath the burden of forced services and sordid payments. Its sons, precious pledges of Mother Church, are seized and carried off; they are compelled to serve the uncleanness of the Gentiles, to deny the name of the living God, and to blaspheme with sacrilegious lips. If they shrink back in horror from the impious commands of the infidels, they are slain by the sword like beasts of sacrifice, and thus become companions of the holy martyrs. To the eye of sacrilege, there is no distinction of place and no respect for persons. Priests and Levites are slain in the sanctuaries; virgins are forced to choose between prostitution and death by torture; nor do matrons reap any advantage from their more mature years.[12]

This was not the first time that Urban II had called for unity among warring Christians, but it was probably the most effective. Describing the cruelties inflicted by Muslims on Christian pilgrims trying to visit Islamic Jerusalem and the defeats suffered by the Byzantine Christians, he called on all of western Christendom to rescue their eastern brethren: 'They should leave off slaying each other and fight instead a righteous war, doing the work of God, and God will lead them. For those that died in battle there will be absolution and the remission of sins.'[13] As Runciman put it: 'Here they were poor and unhappy; there they will be joyful and prosperous and true friends of God.'[14]

The response was overwhelming. The pope's speech was interrupted by cries of 'Deus lo volt' (God wills it). Hundreds flocked to him begging permission to go on the holy expedition. Soon tens of thousands of knights and commoners headed for the Holy Land. Across Europe, preachers called on the faithful to wear the cross on their clothes until they had succeeded in their quest.[15]

The primary reason for the pope's call was the persecution of Christians in Jerusalem. He also requested the Christian west to assist their brothers-in-faith in the Byzantine empire, whose battles with the Seljuks (who had begun an assault on Byzantine-ruled Central Asia after unifying the Muslim Turks in the region) had resulted in the loss of a huge area of Byzantine lands, such as Armenia. There were, of course, mercenaries from Western Europe in the Byzantine army, but they were individuals making a living.[16] But did the Byzantine emperor formally ask the pope to help by sending thousands of knights? None of the six versions of the pope's speech mentions any such appeal. Magdalino suggests that:

> The Latins did not want to admit the 'wretched emperor' had anything but a negative part in their heroic, godly enterprise, and the Byzantines were keen to portray this enterprise as an unsolicited intrusion on imperial space and a masterpiece of imperial damage limitation.[17]

My personal view is that the Byzantine emperor did not ask for a Crusader campaign. The description by Anna Comnena, daughter of Emperor Alexius Comnena, of her father's reaction to the Crusaders' arrival undermines such a claim:

> Before he [Alexius] had enjoyed even a short rest, he heard a report of the approach of innumerable Frankish armies. Now he dreaded their arrival for he knew their irresistible manner of attack, their unstable and mobile character and all the peculiar natural and concomitant characteristics which the Frank retains throughout; and he also knew that they were always agape for money, and seemed to disregard their truces readily for any reason that cropped up. For he had always heard this reported of them, and found it very true. However, he did not lose heart, but prepared himself in every way so that, when the occasion called, he would be ready for battle.[18]

The emperor was obviously less than happy when he learned of the imminent arrival of the Crusaders, and it seems clear that he did not request help from the pope or the Crusader army. On the contrary, the Crusader conquests greatly complicated his attempts to recover lost territory in the east,[19] and ultimately one consequence of the Crusades was a fatal weakening of the Byzantine empire.[20]

In fact, the pope had given other reasons for his call to take up arms and head to the Holy Land:

> This land in which you inhabit shut in on all sides by the sea and surrounded by the mountain peaks, is too narrow for your large population; nor does it bound in wealth; and it furnishes scarcely food enough for its cultivators. Hence it is that you murder one another, that you wage war and that you frequently perish by mutual wounding. Let therefore hatred depart from among you, let your quarrels end, let war cease, and let all dissensions and controversies slumber. Enter the road of the Holy Sepulchre ...[21]

Thus the pope states that France, and even Europe, was limited geographically and in resources, but its population was getting bigger and needed more space. He was also anxious to stop the continual wars between the various kingdoms and principalities by offering them reasonable grounds to forego hostilities. More specifically, he wanted to unite them in what was regarded as a noble enterprise: the liberation of Jerusalem and its holy places from their Muslim enemies. But his desire to stop internecine strife seems to have been a strong motive for the Crusades. As we will see, the condition of the Christians in Islamic Jerusalem was not so desperate that it required thousands of their western brethren to rescue them.

By giving religious sanction to the Crusade, the pope gained a number of benefits. First, the exodus of a large and dedicated army could end the debilitating in-fighting in Europe. Second, occupying the Holy Land would bring it under the control of western Christianity. Third, the success of such an action would enhance the position of the pope and the Roman Catholic Church at a time when he and his priests were under persecution from the German emperor, Henry IV (d. 1106 CE). William of Tyre records how Pope Gregory VII and the priests were persecuted severely by the Emperor Henry because of political and religious conflict between the two parties.[22]

The Situation of Christians in Islamic Jerusalem

Since the first Muslim conquest of Islamic Jerusalem, Christians had been allowed to practice their religion without hindrance and their places of worship were all over the city as well as the region.[23] They enjoyed civil rights and were allowed to move around the Muslim state as freely as Muslims. They also had the right to own property – shops, houses and land – and were allowed to communicate with co-religionists in other Christian countries.[24] Ra'if Mikha'il al-Sa'ati, a local Arab priest, commented on the situation of Christians in Islamic Jerusalem prior to the Crusades, and is quoted by Yusuf:

The fact of the matter is that it is incumbent on us to state that Christian Palestinians lived with their Muslim brethren in peace and harmony. The caliphs would assign high-level positions in government to them. As for the persecution that was meted out to them from time to time throughout history, this was a result of the extreme measures of some rulers, from whom even the Muslims themselves were not safe. If a certain ruler were a tyrant then it would be a great injustice to consider all rulers as such.[25]

Michael Foss, a historian of the Crusades, explains that for more than 350 years, from the time of Caliph 'Umar's Assurance to Patriarch Sophronious in 16 AH/637 CE until 399 AH/1009 CE, when the Fatimid Caliph al-Hakim began to attack Christian and Jews in Egypt, Islamic Jerusalem was welcoming to the west. He even says that the journey from the west to Islamic Jerusalem was no more dangerous than travelling from Paris to Rome at that time.[26] Moreover, the doors were open for Christians to enter government employment without discrimination, except during those periods when Islamic Jerusalem was under hard-line rulers such as al-Hakim or al-Mutawakkil. The right to visit the holy city was granted to Christians, who came on pilgrimage from many countries.[27]

Al-Maqdisi (d. 390AH/1000 CE), a geographer who lived in Islamic Jerusalem all his life, states that Christians and Jews were not under persecution prior to the Crusades, and at times were even the dominant group:

> Everywhere the Christians and the Jews have the upper hand, and these same Christians are rude and without manners in public places ...[28]

Nearly fifty years before the Crusades, the Persian traveller, poet and philosopher Nasir-i-Khusraw visited Islamic Jerusalem in 541 AH/1047 CE and described the religious life of the Christians:

I saw seated in this church [the Holy Sepulchre] great numbers of priests and monks, reading the Scriptures and saying prayers, both by day and by night.[29]

Al-'Arif quotes Guy Le Strange, who said:

We should admit that the Christians were not persecuted and oppressed to the level that the Latin Christians took it as justification to invade the Muslim territory and proclaim the Crusading war.[30]

Finally, Hamilton states that:

The Christians of Jerusalem enjoyed a considerable degree of religious freedom ... they were allowed to hold public processions on great feast days...[31]

From the above accounts it is clear that Christians and Muslims in Islamic Jerusalem lived in a climate of coexistence and suffered much less distress than some in Europe had been led to believe.[32] I conclude that the condition of the local Christians under Muslim rule had not deteriorated to the extent that armed intervention was necessary to liberate them.

The Crusaders in Islamic Jerusalem

The Crusader army approached the walled city in the early days of 492 AH/June 1099 CE. Crusader troops made repeated assaults on the walls and stormed the city successfully the following month (13 *Sha'ban*/15 July). A horrifying massacre followed their entrance into the city. The population was put to the sword, and the Crusaders spent a week massacring Muslims, killing at least 70,000 people. The Jews had taken refuge in their synagogues, where the Crusaders burned them alive. Islamic Jerusalem was emptied of its inhabitants.[33]

There are several accounts of these massacres. William of Tyre says:

It was impossible to look upon the vast numbers of the slain without horror. Everywhere lay bits of human bodies, and the ground was soaked with the blood of the dead. And it was not only the spectacle of the headless bodies and mutilated limbs thrown in all directions that aroused horror in all who saw them. It was still more dreadful to gaze upon the victors themselves, covered in gore from head to foot, a sight that brought terror to everyone they met. It was reported that within the Temple precinct alone 10,000 infidels were killed, in addition to those who lay slain everywhere though the city in the streets and squares, the number of whom was estimated as no less.

Soldiers roamed the streets in search of any wretched survivors who might be hiding from death. When found, these were dragged into public view and slaughtered like sheep. Some of our men formed bands and broke into houses where they laid cruel hands on men, women and children, and whoever else was in the household. The victims were either put to the sword, or thrown from some high place to perish miserably on the stones of the street.

The city was found to be full to overflowing with goods of all kinds. All the soldiers, from the least to the greatest, found an abundance of everything. In the houses were large amounts of gold and silver, valuable stones, and fine clothes. There were stores of grain, wine, oil, and plenty of water, for lack of which the army had suffered so much during the siege. Even our most needy pilgrims and brethren were satisfied with affectionate gifts from the more successful. By the second and third day of the occupation, an excellent public market was established for the sale and exchange of goods. Even the common people had all they needed in abundance. So days passed in joyous celebration, as the pilgrims refreshed themselves with the food and rest they so badly needed.[34]

The extent of the slaughter was quite explicit in Christian sources. The anonymous author of the *Gesta*, who was among the Crusaders who entered the walled city, described events with brutal simplicity:

> Our men killed whom they chose and saved whom they chose. They rushed around the city, seizing gold and silver, horses and mules, plundering every kind of goods from the houses. Then they all came rejoicing and weeping for gladness to worship at the Holy Sepulchre of our Saviour Jesus, and there they fulfilled their vows to Him. Next morning, stealthily they climbed to the roof of the temple and attacked the Saracens sheltering there, both men and women, slashing their heads from their bodies with their swords. Then our leaders ordered that all the Saracen corpses should be thrown outside the gates on account of their dead bodies. The surviving Saracens dragged their fallen comrades out though the gates and piled them in mounds as big as houses. No one has ever seen or heard of such slaughter of pagans. They were burned on pyres like pyramids, and none save God knows how many there were.[35]

This sanctimonious slaughter, and the conjunction between plunder and righteousness, massacre and religious jubilation, was noted by Fulcher of Chartres, who was not present at the fall of the city but received reports of it soon afterwards:

> After this great slaughter, our men went into the houses of the citizens and seized whatever they found. The first to enter the house, whatever his position or rank, had the right to plunder it, and all the Franks acknowledged this. That house or even the palace was his, and he could take whatever he wanted. In this way many poor people became wealthy. They, all the clergy and laity, went to the Sepulchre of the Lord and His most glorious Temple, singing a new canticle to the Lord in voices of exaltation, making offerings and supplications, and joyously visiting the Holy Places as they had so long desired to do.[36]

Raymond D'Aguilers, a Crusader historian, also describes the massacre:

> Some of the pagans were mercifully beheaded, others pierced by arrows plunged from towers, and yet others, tortured for a long time, were burned to death in searing flames. Piles of heads, hands, and feet lay in the houses and street, and indeed there was a running to and fro of men and knights over the corpses.
> Let me tell you that so far these are few and petty details, but it is another story when we come to the Temple of Solomon, the accustomed place for the chanting rites and services. Shall we relate what took place there? If we told you, you would not believe us. So it is sufficient to relate that in the Temple of Solomon and the portico crusaders rode in blood to the knees and bridles of their horses. In my opinion this was poetic justice that the Temple of Solomon should receive the blood of pagans who blasphemed God there for many years.[37]

The fall of Islamic Jerusalem was widely reported in Muslim and Arab sources. According to Ibn al-Athir, the Crusaders killed more than seventy thousand people in the al-Aqsa mosque, among them a large group of Muslim imams, religious scholars, devout men and ascetics, many of whom had left their homelands to live near the holy place.[38] The Coptic historian, Ibn al-'Ibri, confirmed this number when he stated that the Crusaders spent a week in Islamic Jerusalem killing Muslims, and that in al-Aqsa mosque more than seventy thousand were killed.[39]

Ibn al-Jawzi, in his account, states that Islamic Jerusalem was taken by the Franks on Friday 13 *Sha'ban*, 492 AH /15 July 1099 CE. He says that they killed more than seventy thousand Muslims and took forty-odd silver candelabras from the Dome of the Rock, each worth 360,000 *dirhams*, as well as a silver lamp weighing forty Syrian *ratls*, twenty-odd gold lamps, and innumerable items of clothing and other items.⁴⁰ Another historian, Ibn al-Qalanisi (d. 555 A.H /1160 CE), reports:

> The Franks stormed the town and gained possession of it. A number of the townsfolk fled to the sanctuary and a great host were killed. The Jews assembled in the synagogue, and the Franks burned it over their heads. The sanctuary was surrendered to them on guarantee of safety on 22 *Sha'ban* /14 July of this year, and they destroyed the shrines and the tomb of Prophet Ibrahim [Abraham].⁴¹

A new era began in the history of Islamic Jerusalem, lasting 88 years and bringing many changes.⁴²

The Background of Salah al-Din

Yusuf Ibn Ayyub Salah al-Din, known in western literature as Saladin, was born in 532 AH /1137 CE in the town of Takrit, in modern Iraq.⁴³ He was the grandson of Shadhi, who was originally from the village of Dowain in the far south of Azerbaijan.⁴⁴ According to Yaqut al-Hamawi (d. 626 AH /1229 CE), Dowain was in the region of Aran near Tiflis (Tbilisi), the present capital of Georgia.⁴⁵ The family belonged to the al-Rawadiyya Kurds.⁴⁶ During his youth in Dowain, Shadhi had a very close friend, Mujahid al-Din Bahruz, a white Greek slave.⁴⁷ As a young adult, Bahruz left Dowain for the court of the Seljuk king, 'Ghayyath al-Din Muhammad Ibn Malikshah', in Baghdad. There he found employment as a servant.⁴⁸ Because of his ability he was offered higher positions and was finally elevated to the court staff.

Mujahid al-Din Bahruz did not forget his old friend Shadhi, and summoned him from his village 'to see the success and prestige he had achieved, and to share what God had bestowed upon him'.⁴⁹ While Shadhi and his family – his two sons, Najm al-Din Ayyub (Salah al-Din's father) and Asad al-Din Shirkuh (Salah al-Din's uncle) – were in Baghdad under Bahruz's care, the Seljuk king decided to appoint Bahruz governor of Baghdad.⁵⁰ Some time later the king entrusted Bahruz with the citadel of Takrit. Bahruz then appointed Shadhi to the position of *dazdar* (guardian of the citadel) of Takrit,[51] and Shadhi and his family moved to that city.

A few years later Shadhi died. His position of master of the citadel of Takrit was given to his son, Najm al-Din Ayyub. At the time, 'Imad al-Din Zanki was ruling al-Musil (Mosul) and much of its surrounding region. His attempt to capture Baghdad from Bahruz failed, and he was obliged to retreat, wounded, to al-Musil. He passed by Takrit and was received with courtesy by Najm al-Din Ayyub.[52] Ibn Kathir reports that Zanki, although an enemy of Bahruz, was a good friend of Najm al-Din and spent 15 days in his care until his wounds were healed.[53] Both Abu Shama and Ibn Khalikan say that Najm al-Din Ayyub built ships for Zanki, enabling his followers to cross the river and join him.[54]

Bahruz, was infuriated when news reached him of the collaboration between Najm al Din Ayyub and Zanki, as Bahruz had always been generous to Najm al-Din and had helped him in time of need. In spite of that, he expressed his anger courteously, saying: 'Your father was devoted to me. We were bound together by kindness, and I cannot punish you, but I would like you both to leave Takrit, and find another place to make your living.'[55]

In Ibn Khalikan's account, this event was compounded by the killing of a man in Takrit by Najm al-Din's brother Shirkuh in an argument.[56] Bahruz, already angered by Zanki's escape, was not prepared to overlook Shirkuh's violence. He ordered the family to leave the territory immediately. On the day of their departure Salah al-Din was born, and the family considered this a bad omen.[57] They went to al-Musil and offered their services to Zanki. During their time in al-Musil, Salah al-Din's father, uncle and other family members were appointed to prominent government and military positions under the Zanki dynasty,[58] whose sphere of control extended to Damascus and Aleppo.

Another feature of Salah al-Din's life was that as a child he vigorously studied the Qur'an. This was later followed by long hours of scholarly study. Throughout his life he made strenuous efforts to be a devout Muslim, even when preoccupied with *jihad*.

At the young age of 14 Salah al-Din began to learn the art of fighting, and soon stood out among the troops of Nur al-Din[59] (the son and successor of 'Imad al-Din Zanki), who was based in Damascus. Like his father, Nur al-Din was vying with the Crusader kingdom of Jerusalem, and both were attempting to take over Egypt. In several campaigns to Egypt between 558 and 564 AH (1163–69 CE) Salah al-Din performed impressively, outstripping his peers. He served under his uncle Shirkuh, who was commander-in-chief of the Syrian army. In the third campaign the two men led the Syrian forces to Egypt at the request of Shawar, the powerful *wazir* (prime minister) of the Fatimid Caliph al-'Adid in Cairo, to help Egypt resist the Crusaders. When Shawar was killed, al-'Adid appointed Shirkuh as *wazir* of Egypt – effectively its ruler, as under the weak Fatimids power was in the hands of the *wazir*. Two months later Shirkuh died unexpectedly and was succeeded by Salah al-Din. It was still 564 AH/1169 CE,[60] a significant year for the 32-year-old commander.

Salah al-Din had little regard for al-'Adid, and on the caliph's death in 567 AH/1171 CE he immediately seized power, not as caliph, but in the name of Nur al-Din, who recognized the Abbasid caliphate in Baghdad. Salah al-Din began to reform Egypt and to turn it into a powerhouse, restoring the Sunni school of *fiqh* and becoming the country's unquestioned ruler.[61] After Nur al-Din's sudden death in 569 AH/1174 CE, leaving a 12-year-old son, al-Malik al-Salih Isma'il, Salah al-Din asserted his right to the succession on grounds that al-Salih would not be able to shoulder the burden of kingship or defend the lands against the Crusaders. It was also apparent that the unity Nur al-Din had achieved between the various emirates in al-Sham was in danger of fragmenting.[62]

The following year Salah al-Din proclaimed himself sultan (ruler) of Egypt and al-Sham – those parts of it that he now held. Two months later the Abbasid caliph in Baghdad, al-Mustadi' Bi'amrillah (d. 576 AH/1180 CE) formally confirmed

Salah al-Din as sultan of the combined governments of Egypt, Yemen and al-Sham. The caliph told him not to covet al-Salih's fiefdom of Aleppo and to maintain good relations with the youth.[63] However, al-Salih died in 577 AH/ 1181CE.

Western writers regard Salah al-Din as a remarkable man. For instance, the most impressive feature of Lane-Poole's book is its enthusiastic admiration for the personality of Salah al-Din. 'Gentleness was the dominant note of his character', wrote Lane-Poole:

> We search the contemporary descriptions in vain for the common attributes of Kings. Majesty? It is not mentioned, for the respect he inspired sprang from love, which 'casteth out fear.' State? Far from adopting an imposing mien and punctilious forms, no sovereign was ever more genial and easy of approach. He loved to surround himself with clever talkers, and was himself 'delightful to talk to'. He knew all the traditions of the Arabs, the 'Days' of their ancient heroes, the pedigrees of their famous mares. His sympathy and unaffected interest set every one at his ease, and instead of repressing freedom of conversation; he let the talk flow at such a pace that sometimes a man could not hear his own voice. Old-fashioned courtiers regretted the strict propriety of Nur al-Din levees, when each man sat silent, 'as if a bird were perched on his head,' till he was bidden to speak. At the Saladin court all was eager conversation – a most unkingly buzz. Yet there were limits, which no one dared to transgress in the Sultan's presence. He suffered no unseemly talk, nor was there any flippant irreverence or disrespect of persons permitted. He never used or allowed scurrilous language. He kept his own tongue, even in great provocation, under rigid control, and his pen was disciplined: he was never known to write a bitter word to a Muslim.[64]

Salah al-Din and the Christians in Egypt

The Muslim treatment of Christians during Salah al-Din's reign was quite different from that of Caliph 'Umar Ibn al-Khattab in an earlier century. The political situation was also very different. In the time of 'Umar there was one Muslim state, with a central government in Madinah controlling the whole of the state and its subjects. In Salah al-Din's day there was more than one Muslim government. The caliph in Baghdad represented the Sunnis, but was very weak and had no control over the many rival emirates in al-Sham. Up till the time Salah al-Din took power, the other caliph in Cairo, who was dominated by his *wazir*, represented the Shi'is. The security situation in both caliphates was unstable, and Jerusalem and large tracts of former Muslim land in al-Sham were in the hands of the Crusaders.

Some historians writing at the time reported that Salah al-Din's relations with the Christians in Egypt began uneasily and then deteriorated further. For instance, Sawirus Ibn al-Muqaffa', the Coptic historian, states that the churches in Egypt suffered extreme destruction, particularly after Salah al-Din became *wazir* and at the beginning of his Ayyubid sultanate.[65] He records that all wooden crosses on the tops of basilica domes and churches in Egypt were removed on Salah al-Din's orders. Churches with white exteriors were painted black. The ringing of bells was prohibited throughout the country, and the Christians were not allowed to pray in public. On Palm Sunday (*sha'anin*) the Christians were not allowed to hold their traditional procession in the streets of Egyptian towns and villages, or to carry olive branches and crosses.[66]

Sawirus also says that at the beginning of his reign Salah al-Din promulgated harsh social restrictions on the *dhimmis*, ordering the Christians to wear clothes that distinguished them from the Muslims and waist belts of a different colour, not to ride horses or mules, but only donkeys, and not to drink alcohol in public.[67] Salam, an Egyptian historian, confirms that the Coptic patriarch and priests suffered greatly in the early years of Salah al-Din's rule.[68]

While he was still *wazir*, Salah al-Din ordered the Armenian patriarch of Cairo to close down his court in the al-Zuhri area of the city in 564 AH /1169 CE, and to move to the John the Baptist church in the Zuwayla neighbourhood.[69] Four years later, when Salah al-Din tightened his grip on Armenia, the Armenian patriarch left Cairo of his own accord for Jerusalem.[70] Abu Salih al-Armani (d. 606 AH/ 1209 CE) says the sultan allowed the patriarch to take all the religious books he could carry, as well as the church utensils and some gold *dinars*. The patriarch appointed a priest to stay behind and lead the prayers in the John the Baptist church. Abu Salih adds that Salah al-Din allowed the Armenian Christians to carry out their religious duties freely in spite of their participation in the conspiracy against him[71] (see below).

Salah al-Din's change of attitude
Salah al-Din's harshness towards the Christians did not, however, continue. After about five years, when the situation had settled down and he had developed more confidence in the Christians, he allowed them become clerks in the army and to hold higher positions than before. They were also permitted to ride horses and mules and to wear shoes and garments similar to those of Muslims.[72]

Overall, Salah al-Din displayed tolerance towards the *dhimmis* of Egypt. He gave generously to them and to *dhimmis* in surrounding areas, and allowed them certain benefits. The Coptic patriarch, Marcus Ibn Qunbur, was greatly pleased by the favours bestowed by the sultan on the Copts and their church.[73] Evidence of Salah al-Din's more benign attitude to churches and monasteries is that between 570–75 AH /1174–79 CE, soon after he became sultan, Egypt witnessed a large building and renovation programme of Christian churches.[74] Later in Salah al-Din's reign the Christians were able to celebrate Palm Sunday and other festivals in the atmosphere of greater religious tolerance.[75] Salah al-Din placed great importance on allowing freedom of religious practice in Christian places of worship. When Qadi Shihab al-Din al-Tusi, a Muslim judge, ordered some restrictions on the Christians and closed down two churches in Cairo in 582 AH /1186 CE,[76] the Christians raised the matter with al-Malik al-'Adil, Salah al-Din's brother. Salah al-Din ordered that the churches be opened immediately.

Salah al-Din's tolerance extended to the *dhimmi* peasants. Sawirus mentions that Coptic farmers, like all inhabitants, benefited from the justice and tolerance of Salah al-Din's era. The farmers were grateful that their land was safe from confiscation.[77] Sawirus comments that the religious officials had complete freedom from government interference when collecting the proceeds from farms belonging to the church and from lands endowed to churches and monasteries.[78]

Nor did Salah al-Din intervene in matters of church leadership. For example, when the Coptic patriarchate became vacant in 584 AH /1188 CE on the death of Marcus Ibn Qunbur, the 73rd patriarch of Alexandria, the Coptic community chose Yunus Ibn Abi Ghalib as the 74th patriarch.[79] Salah al-Din did not oppose this appointment and made no attempt to confiscate the great wealth of the new patriarch, which was spent on building churches and paying alms to poor Christians.[80] His attitude was similar to that of 'Umar in Islamic Jerusalem, who took no part in the appointment of a new patriarch in the holy city (see chapter 3).

The variation in Salah al-Din's policy towards the *dhimmis* during his rule was illustrated by Hillenbrand, who argues that the Copts enjoyed mixed fortunes under Salah al-Din and his family. At one point they were dismissed from office because of alleged links with the Crusaders, and their churches were destroyed. However, some Copts were still appointed to high positions. She gives the example of Ibn Sharafi, who was appointed private secretary to Salah al-Din himself. Moreover, al-'Adil, Salah al-Din's brother, appointed the Copt Ibn al-Miqat to head the army bureau *(diwan al-jaish)*. She concludes that the appointment of Christians to such powerful positions in wartime and in an area that was militarily so sensitive speaks for itself.[81]

Another example is from Ibn Jubayr (d. 614 AH /1217 CE), an Andalusian Muslim traveller who visited Egypt during Salah al-Din's reign and passed through several cities and villages, including the city of Akhmim. He says that he saw churches populated by Coptic Christians.[82] Salam regards Ibn Jubayr's report as evidence that Christians enjoyed freedom of religion under Salah al-Din.[83]

Reasons for the harsh policies
The question arises of why Salah al-Din imposed strict restrictions on the *dhimmis*, and whether his treatment of Egypt's Christians bore any relation to the occupation of Jerusalem by the Crusaders. An answer is found in the circumstances in which he became *wazir*. As we have seen, Salah al-Din succeeded his uncle Shirkuh as *wazir* on the latter's untimely death in 564 AH/1169 CE. Within the next three years he consolidated his power base, and on al-'Adid's death he overthrew the Fatimid caliphate and became the country's sole ruler.[84]

Both the Fatimids and some *dhimmis* strongly opposed these events. Salah al-Din therefore faced threats from Fatimid supporters; from the large number of Armenian soldiers who had held positions of authority and had been exempted from the *jizyah* tax,[85] a privilege now denied them; and from Christian and Jewish activists who had played a significant role in the disturbances and plots against his new government.[86] Al-Maqrizi reports that the Armenians had fiercely resisted Salah al-Din's army in 564 AH /1169 CE[87] when it challenged the rebellion by Mu'taman al-Khilafah, one of the powerful civilian controllers of the Fatimid palace in Cairo.[88]

Understandably, Salah al-Din took harsh measures to protect himself and his new regime. His uncle Shirkuh had taken ruthless measures against the Christian and Jewish *dhimmis* of Egypt, forcing the Christians to change the colour of their dress and wear distinctive waist belts, and dismissing *dhimmis* from government departments.[89] Salah al-Din seems to have followed his example.

Abu Shama (d. 665 AH /1283 CE) and Ibn Wasil (d. 679 AH /1297CE) confirm that savage punishments, including death and crucifixion, were meted out to Jewish and Christian participants in the conspiracies against Salah al-Din in 564 and 568/69 AH (1169 and 1173/74 CE). The plotters were also found guilty of a secret connection with the Crusaders, whom they had contacted to ask for help in overthrowing Salah al-Din.[90] Salam, too, reports that Salah al-Din imposed severe restrictions on the *dhimmis* because Christians and Jews had been very active supporters of the Fatimids and had conspired to overthrow Salah al-Din and revive Fatimid rule.[91]

It seems clear that the unstable political and security situation was the reason for the harsh rules and regulations,[92] as it was at the time of the Pact of 'Umar. Salah al-Din's restrictions would, first, compel the Christians to submit to his rule, since they were his subjects, and second, would control them and restrict their freedom. This would make it easier for him to assert his authority, and if the *dhimmis* breached the regulations they would be accountable to him. Some scholars argued that Salah al-Din went further, ordering the Christians to obey the restrictions laid down in the Pact of 'Umar. 'Abd al-Mun'im, an Egyptian historian, concluded that all this was a result of the *dhimmis'* conspiracy against Salah al-Din.[93]

The turning point came when Salah al-Din abandoned these oppressive rules after four to five years. It was not a sign of weakness on his part. The conspiracies had been suppressed and the situation had calmed down. Salah al-Din was now the sole ruler of Egypt, supported by the army that had accompanied his uncle Shirkuh from al-Sham, as well as by many Egyptians who had been opposed to the Fatimid caliphate.

From the historical record it is evident that Salah al-Din's actions against the Christians in Egypt were in no way related to the Crusader occupation of Jerusalem, but were a direct response to the rebellion of local Christians against him. Furthermore, the relationship between the Latin Crusaders and the Egyptian Orthodox Copts was not good. The latter had been banned from the holy city ever since the establishment of the Latin kingdom of Jerusalem, nearly ninety years, because the Crusaders regarded them as heretics and atheists.[94]

The Importance of Islamic Jerusalem to Salah al-Din

Islamic Jerusalem occupied a very distinctive position in the mind of Salah al-Din.[95] There is no doubt that he saw the liberation of the city as a top priority, and between his appointment as *wazir* and his eventual departure to recover Islamic Jerusalem from the Crusaders he spent time consolidating the Muslim armies and uniting Muslim territory, as well as reminding Muslims of the importance of this holy region. In a speech to his fellow Muslims, reported by 'Imad al-Din al-Asfahani (Salah al-Din's secretary), Salah al-Din said:

> If God blesses us by enabling us to drive His enemies out of Islamic Jerusalem, how fortunate and happy we are going to be! For the enemy has controlled Islamic Jerusalem for ninety-one years, during which time God did not accept any deeds from us. At the same time, the zeal of the Muslim rulers to deliver it faded away. Time passed, and so did many generations, while the crusaders succeeded in rooting themselves strongly there ...[96]

Thus, recovering Islamic Jerusalem was Salah al-Din's ultimate target. His biographer, Baha' al-Din Ibn Shaddad, heard Salah al-Din say: 'When God enabled me to gain Egypt, I realised that he willed the conquest of the coast (Syrian coast), because he had put the idea in my mind.'[97] It seems that Salah al-Din considered the recovery of Islamic Jerusalem and the Syrian coast, as well as his rule over Egypt, to be a divine command that he was obliged to fulfil. These two objectives were not new; they were the common ambition of all Muslims, and he had grown up with them. But given his position, Salah al-Din felt more responsible than other Muslims for achieving these goals because he had the power to do so.

After the death of Nur al-Din in Damascus in 569 AH /May 1174 CE, leaving a 12-year-old son with no institutional procedure for succession, the political situation was very dangerous; the Sultanate could not be governed by a young child. A struggle for succession between its most powerful commanders threatened the stability of the region and plunged al-Sham into a civil war that destroyed all that Nur al-Din had achieved. Salah al-Din received many invitations from commanders, religious leaders and Muslim thinkers asking him to come to al-Sham to resolve the situation. 'Imad al-Din al-Asfahani wrote informing him of the situation in al-Sham, the danger that this posed to the Muslim nation, and urging him to intervene to prevent the country being fragmented by power struggles.[98] Five months after the death of Nur al-Din, Salah al-Din set off for al-Sham. According to Ibn Shaddad:

> When Salah al-Din received confirmation of Nur al-Din's death, and as he was aware that his son was a child unable to shoulder the burdens of kingship and incapable of taking on the defence of the lands against God's enemies, he made his preparation to march to Syria, since it was the cornerstone of Muslim territory ... Salah al-Din arrived in Syria demanding that he himself should take on al-Salih's guardianship, direct his affairs and set straight what had gone awry. Salah al-Din reached Damascus, without having renounced allegiance, and entered the city after a peaceful handover on Tuesday, the last day of *Rabi' al-Thani* 570 AH (27 November 1174 CE), and he took over the citadel.[99]

It seems that Salah al-Din was certain that what he did was an essential step towards recovering Islamic Jerusalem. He realized that uniting Muslim ranks and saving Nur al-Din's kingdom would allow the Crusaders further south to be effectively resisted, and would ensure that he would not be attacked from the rear.

The profound significance of Islamic Jerusalem to Salah al-Din was shown after he conquered the city, in the care he took over the sermon to be preached in the al-Aqsa mosque on the first Friday after the city's liberation. He invited the greatest Muslim preachers to submit draft sermons to him. His final decision was determined by the strength and intensity of the ideas he wanted conveyed to Muslims about the significance of the holy city.[100]

Conclusion

Salah al-Din's personality, education and background played a substantial role in his policies towards the Christians in Egypt. In addition to being a military leader, he was a well-educated religious man, and this had a bearing on his dealings with the Christians as *dhimmis*. Initially, Salah al-Din's treatment of the Christians was harsh, because of Christian participation in conspiracies against him and their links with the Crusaders in Islamic Jerusalem in a plot to overthrow him. Even so, there was no religious connection between Salah al-Din's policies against the Christians in Egypt and the Crusader kingdom in Jerusalem. After Salah al-Din had overcome his enemies, he became notably more tolerant to the Egyptian Christians. Before the Crusader occupation the Christians in Islamic Jerusalem were treated as *dhimmis*, but their rights were fully guaranteed. This refutes the claim of Pope Urban II that armed intervention was needed to rescue the Christians of Islamic Jerusalem and save them from massacre.

5

SALAH AL-DIN AND THE CHRISTIANS OF ISLAMIC JERUSALEM

After his success in uniting Muslims under his leadership and in his administrative reforms, Salah al-Din and his army proceeded towards Islamic Jerusalem. This chapter discusses the steps he took in liberating the city and offers a reassessment. It examines the communications between Salah al-Din and the Crusader leaders, his attitude towards the Christians in Islamic Jerusalem – both the indigenous Christians and their holy places and the Crusaders who were in the city before and after its capture; and the peace negotiations between Salah al-Din and Richard I ('the Lion-heart'), king of England.

The Road to Islamic Jerusalem
As the Muslim army marched south from Damascus they won a number of victories over the Crusaders, but the most important and decisive battle was that of Hittin[1] (known in western literature as Hattin, or the Horns of Hattin), on 24 *Rabi' al-Thani* 583 AH /4 July 1187 CE[2] near the Sea of Galilee. Here the Muslim forces heavily defeated a combined Christian army, killing or capturing a huge number of them. Among those taken were Guy of Lusignan, king of the Latin kingdom of Jerusalem; his counsellors; his brother Amaury, the constable of the kingdom; the grand masters of the Knights Templar and the Hospitallers (the Knights of the Order of the Hospital of St

John of Jerusalem); and many knights from these two military-religious orders. The only surviving leaders, who fled to safety through Muslim lines, were Raymond of Tripoli, Reynald of Sidon and Balian of Ibelin (referred to in Arabic sources as Balian Ibn Barzan). These men had enjoyed friendly relations with Salah al-Din and were suspected by the Crusaders of complicity with him.[3] The common soldiers taken at Hittin were sold in the slave market at Damascus.

Salah al-Din camped on the field of battle and ordered the leaders of the captured soldiers to be brought before him. This encounter received wide coverage from Muslim historians, such as Ibn Shaddad,[4] 'Imad al-Din,[5] Abu Shama,[6] Ibn al-'Adim,[7] Abu al-Fida',[8] al-Hanbali[9] and from non-Muslim historians like Runciman, who wrote:

> There Saladin received King Guy and his brother the Constable Amalric, Reynald of Chatillon and his stepson Humphrey of Toron, the Grand Master of the Temple, the aged Marquis of Montferrat, the lords of Jebail and Botrun, and many of the lesser barons of the realm. He greeted them graciously. He seated the King next to him and, seeing his thirst, handed him a goblet of rose water, iced with the snows of Hermon. Guy drank from it and handed it on to Reynald who was at his side. By the laws of Arab hospitality to give food or drink to a captive meant that his life was safe; so, Saladin said quickly to the interpreter: 'Tell the King that he gave the man drink, not I.' He then turned on Reynald whose impious brigandage he could not forgive and reminded him of his crimes, of his treachery, his blasphemy and his greed. When Reynald answered truculently, Saladin himself took a sword and struck off his head. Guy trembled, thinking that his turn would come next. But Saladin reassured him. 'A king does not kill a king,' he said, 'but that man's perfidy and insolence went too far.' He then gave orders that none of the lay barons was to be harmed but that all were to be treated with courtesy and respect during their captivity. But he would

not spare the knights of the military orders, save only the Grand Master of the Temple ...[10]

This established the pattern for Salah al-Din's treatment of the Crusaders – both in his magnanimity towards King Guy and his harshness toward Reynald. Ibn Shaddad justified the latter, saying that Salah al-Din had vowed to kill Prince Reynald if he had him in his power. The reason was that a caravan from Egypt had passed through Reynald's territory at Shawbak during a time of truce. They had halted there under conditions of safe conduct, but Reynald had killed them. Salah al-Din heard of this and swore in the name of God that if he captured Reynald he would kill him.[11]

Salah al-Din's goal was to move towards Islamic Jerusalem. To open the way, he first had to conquer the cities in the region. The Crusader losses at the battle of Hittin had added to their serious manpower shortage. Within a period of two months, from July to September that year, Salah al-Din had recovered all the inland cities and fortresses except the walled city of Islamic Jerusalem.[12] He also conquered all major ports between 'Asqalan (Ashkelon) and Jubayl except for Sur (Tyre).[13] As a result, the land route between Palestine and Egypt was cleared for the movement of the Muslim army. Salah al-Din then established his fleet in the Mediterranean between Alexandria and Acre. His ships went into action on *Jumada al-Thani*, 583 AH/September 1187 CE and blocked the movement of Crusader ships in the area under its control. It was essential for Salah al-Din to deny easy bridgeheads to potential Crusader support forces from Europe, and he spent the ensuing weeks capturing as many coastal towns from the Crusaders as possible.

Having gained 'Asqalan on 16 *Jumada al-Thani*, 583 AH /5 September 1187 CE and arranged for its administration, Salah al-Din summoned all his troops, who were scattered along the coast. He then marched on Islamic Jerusalem.[14] On reaching the walled city, the sultan enquired about the location of the al-Aqsa mosque and the shortest route to it,[15] which he described as 'the shortest route to Heaven.'[16] As 'Imad al-Din reports, he swore to restore the sacred shrines to their old grandeur and vowed not to leave Islamic Jerusalem until he had recovered the 'rock on which the Prophet had set foot,' had visited it personally and raised his flag on its highest point.[17]

According to Muslim chronicles, Salah al-Din and his army approached Islamic Jerusalem from 'Asqalan[18] on the western side of the walled city on Sunday 15 *Rajab* 583AH /20 September 1187 CE.[19] Lane-Poole says that Salah al-Din stationed his forces opposite the western wall between Jaffa's Gate (*Bab al-Khalil*) and Damascus Gate (*Bab al-'Amud*), and began to besiege the city.[20] Muslim historians do not give the exact location of the Muslim army in these first few days of the siege.

The Crusaders were worn down by two weeks of unremitting assault, with arrows raining down on them. On 21 *Rajab*/26 September Salah al-Din ordered his camp to be quietly moved. When the people of Jerusalem saw this they relaxed, but Salah al-Din had only spread out his camp across the nearby hills. He then ordered assault engines (mangonels)[21] to be built, and formed a group of 10,000 cavalry and 10,000 archers.[22]

On Friday 20 *Rajab*/25 September, Salah al-Din set up his mangonels and commenced his final attack on the city. Ibn Shaddad gives a brief account of the battle, stating that Salah al-Din pressed his attack until a hole was made in the wall overlooking the valley of Hinnom (*Wadi Jahannam*). Realizing the inevitability of their defeat, the besieged Crusaders conferred and agreed to surrender Jerusalem to Salah al-Din and to seek safe conduct for themselves. They sent messengers asking the Muslim leader for a settlement, and an agreement was reached soon after.[23]

Ibn al-Athir's account of the battle is more detailed. According to him, on the night of 20 *Rajab*/25 September Salah al-Din installed his mangonels and by morning these machines were in operation. The Crusaders set up their own mangonels on the wall and began firing catapults. Both sides fought bravely, each considering the struggle to be in defence of its faith. The Crusader cavalry emerged from the city daily to engage in combat with Salah al-Din's forces, and both sustained casualties.[24] In one of these battles, Ibn al-Athir says that the Crusaders killed 'Izz al-Din Isa Ibn Malik, a Muslim commander. His death so grieved the Muslims that they violently charged the Crusaders, forcing them from their positions and pushing them back to the city wall. The Muslims then crossed the moat and reached the wall. Their sappers[25] prepared to destroy it, while archers gave cover and mangonels continued their bombardment.

Ibn al-Athir agrees with Ibn Shaddad that the Crusader leaders, realizing that they were on the verge of perishing, met in council and agreed to surrender Jerusalem to Salah al-Din and ask him for safe conduct. But Salah al-Din turned their delegation away, saying he would deal with them in the same way they had dealt with the city's inhabitants in 492 AH/ 1099 CE – by killing and the taking of prisoners.[26] However, different chroniclers give four different accounts of the communications between Salah al-Din and Jerusalem's rulers about surrender.

The four accounts of negotiations
According to Runciman, on 2 October Balian of Ibelin (Balian Ibn Barzan) left Jerusalem to discuss the future of the city and its people with Salah al-Din.[27] This was not, it seems, the first attempt at communication but had been preceded by four others. The first of these was reported by Abu Shama, who quoted Ibn al-Qadisi's story that Salah al-Din, in a letter to his relatives, had said that the king of Jerusalem had contacted him during his attack on Tyre, in 583 AH / 1187 CE, to ask for safe conduct (*aman*) and that Salah al-Din had responded, 'I will come to you in Islamic Jerusalem'.[28] Ibn al-Qadisi adds that the astrologers had informed Salah al-Din that the stars indicated he would enter Islamic Jerusalem but would lose one eye. To which Salah al-Din replied, 'I would accept becoming blind if I took the city.'[29] At that time only the siege of Tyre prevented the sultan from going to Jerusalem.

The second attempt at negotiation was reported by Lane-Poole, who quoted Ernoul, the Crusader chronicler who was in

Jerusalem during Salah al-Din's siege. Ernoul provided details that did not appear in Arabic sources. He indicated that on the day the Muslims took 'Asqalan, a delegation from Jerusalem went to ask Salah al-Din for a peaceful solution for their city. On the day of the meeting there was a solar eclipse, which the Crusader delegates considered a bad omen. Salah al-Din was keen to spare the holy city the misery of a siege, because 'Jerusalem is the house of God, as you also believe, and I will not willingly lay siege to the house of God or put it to the assault'. He offered them generous terms: they would be allowed to remain in the city temporarily; they could retain the surrounding land within a radius of five leagues, and they would receive the supplies of money and food they needed until the following Pentecost. If the inhabitants of Jerusalem had any prospect of being rescued by an external force, they should keep the holy city, but if not, they were to surrender it and Salah al-Din would conduct them and their possessions safely to Christian lands. The delegation refused this offer without hesitation, saying: 'if God pleases, [we] would never surrender the city where the Saviour died for [us]'. Salah al-Din then vowed that he would never take Islamic Jerusalem except by force, and commenced his march against the city.[30]

The third attempt was reported by 'Imad al-Din, who says that when Salah al-Din was at Tyre, he brought the captured king of Jerusalem – Guy of Lusignon – and the grand master of the Templars before him and promised them freedom if they would help him secure the surrender of other cities.[31] In fact, they did help him later to obtain the surrender of 'Asqalan and Gaza.

The fourth account is reported by Runciman. He says that Balian of Ibelin, who was with the Frankish (Crusader) refugees at Tyre, contacted Salah al-Din and asked for a safe conduct to enter the city of Jerusalem in order to rescue his wife Queen Maria (he had married the widow of Amalric, king of Jerusalem), who had retreated there from Nablus with her children, and whom he wished to bring to Tyre. Salah al-Din granted this request on condition that Balian spends only one night in the city and did not carry arms.[32] By acceding to Balian's request, it seems that Salah al-Din hoped to use him as his chief negotiator in Jerusalem's surrender. Balian ultimately did negotiate the surrender of the city, but only after he had broken his agreement with Salah al-Din and had played a dramatic role in the city's defence.[33]

When Balian arrived in Jerusalem, Patriarch Heraclius and the officers of the military orders insisted that he should stay and lead the city's defence. At first Balian refused, saying that he would keep his commitment to Salah al-Din. But at the insistence of the patriarch, Balian, deeply embarrassed, wrote to Salah al-Din to explain the violation of his oath. Runciman says that Salah al-Din was always courteous to an enemy whom he respected. He not only forgave Balian but sent an escort to convey Queen Maria and her family to Tyre. Salah al-Din is said to have wept when he saw these children, heirs to vanished grandeur, passing through his camp into exile.[34] Balian finally consented to accept the leadership of the city and immediately began to consolidate the Crusader forces and plan the defence.[35]

Balian's threat to destroy the city
It seems that Balian came to the conclusion that the massacre committed by the Crusaders against the Muslims when they first entered Islamic Jerusalem would sooner or later be repeated against them, and that all the Christians (both the Crusaders and indigenous Christians) in the city would be killed or captured. Most probably they would be killed. Balian concluded that the only solution was to threaten Salah al-Din. Ibn al-Athir, Abu Shama, Ibn Shaddad, Abu al-Fida', Ibn Kahir, Ibn al-'Ibri and other Muslim and non-Muslim chroniclers are unanimous about the content of Balian's speech to Salah al-Din:

> O Sultan, he said, know that we soldiers in this city are in the midst of God knows how many people, who are slackening the fight in the hope of thy grace, believing that thou wilt grant it then as thou hast granted it to the other cities- for they abhor death and desire life. But for ourselves, when we see that death must needs be, by God

we will slaughter our sons and our women, we will burn our wealth and our possessions, and leave you neither sequin nor smallest amount to loot, nor a man or a woman to enslave; and when we have finished that, we will demolish the Rock and the al-Aqsa Mosque, and the other holy places, we will slay the Muslim slaves who are in our hands – there are 5000 such, and slaughter every beast and mount we have; and then we will go out in a body to you, and will fight you for our lives: not a man of us will fall before he has slain his like; thus shall we die gloriously or conquer like gentlemen.[36]

It can be seen from this that if Salah al-Din would not grant the people of Jerusalem fair terms of surrender, Balian would order them to fight to the death and to destroy much of the city. Balian and his soldiers were therefore prepared to violate the sacredness of Muslim holy places by destroying the Dome of the Rock and massacring Muslim prisoners of war, who were estimated to number in the thousands. There is no doubt about the dramatic impact of this message.

Regan comments that Salah al-Din was forced to reconsider.[37] The sultan had sworn to take the city by force and to repay the Crusaders for their massacre. However, becoming master of a ruined city, with its holy sites destroyed, would have been a tragic end to the holy war. Regan questions whether a voluntary surrender by the defenders would have violated Salah al-Din's oath. He adds that the siege had already been bloody enough. He suggests that it was generous terms, rather than military might, that had facilitated the surrender of other cities. Moreover, conquering Islamic Jerusalem by force would take longer and would affect the capabilities of Salah al-Din's forces. He concludes that Salah al-Din understood that generosity was his most potent weapon.[38]

Salah al-Din discussed the situation with his commanders, and was at first told that the right approach was to cause humiliation by taking the enemy and their families as prisoners of war. But after lengthy negotiation with Balian,[39] terms of surrender were finally agreed. The city was to surrender unconditionally, but the Crusaders were granted safe conduct to leave, provided that they paid a ransom fixed at ten *dinars* for a man, five for a woman, and two for a child.[40] Seven thousand of the poor would be freed for a lump sum of 30,000 *dinars*.[41]

Salah al-Din saw this as an excellent opportunity to capture Islamic Jerusalem without further bloodshed. All those who paid their ransom within 40 days were allowed to leave, while those who could not pay it would be enslaved. The Crusaders were allowed to take with them any movable property. However, they were encouraged to sell as much as possible to the Muslims, either to merchants in Salah al-Din's army or to local Christians,[42] in order to raise their ransom. 'Imad al-Din reports that Balian promised to pay 30,000 *dinars* to free the poor. He says the offer was accepted, and that Balian fulfilled this promise.[43]

The Surrender of Islamic Jerusalem

The walled city of Jerusalem surrendered on Friday 27 *Rajab* 583 AH/2 October 1187 CE, and according to 'Imad al-Din al-Asfahani it contained more than one hundred thousand people, including Christian men, women and children.[44] Salah al-Din entered the city and freed it from 88 years of Crusader rule. The 27 *Rajab* was the same date on which the Prophet Muhammad had been supernaturally transported from Makkah to Islamic Jerusalem in a single night, known as the Ascent, on the eve of *al-Mi'raj*, as recorded in the Qur'an.[45] Ibn Shaddad says that God facilitated this remarkable coincidence of restoring Islamic Jerusalem to Muslim hands on the anniversary of the Night Journey and the Ascent of the Prophet Muhammad.[46] He adds that a large number of people from all over the Muslim world had come to the region after hearing about the conquest of the coastal lands, hoping for the capture of Islamic Jerusalem. Many notables from Egypt and Syria witnessed the liberation, so that when Salah al-Din entered the city he was surrounded by scholars, jurists, Sufis and poets, as well as by a crowd of civilians and military officers. On the day of the conquest the huge cross that had been placed over the Dome of the Rock was pulled down and Salah al-Din released all Muslim prisoners, who, according to Ibn Shaddad, numbered close to three thousand.[47]

The Patriarch Heraclius and his priests each paid their ten *dinars* and left the city laden with gold and silver jewellery, relics by the cartload and other artifacts from the church of the Holy Sepulchre. According to 'Imad al-Din, the Crusaders stripped the ornaments from their churches, carrying with them vases of gold and silver, silk- and gold-embroidered curtains and other church treasures.[48]

Salah al-Din's brother, al-Malik al-'Adil, was so moved by this scene that he asked for a thousand captives. Salah al-Din granted his request, and al-'Adil immediately set them free. Salah al-Din himself set free all the aged prisoners.[49] An example of his magnanimity is that he sent his guard to proclaim throughout the streets of Islamic Jerusalem that all old people who could not pay the ransom would be allowed to leave the city. Lane-Poole says that they came forth from the Postern of S. Lazar, and their departure lasted from the rising of the sun until night fell.[50]

'Imad al-Din, Ibn al-Athir and Abu Shama were among historians who reported the gracious conduct of Salah al-Din towards many noble women of the city, allowing them to leave without ransom. For example, a Byzantine queen, who had led a monastic life in Jerusalem, was not only allowed to leave without ransom, but was permitted to take all her belongings and whatever else she wanted.[51] Another example was the wife of the captured King Guy, who was allowed to leave the city unhindered, with her retinue and associates. Salah al-Din even granted her safe conduct to visit her captive husband in Nablus.[52] Some of Salah al-Din's commanders (for example, the ruler of al-Bira) asked for the freedom of 500 Armenians, as they were from his country. Muzaffar al-Din Ibn 'Ali Kuchuk requested the release of 1,000 captives, claiming that they had come from his home town of al-Ruha (Urfa). Salah al-Din granted his request.[53]

Runciman reports that some of the Crusader ladies who ransomed themselves came to Salah al-Din in tears and asked what was to happen to them, as their husbands or fathers had been slain or taken captive. He replied by promising to free those of their husbands who were in captivity, and to the widows and orphans of men who had been slain he gave money and gifts from his own treasury according to their need.[54] Runciman commented that this incident was in contrast to the deeds of the conquerors of the First Crusade.

In order to control the departing population Salah al-Din ordered that all the gates of walled city be temporarily closed. At each gate a commander was appointed to monitor the movements of the Crusaders and to ensure that only those who had paid a ransom could leave. Others were employed inside the city to take a census.[55] 'Imad al- Din says that Egyptian and Syrian officers were appointed to collect the payments and to give the departing people receipts that had to be submitted at the gates.[56] The grand masters of the Templars and Hospitallers were approached to donate money for the release of poor Crusaders. When they resisted, a riot almost erupted and they were forced to contribute to the ransoms.[57]

As the Crusaders were leaving, Salah al-Din assigned officers whose job was to ensure their safe arrival in territories held by the Christians.[58] Regan quotes an unnamed chronicler who gave Salah al-Din's officers credit for their humane treatment of the refugees:

> [The officers] who could not endure the suffering of the refugees, ordered their squires to dismount and set aged Christians upon their steeds. Some of them even carried Christian children in their arms.[59]

After the exodus, the 15,000 people who remained in the city were enslaved, as they could not pay the ransom. According to 'Imad al- Din, 7,000 were men and 8,000 were women and children. 'Imad al- Din was amazed at the amount of treasure that was carried away by the Crusaders. He reported to Salah al-

Din that it could be valued at 200,000 *dinars*. He reminded the sultan that his agreement was for safe conduct to the departing Crusaders for themselves and their personal property, but not for the property of the churches, and he advised that such treasures should not be left in their hands. But Salah al-Din replied:

> If we interpret the treaty [now] against their interest, they will accuse us of treachery. Let us deal with them according to the wording of the treaty so they may not accuse the believers of breaking the covenant. Instead, they will talk of the favours that we have bestowed upon them.[60]

In the words of Esposito:

> The Muslim army was as magnanimous in victory as it had been tenacious in battle. Civilians were spared; churches and shrines were generally left untouched ... Salah al-Din was faithful to his word and compassionate toward non-combatants.[61]

Salah al-Din's magnanimity contrasts sharply with the attitude of the victorious Crusaders in 492AH /1099 CE. He was chivalrous and fair-minded to his enemies, and his generosity was recognized by Muslim and Christians alike.

Hillenbrand says that the propaganda value of Salah al-Din's bloodless conquest of [Islamic] Jerusalem counts for much more than the temptations, soon overcome, to exact vengeance. She adds that it was important for Muslim chroniclers like Ibn al-Athir to display the magnanimity of Salah al-Din's conduct not just as a personal characteristic, but as a demonstration of the superiority of Muslim conduct over Christian conduct, and of Islamic values over Christian values.[62] Salah al-Din was steeped in Islamic teaching, and his treatment of the Christians reflected the original Muslim vision for the treatment of non-Muslims that was established in the Qur'anic verse:

God forbids you not, with regard to those who fight you not for [your] Faith nor drive you out of your homes, from dealing kindly and justly with them: for God loves those who are just.[63]

The instructions of Islam restrained him from barbaric acts, and it is likely that the concept of 'forgiveness with capability' (*al-'Afu 'ind al-Maqdirah*) was in his mind at the time.

Salah al-Din and the Holy Places

The first action that Salah al-Din took towards the church of the Holy Sepulchre, the holiest place in the world for Christians, was to ordered it to be closed for three days.[64] This allowed the situation to calm down and life to return to a semblance of normality.[65] The closure was also gave the sultan and his advisers time to discuss the church's future after a long and tiring war. Some of his advisers wanted him to destroy the church and put an end to Christian interest in Islamic Jerusalem, so that they would no longer come for visits and pilgrimages. 'Imad al-Din says that:

> Salah al-Din discussed with his people the issue of the church of the Holy Sepulchre. Amongst them were those who advised that its structures should be demolished, its traces should be blotted out, the way to visiting it should be blinded, its status should be removed, its candelabras should be extinguished, its gospels should be destroyed, its seductions should be removed and its pronouncements should be exposed as lies ...[66]

However, most of the advisers rejected this, arguing that it was the site and not the building that mattered; Christians would still make pilgrimage because of the sanctity of the place. They also reminded the sultan that when Caliph 'Umar Ibn al-Khattab conquered the city he did not destroy the holy places, but had confirmed the right of Christians to them.[67] Why should the conquering Muslims now destroy the Holy Sepulchre? Salah al-

Din was persuaded by this majority opinion and 'Umar's example. After three days of closure he ordered the church reopened and granted Christians freedom of worship in it. However, Crusader pilgrims would be admitted only on payment of a fee.[68]

Salah al-Din introduced some structural changes in the course of restoring the Muslim holy places. As mentioned, the golden cross that had dominated the Dome of the Rock was taken down.[69] The al-Aqsa mosque was cleared of Christian furnishings[70] and fitted with beautiful oriental carpets. Its walls were illuminated with texts from the Qur'an and rich candelabra were hung from the ceiling.[71] Salah al-Din also installed a *minbar* (carved pulpit) in the mosque. According to Abu Shama, this *minbar* had been prepared by Nur al-Din, to accompany him to Islamic Jerusalem should the city be liberated during his lifetime.[72]

After discussion with Muslim scholars (*'ulama*), Salah al-Din established new religious institutions in buildings previously used by Christians. It was argued that these Christian places had been Muslim prior to the Crusades.[73] For example, *al-madrasa al-salahiyya*, a school for teaching shafi'i *fiqh*, was set up in the church of St Anne. *Al-khanqah al-salahiyya*, a monastery (*ribat*) for Sufis, was placed in the former residence of the patriarch of Jerusalem, adjacent to the church of the Holy Sepulchre.[74] A hospital, *al-bimaristan al-salahi*, was established in a church in the Tanners quarter (*hayy al-dabbagha*) near the Holy Sepulchre. Rich endowment was arranged to service the hospital, which apparently also functioned as a medical teaching centre.[75]

Salah al-Din and the Local Christians

In his treatment of the Christians in Islamic Jerusalem, Salah al-Din made a distinction between two groups. On the one hand were the Crusaders, invaders who had instigated a horrific massacre after their conquest of the city, and on the other hand were the indigenous Christians, who were both Arab and non-Arab followers of the Greek Orthodox Church – eastern

Orthodox Christians as opposed to the Latin (Roman Catholic) Crusaders.

According to 'Imad al-Din, Salah al-Din's secretary, the local Christians now requested permission to remain in the city, which Salah al-Din granted with conditions: after paying their ransom they should pay the *jizyah* tax, agree to be his subjects and accept the role of *dhimmis*. However, the poorer classes, who did not have money, were exempted from the *jizyah*.[76] At the same time, Salah al-Din ordered the Crusader Christians to leave Islamic Jerusalem. The Orthodox Christians and the Jacobites (Syrian Orthodox) were allowed to remain and to worship as they chose. 'Imad al-Din says that Salah al-Din even allowed them to work in his service and in the government, although he gives no examples. Arnold agrees with Imad al-Din[77] that the local Christians were satisfied with their Muslim employers.[78]

Salah al-Din's attitude to the local Christians seems to have been partly due to the warm relations he enjoyed with the Byzantine emperor, Isaac Angelus. Runciman reports that Salah al-Din received a message from the emperor just after the liberation of Islamic Jerusalem, congratulating him on his victory over the Crusaders and requesting that he convert the churches in the city back to the Orthodox Church, and that all Christian ceremonies in the city be conducted according to the Greek Orthodox liturgy. His request was later granted, although the rights of other sects were protected.[79] Salah al-Din allowed the local Christians to pray freely in their churches, and handed over control of Christian affairs to the Byzantine patriarch. Regan suggests that Salah al-Din saw this as a good opportunity to foster the disagreements between the followers of the Roman and Orthodox Churches,[80] in a divide and rule strategy. There is no doubt that the Orthodox Christians and their priests benefited greatly from the departure of the Catholics from Islamic Jerusalem, as they were able to recover sovereignty over the Christian holy places.[81]

During the siege of the city, the attitude of the indigenous Christians towards Salah al-Din was one of collaboration. Some argue that Salah al-Din would not have been able to conquer the city without their help. They maintained secret contact with Salah al-Din though Yusuf Batit,[82] an Arab Orthodox scholar from the city. They were ready to help the sultan and his army liberate Jerusalem by opening the gates at an agreed time. It is undeniable that there was some sort of collaboration between the two sides.

Regan argues that one reason behind the requests of Balian and the patriarch proposing the city's surrender and asking for safe conduct is that they doubted the loyalty of the local Christians. It was well known to the Crusaders that thousands of Greek Orthodox Christians in Islamic Jerusalem would welcome a Muslim conquest to liberate them from the domination of the Church of Rome.[83] At the beginning of the Crusades, these local Christians were excluded from living in the city. Later, during the time of Baldwin I (king of the Latin kingdom of Jerusalem 1100–18 CE), the Crusaders allowed considerable numbers of them to return, mainly to populate the city and ensure that there were enough people to carry out the necessary business of the realm. According to Runciman, these local Orthodox Christians were made to attend ceremonies in which the language and rituals were alien to them. He adds that they were the majority and resented the domination of the Catholic Crusaders,[84] and looked back with nostalgia to the days under Muslim rulers such as Caliph 'Umar, when they could worship freely.[85] Arnold confirms their greater religious security under the Muslims:

> The Native Christian certainly preferred the rule of the Muhammadans [Muslims] to that of the Crusaders, and when Jerusalem fell finally and ever into the hands of the Muslims (A.D. 1244), the Christian population of Palestine seems to have welcomed the new masters and to have submitted quietly and contentedly to their rule.[86]

However, it seems that Salah al-Din's recovery of Islamic Jerusalem took place without physical intervention of the Orthodox Christians.

In contrast to the religious exclusivism of the Crusaders, Salah al-Din made Islamic Jerusalem an open place to all Christian denominations and sects and allowed them to practice their rituals as they wished. He returned to the Coptic priesthood all former Coptic churches, monasteries and other property taken by the Crusaders. It was reported that he also granted the Copts a place in Islamic Jerusalem known as *dayr al-Sultan* (monastery of the sultan). Ever since the establishment of the Latin kingdom of Jerusalem – almost ninety years – Egyptian Orthodox Copts had been banned from the holy city because they were regarded by the Latins as heretics and atheists.[87] However, Salah al-Din allowed them to visit the church of the Holy Sepulchre and other Christian sites. He also exempted them from paying fees to enter Islamic Jerusalem, largely on the basis that they were his subjects.[88]

Interestingly, Salah al-Din also treated the Christians of Habsha (Abyssinia) generously, particularly in exempting them from fees when they visited the holy places.[89] 'Ashur adds that Salah al-Din showed respect to their monasteries and kindness to the Habashi priest who took care of these places.[90] It is evident that Salah al-Din succeeded in allowing different religions and sects to co-exist in Islamic Jerusalem, and did not impose new practices or regulations when he conquered the city. For him, the principles contained in 'Umar's Assurance of Safety were the most appropriate guide, as the above examples show.

Muslims, Christians and the Third Crusade[91]

The fall of Jerusalem was followed by several campaigns and another major effort to regain it. The Third Crusade (1189–92 CE) was led by three of medieval Europe's most famous monarchs: Emperor Frederick Barbarossa of Germany, King Philip II of France and King Richard I of England. The Crusaders started strongly, but soon weakened. Frederick Barbarossa accidentally drowned while he was marching towards Jerusalem,[92] which halted his army's momentum. As a result, most of the troops trudged back to their German homes. Salah al-Din attributed the emperor's death to the will of God, for he had feared the strength of Frederick's army. Philip was taken ill during the siege of Acre and may not have fully recovered. He was probably also weary of fighting and had disagreed with Richard and the other leaders, and decided to go back home. Although Richard enjoyed military successes and won back a considerable portion of the region, he failed to take Islamic Jerusalem. The third Crusade ended in peace with the al-Ramla peace treaty, in effect a Muslim victory, but with both Muslim and Christian sides exhausted.

The following discussion will focus on the relationship between the English king and the Muslim sultan. Richard and Salah al-Din led all the negotiations between Crusaders and Muslims, apart from a long letter sent by Frederick Barbarossa when he was still in Germany, threatening Salah al-Din and demanding that he hand over Jerusalem and the Holy Land, or else Frederick would go to war against him. Salah al-Din replied to him, but this appears to have been the only communication between the two leaders.[93]

After the Crusaders moved their forces to Acre they besieged the city for almost two years, during which thousands died on both sides. At this point, channels of communication between the Muslim and Crusader leaders were established. According to Ibn Shaddad, although the fighting was extremely fierce and violent, the Muslims remained steadfast. This surprised the Crusaders, and Richard sent a messenger first to al-Malik al-'Adil asking for a meeting with the sultan. Salah al-Din himself replied:

> Kings do not meet unless an agreement has been reached. It is not good for them to fight after meeting and eating together. If he wants this, an agreement must be settled before it can happen. We must have an interpreter whom we can trust to act between us, and who can make each of us understand what the other says. Let the envoy be our mutual interpreter. If we come to an agreement, the meeting can happen later, God willing.[94]

Richard agreed about the interpreter and sent another messenger asking for a time to meet on the plain, with their troops surrounding them. Salah al-Din agreed, but the meeting did not take place on account of Richard's sudden illness, and he sent a messenger to Salah al-Din explaining the reason for his absence.[95] It was also reported that the Frankish princes had expressed to Richard their disapproval of his actions, in the belief that he was endangering Christianity.

After a while, when it became clear to the Muslim defenders of Acre that there was no hope of Salah al-Din's army reaching the city to relieve them, they agreed surrender terms with the Crusaders.[96] To ensure that these were fulfilled, the Crusaders took hostage 3000 prisoners. Ibn Shaddad describes the surrender terms:

> They would give up the city and all the engines, equipment and ships it contained and hand over 200,000 *dinars*, 1500 prisoners of common, unremarkable background and 100 prisoners to be specified by the Franks, whom they would select, and additionally the Holy Cross that was taken by the Muslims. These would be granted, provided that the Muslims could leave in safety, taking with them their personal wealth and goods and their children and womenfolk. They guaranteed to the marquis (for he had been reconciled and had returned) 10,000 *dinars* because he was the intermediary, and 4000 *dinars* to his men. On that basis an agreement was concluded between them and the Crusaders.[97]

Under this agreement, Salah al-Din was supposed to hand over the money, Christian prisoners were to be exchanged for Muslim hostages and the Holy Cross (captured at the battle of Hittin) was to be restored to the Crusaders. However, progress was slow because Salah al-Din suspected that if the Crusaders received the money, the Cross and the prisoners while still holding Muslim hostages, they would act treacherously and the Muslims would sustain a loss too great to repair.[98] Richard lost patience and massacred some 2700 Muslims within the sight of Salah al-Din's army.[99] Ibn al-'Adim asserts that he killed 2200 and spared the rest.[100] Hallam comments that later chronicles contrast this incident with Salah al-Din's more chivalrous treatment of Frankish prisoners.[101] Lane-Poole says that there was 'no imaginable excuse or palliation for the cruel and cowardly massacre that followed'.[102] He quotes an account of it:

> Orders were then given to cut off the heads of the hostages with the exception of a few of the nobler prisoners, who perhaps might yet be relieved or exchanged for captive Christians. King Richard, always eager to destroy the Muslims, to confound the law of Muhammad utterly, and vindicate that of Christ, on the Friday after the Assumption bade 2700 Muslim hostages led out of the city and beheaded. Nor was there any delay. The king's followers leapt forward eager to fulfil the commands, and thankful to the Divine Grace that permitted them to take such vengeance for those Christians whom these very [captives] had slain with bolts and arrows.[103]

After the Crusaders had captured Acre they marched south along the coast, with Salah al-Din not far behind. King Richard asked al-'Adil, who came up to the advance guard, for a meeting and this was granted. However, it did not go well. Richard started talking about peace, and according to Ibn Shaddad, al-'Adil said:

> You desire peace but you do not mention your demands that I might mediate your differences with the sultan'. The King of England replied, 'the basic condition is that you should restore all the lands to us and return to your countries'. Al-'Adil gave a harsh answer and a quarrel followed which led to the enemy's departure after the two of them had separated.[104]

Richard's reply made it clear that he saw the Muslims as invaders who had no rights, not only in Jerusalem but in the whole region. He believed that the Christian Crusaders were the real owners of those lands and that Muslims should leave the area. As a result, negotiations were unsuccessful, and were followed by a battle fought near Arsuf on 14 *Sha'ban* 581 AH/ 7 September 1191 CE, in which Richard was victorious. The Crusaders then headed to the port of Yafa (Jaffa) and conquered it as well.

Negotiations for peace
Yet it seems that Richard realized that his last meeting with al-'Adil had not been a proper basis for peace negotiations. On 26 *Ramadan* 581 AH /18 October 1191 CE he met al-'Adil at Yazur, and they talked for a long time. Richard made a proposition and asked al-'Adil to send it to Salah al-Din. It is regarded as the most important letter between Salah al-Din and Richard, and deals directly with Islamic Jerusalem:

> You will greet him and say, the Muslims and the Franks are done for. The land is ruined, ruined utterly at the hands of both sides. Property and lives on both sides are destroyed. The matter has received its due. All we have to talk about is Jerusalem, the Holy Cross and these lands. Now Jerusalem is the centre of our worship, which we shall never renounce, even if there was only one of us left. As for these lands, let there be restored to us what is this side of Jordan River. The Holy Cross is a piece of wood that has no value for you, but it is important for us. Let the sultan bestow it upon us. Then we can make peace and have rest from this constant hardship.[105]

Salah al-Din consulted the leading men in his council about this message. His famous reply was as follows:

> Islamic Jerusalem is ours as much as it is yours. Indeed, for us it is greater than it is for you, for it is where our Prophet

came on his Night Journey and the gathering place of the angels. Let not the king imagine that we shall give it up, for we are unable to breathe a word of that amongst the Muslims. As for the land, it is also ours originally. Your conquest of it was an unexpected accident due to the weakness of the Muslims there at that time. While the war continues God will not enable you to build up one stone there. From the lands in our hands we, thanks be to God, feed on the produce and draw our benefit. The destruction of the Holy Cross would in our eyes be a great offering to God, but the only reason we are not permitted to go that far is that some more useful benefit might accrue to Islam.[106]

It is evident from the above exchange how important Islamic Jerusalem was to both sides and how each had their reasons for claiming it. As events confirmed, both would make the utmost effort to keep control of the city. Richard was exhausted by war and sought to persuade Salah al-Din to agree to peace. His demands became less; he now discusses only Jerusalem, whereas previously he had referred to the whole region. However, he continues to insist that Jerusalem belongs first and foremost to Christians and is not to be shared with Muslims. Salah al-Din, on the other hand, denies that the Muslims are invaders. More importantly, he asserts the Muslim right to Islamic Jerusalem while acknowledging the Christian claim to the city – his vision is inclusive.

Richard tried hard to reach peace with Salah al-Din. On 29 *Ramadan* 581 AH /21 October 1191CE he proposed the following terms: al-'Adil (who was, after all, Salah al-Din's brother) would marry his sister Joan (the widowed Queen of Sicily); the couple would live in Islamic Jerusalem; and Salah al-Din would give al-'Adil all the coastal lands he held and make him king of the littoral region. In addition to the lands and fiefdoms (*Iqta'at*) already in Salah al-Din's hands, al-'Adil and Joan should together rule the land (that is, they would replace Salah al-Din); the Holy Cross was to be returned to the

Crusaders; prisoners from both sides were to be freed; and the Templars and Hospitallers were to be given villages. If these terms were agreed, Richard would return to England.[107]

When Salah al-Din received these proposals he expressed approval, but at the same time treated them as a joke on Richard's part. He believed that the English king would not in the end agree to any of these conditions and that they were meant to mock and deceive the Muslim leader. In part, Salah al-Din's expectations were correct. After receiving Salah al-Din's approval to the marriage condition, Richard had to apologize, saying that his sister had utterly rejected the idea and sworn in the name of the Lord that she would never marry a Muslim. Richard then suggested that the marriage condition could be fulfilled if al-'Adil became a Christian.[108]

Since his approaches to Salah al-Din had been unsuccessful, Richard took the dramatic step of marching towards Islamic Jerusalem in the hope of recovering the city and achieving the Crusade's objective. On the 27 *Jumada al-Thani* 588 AH /6 June 1192 CE, Crusader forces under the king's leadership arrived at the village of Bayt Nuba, west of Jerusalem, which he chose as the base for an assault on the holy city. Richard examined the situation carefully in terms of the forces available on both sides and the outcome of such a military campaign. He realized the difficulty of the situation, and it soon became clear to him that a military assault was not viable. He could spend years besieging the walled city and then, when he conquered it, could find it virtually impossible to hold. He had enough troops and strength to maintain a siege, but could not keep up supplies of food and water for a protracted war. Richard told his generals that he would never desert them, but that he would proceed to the city as a comrade and not as a commander. He asked if anyone would volunteer to lead them. They all agreed that if Richard was not willing to be their leader, neither were any of them.[109] Therefore the king once again made overtures for peace.

From reading the different sources it seems that Richard's reasons were three-fold. First, his health appeared to deteriorate shortly after the capture of Acre, and the intense heat of the local climate would not have helped. During the summer of 588 AH /1192 CE, at Bayt Nuba, Richard's health deteriorated further. Second, he assessed the strength and power of the Muslim army as greater than he had expected. Because he had gathered a large army from several European countries, he had assumed that he would easily defeat Salah al-Din's forces. Third, the unstable political situation in England required his return, because his brother John was planning to overthrow him and seize the throne.

The failure of Richard and his army to recover Islamic Jerusalem led to a disagreement among the Crusaders about whether to march on the holy city or return to their own lands.[110] The French troops were in favour of marching on, saying, 'the only reason we came was Jerusalem and we shall not return without it'.[111] However, Richard asked how they were going to get clean water to drink, as the wells around the city had been poisoned on Salah al-Din's orders.[112] A meeting was held, and the decision was made to depart. In the early morning of 21 *Jumada al-Thani* 588 AH /4 July 1192 CE, Richard and his army set out in the direction of al-Ramla, retreating the way they had come.[113]

Final negotiations for peace
On 26 *Jumada al-Thani*/9 July Richard sent another messenger to Salah al-Din. Ibn Shaddad reports it as follows:

> The king of England desires your love and friendship. He does not wish to be a Pharaoh ruling the earth and he does not think that of you. 'It is not right' he says, 'for you to ruin all the Muslims, nor for me to ruin all the Franks. Here is my nephew, Count Henry, whom I have made ruler of these lands. I hand him and his troops over to your authority. If you were to summon them for execution they would hear and obey. Many monks and men of religion have asked you for churches and you have not grudged them what they asked. Now I ask you for a church. Those matters which annoyed you in the negotiations with al-'Adil

I have declared that I give them up. I have renounced them. Were you to give me a very small village, I would accept it.'[114]

Ibn Shaddad continues:

When the Sultan had heard this message, he gathered his advisers and counsellors and asked them what the reply to this message should be. There was no one who did not advise conciliation and a conclusion of peace because of the fatigue, exhaustion and burden of debts from which the Muslims suffered. It was agreed to make this response: 'if you make this sort of overture to us, goodwill cannot be met with other than goodwill. Your nephew will be to me like one of my sons. You shall hear how I shall treat him. I shall bestow on him the greatest of churches, the Holy Sepulchre, and the rest of the land's upland castles that are in our hands shall remain ours. What is between the two regions shall be considered condominium. 'Asqalan and what is beyond shall be left in ruins, neither yours nor ours. If you want its villages, let them be yours.[115]

Richard's message shows how desperate he was to finish his mission by almost any means, and wished to reach an arrangement in a conciliatory spirit. It also shows how far his concessions had gone, in that he was willing to accept just a small village, in contrast to earlier negotiations when he had asked Salah al-Din's army to return to their countries and leave Jerusalem to him. This time the king acknowledged Salah al-Din's overall sovereignty, in recommending his own nephew to the sultan's good graces. Salah al-Din's reply was one of peace. He promised, first, that he would treat the king's nephew as a son; second, he would hand him the most important church in Islamic Jerusalem; and finally, he would divide the country between Muslims and Christians.

The next day, 29 *Jumada al-Thani* 588 AH/12 July 1192 CE, another messenger was sent by Richard to Salah al-Din, conveying his thanks and making a new request:

> What I request from you is that we should have twenty persons in the citadel of Jerusalem and that the local Christians and Franks who live in the city should not be harassed. As for the rest of the land, we have the coastal plain and the lowlands and you have the hill country.[116]

This time Richard's messenger, on his own initiative, revealed that winning Jerusalem was no longer the king's intention. He had given up all talk of the city apart from permission to make pilgrimage there. His aim was to reach a peaceful agreement and return home. Salah al-Din's reply was: 'you will not have anything at all to do with Islamic Jerusalem, apart from making a pilgrimage visit.' The messenger replied, 'but the pilgrims would have nothing to pay.' Ibn Shaddad says it was understood from these words that the king accepted the reduced terms.[117]

These negotiations took place while the conflict continued in various places. During the fighting in Yafa, Richard asked to meet Salah al-Din's chamberlain (*al-hajib*), Abu Bakr. At this meeting, according to Ibn Shaddad, he said:

> This Sultan of yours is a great man. Islam has no greater or mightier prince on earth than him ... By God, he is great ... Greet the sultan for me and say for God's sake grant me what I ask for to make peace. This is a matter that must have an end. My lands over the sea have been ruined. For this to go on is no good for us nor for you.[118]

While negotiations were still going on the king's health deteriorated, and he had a burning fever. He craved fruit and ice and had a yearning for pears and plums. In a goodwill gesture, Salah al-Din supplied these fruits with refreshing snow from the mountain.[119] It seems there were two reasons for this. First, Richard's sickness seems to have softened the heart of Salah al-

Din towards him;[120] and second, the sultan could gain intelligence by the coming and going of messengers.[121] Richard asked Abu Bakr to thank Salah al-Din for the fruit and ice. He also asked al-'Adil's advice on how he could influence Salah al-Din to make peace and to give him the city of 'Asqalan. In return, Richard would agree to leave, but would leave behind a small band of soldiers, so that Salah al-Din would be able to take the land from them. All he sought, on his departure, was to consolidate his reputation among the Crusaders.

Salah al-Din responded that if they agreed to give up 'Asqalan, then a peace treaty would be concluded, as his army was weary of constant fighting and campaigning and their resources were exhausted.[122] Salah al-Din wanted to rest his troops for a while so that they could recover strength. Furthermore, he wanted to make the land productive again, and capable of supplying Islamic Jerusalem with more weapons to fortify his defences.[123] The al-Ramla peace treaty between the two leaders was finally negotiated and signed on 23 *Sha'ban* 588 AH /2 September 1192 CE.[124] It stipulated a duration of three years and eight months,[125] or three years and five months according to Ibn al-'Adim[126] (d. 660 AH /1262 CE), while Abu al-Fida' (d. 732 AH /1332 CE) and al-Maqrizi (d. 845 AH /1442 CE) says it was three years and three months.[127]

The conditions included the destruction of 'Asqalan and a three-year prohibition on its rebuilding (after the three years whoever was the stronger would get 'Asqalan). Salah al-Din would give the Crusaders Yafa, its environs, the sea coast and the mountains, and they would retain a narrow strip of coast between Tyre and Yafa. Salah al-Din was to keep Islamic Jerusalem, provided that he allowed free passage into it without tribute and the freedom to sell goods to any land exercising free commerce. Both parties signed the treaty.[128] Immediately afterwards, Salah al-Din ordered his herald to make a loud proclamation in the encampments and in the markets:

> Listen all! Peace has been arranged. Any person from their lands who wishes to enter ours may do so and any person

from our lands who wishes to enter theirs may also do so. The sultan [also] announced that the pilgrim route from Syria was now open.[129]

Salah al-Din adhered to the terms of the peace treaty, including freedom of religion, so that Christians were allowed to visit Islamic Jerusalem and to carry out pilgrimages. Salah al-Din even gave them assistance in the form of escorts, who protected them until they were taken back to Yafa.[130] This was mainly to ensure the completion of their pilgrimage and that they returned satisfied to their own lands. He also offered them food and treated them with kindness. Richard, however, was angered at seeing the large number of Frankish pilgrims visiting Islamic Jerusalem. He sent a letter to Salah al-Din asking him not to allow Christians to visit the city unless they had written permission from the king.[131] Salah al-Din refused, saying that if people had travelled long distances it would be unacceptable to prevent them from visiting the holy sites.[132]

Salah al-Din was undoubtedly aware that if he stopped these pilgrims they would go back home and tell others. As a result, people would be outraged and might start a new crusade. The sultan's decision also effectively prevented Richard from having any control of Islamic Jerusalem, even if only a spiritual influence over Christian holy places. Salah al-Din turned the situation to his own advantage, informing visitors of Richard's dissatisfaction, but telling them they could still perform their pilgrimages.

An encounter between Salah al-Din and Hubert Walter, the bishop of Salisbury, during the bishop's visit to Islamic Jerusalem demonstrates the sultan's attitude. The bishop had brought pilgrim caravans to the holy places. Salah al-Din welcomed them warmly and a meeting took place between the two men, where several issues were discussed including the character of King Richard. Salah al-Din asked the bishop what he would like as a present. The bishop requested a day to think carefully about it. The next day he told the sultan that he would like two Latin (Roman Catholic) priests and two Latin deacons to be permitted to celebrate divine service with the Syrian Orthodox priests at the Holy Sepulchre church. They were to be supported out of the pilgrim offerings. He asked the same for Bethlehem and Nazareth. Salah al-Din granted this request.[133]

The Third Crusade, which lasted nearly five years, ended with Richard and Salah al-Din parting on good terms. In general, each had shown respect for the other, at times exchanging generous gifts even in the heat of battle. Ibn Shaddad described Richard as 'a very powerful man of great courage and spirit.'[134] King Richard sailed out of Acre in October 1192 CE, aware that more enemies awaited him on his journey home.

The last days of Salah al-Din
Salah al-Din returned from al-Ramla to Islamic Jerusalem, to prepare to restore the city and look after its welfare. On being assured that Richard had left the country,[135] the sultan began to make plans for a *hajj* (pilgrimage to Makkah).[136] His intention was to inspect the coastal areas and make sure everything was in good order,[137] and go to Damascus for a few days. Before travelling to Egypt he would return to Islamic Jerusalem to establish its government and take steps to further its prosperity.[138] Salah al-Din left Islamic Jerusalem for Damascus on 6 *Shawwal* 588 AH /15 October 1192 CE. Shortly after, he fell ill with a severe fever for nearly ten days. He died in Damascus on 27 *Safar* 589 AH /4 March 1193 CE, six months after the end of the Third Crusade.[139]

Lane-Poole emphasizes that 'the secret of Salah al-Din's power lay in the love of his subjects: 'What others sought to attain by fear, severity, and majesty, he accomplished by kindness.'[140] The legacy and legend of Salah al-Din grew after his death. Respected by those who fought against him as well as by those who surrendered to his mercy, he found a lasting place in the hearts of the Muslim people and achieved a fame rarely given in Western society to a non-Christian enemy. Yet it was Salah al-Din's adherence to ideals of justice and magnanimity – ideals that were similar to those espoused by Latin knights in their code of chivalry – as well as his military expertise that have given him a unique place among historical heroes.

This chapter is best concluded with a story that shows the kindness of Salah al-Din towards his enemies, even in the heat of war. The story has been quoted by many historians including Ibn Shaddad, who says that even Salah al-Din's enemies testified to his generosity and compassion:

> During the siege of Acre, a Crusader mother missed a child as Muslim thieves had entered her tent and had taken her unweaned infant of three months old and she spent all night pleading and shouting for help and crying. Her case came to the notice of the crusade's princes, who advised her to go and seek the help of Salah al-Din as he had a merciful heart. The princes said to her 'Go and ask Salah al-Din for the child and he will bring him back to you'. She went out to ask the Muslim advance guard for assistance, telling them of her troubles through an interpreter. They sent her to Salah al-Din. She came to him when I [Ibn Shaddad] was serving the sultan. She was sobbing and beating her breast and besmirched her face with soil. After he asked about her case and it had been explained to him, he had compassion for her and, with tears in his eyes, he ordered the infant to be brought to him. People went and found that it had been sold in the market. The sultan ordered the price to be paid to the purchaser and the child was taken from him. He himself stayed where he was and did not move until the infant was brought and handed over to the woman who took it, wept mightily, and hugged it to her bosom, while people watched her and wept with emotion also. She looked heavenward and began to utter incomprehensible words. Then he ordered that she and the infant be taken on horseback and be restored to her camp.[141]

Conclusion

It can be said that Salah al-Din was a model of chivalry. He was generous to his defeated enemies, kind to Crusader women and humane to captured prisoners of high rank. Once he had taken Islamic Jerusalem he opened the city to pilgrims of all faiths. Salah al-Din was also a determined fighter and a good strategist. His attitude towards Christians was vastly different from that of the Crusaders to Muslims. Although he had the power to do so, Salah al-Din did not kill thousands of them when he took Islamic Jerusalem, as the Crusaders had done to Muslims and Jews. His treatment of Christians and non-Muslims in Islamic Jerusalem was characterized by tolerance, respect and generosity.

CONCLUSION

Because of the current conflict over Jerusalem, its turbulent history and the important place that it holds in the hearts of the three monotheistic religions, it is easy to forget the long period of peace and tolerance that the city enjoyed under Muslim rule. If we wish to discuss Islamic Jerusalem in depth, we should look beyond the tensions of recent years and learn from that historical era.

This book demonstrates that Muslim tolerance of the Christians who lived in Islamic Jerusalem stemmed from a solid understanding of the guidelines laid down in Islam. A discussion of the juristic principles of the Qu'ran and other texts confirms that Islam has well-established ways of how non-Muslims should be treated. These teachings are regarded as eternal legislation until the Day of Judgment, but can be adapted to time and place. They affirm the concern of Islam for Jews and Christians, who are the People of the Book – a term that signifies the honour due to people whose faith is derived from revealed Scriptures.

The Qur'an urges Muslims to base their treatment of the People of the Book on peaceful cooperation, mutual respect and kindness. It warns them against breaking covenanted rights, especially towards those who are peacefully disposed towards Muslims. Deviation from these rules is justified only in certain exceptional circumstances. Muslims should not persecute others, take away their rights or hurt them simply because they are non-Muslims. Justice (*'adl*) should be meted out regardless of colour, race and religion. Another key concept is '*al-Birr*', used in the Qu'ran of parent/child relationships and indicating the affectionate care that Muslims should exercise in their dealings with non-Muslims. In a Muslim state, the protection, rights and security of non-Muslims are also based on the principle that all mankind is the creation of God without discrimination and that differences among people are the will of God. Maintaining human unity is another important concept, and Muslims are not entitled to judge non-Muslims for their disbelief in Islam.

My research has clarified one of the most troublesome concepts – the prohibition of alliance with non-Muslims. It established that this is not open-ended but conditional, and that understanding the reasons for the revelation of these Qur'anic verses helps Muslims to avoid disobeying other Qur'anic injunctions requiring good behaviour towards the peace-loving peoples of any religion. It was also noted that fair treatment of and cooperation with non-Muslims are not the same as loyalty, but are practical ways of promoting good and combating evil. The type of loyalty that the Qur'an warns against is supporting non-Muslims against Muslims.

The Sunnah sets out clear guidelines for the treatment of non-Muslims. In the constitution of Madinah, which reveals the high level of organization achieved by the Prophet, the Jews in that city were guaranteed rights as citizens of the Muslim state. The constitution placed principles of justice above religious solidarity and affirmed the right to justice irrespective of tribal or religious affiliation. It established a pattern for future relations with non-Muslims within the Muslim state. Religious tolerance, non-interference in the religious affairs of a non-Muslim group and freedom of religion for all citizens are an essential part of this.

Similarly, the Prophet's treaties with various non-Muslim kings and chiefs became an example for Muslim leaders in their dealings with *dhimmis*. These agreements demonstrated the Prophet's practical application of the concepts of tolerance and religious freedom. Under a *dhimma* pact, the non-Muslim automatically becomes a citizen of the Muslim state, benefits from its protection and shares the basic rights of a Muslim. The category of ethnic minority has no place in Muslim law.

The concepts of the *dhimma* pact and the *jizyah* tax have led to much confusion and inaccurate interpretation among western writers. However, the *dhimma* pact is a contract like any other between citizens and the state, and the *jizyah* tax is no more than an economic arrangement for a group of citizens to provide revenue to the state. It covers the expenses of protecting non-Muslims from outside attack and the cost of their exemption from military service. The poor, females, children, slaves, monks and hermits were exempted, and the level of the tax varied according to time, place and economic circumstance. Islam does not impose the *jizyah* tax to compensate for the failure of non-Muslims to believe in Islam, and *dhimmis* do not have to pay the *zakah* tax that is obligatory for Muslims.

My research concluded that *jihad* is a means and not an end in Islam. It is the last resort, used only when all other measures fail. The purpose of *jihad* is to remove injustice and aggression. Even when *jihad* is inevitable, Muslims are enjoined not to exceed the limits, for example, not to fight those who do not fight against Muslims.

I attempted to convey the religious tolerance that prevailed in Islamic Jerusalem during the two important periods of Muslim rule under Caliph 'Umar Ibn al-Khattab and Sultan Salah al-Din. There were similarities between these two leaders' treatment of non-Muslims, because both were devout men who observed the teachings of the Qur'an and the Sunnah. However, one major difference was that in 'Umar's time the Muslim state was strong, with the central government in Madinah controlling an extended state that was rapidly expanding through Muslim conquest. A very large number of non-Muslims, mostly Christians, became subjects of the state and were treated as *dhimmis*. In the early years of Salah al-Din's leadership, however – until the death of the Fatimid Caliph al-'Adid in 567 AH/1171 CE – there were two caliphates, in Baghdad and Cairo. The Crusaders occupied large areas of former Muslim territory, and security in both caliphates was unstable.

This book refutes allegations of injustice towards Christians on the part of Caliph 'Umar, such as in the peace treaty with the Banu Taghlib tribe or in the so-called Pact of 'Umar. It was concluded that 'Umar himself was not responsible for the conditions in the Banu Taghlib treaty. They were issued by the Prophet Muhammad himself at the request of the Muslims in this Christian tribe, to protect their children especially in times of war. It was also found that, to save face, this tribe opted to pay *jizyah* in the form of *sadaqa*, although its amount was doubled. Obviously, *jizyah* can be collected under any name as long as non-Muslims pay the agreed amount and it ends up in the Muslim treasury.

The so-called Pact of 'Umar appeared after Caliph 'Umar's reign and is not relevant to the first Muslim conquest. The humiliating conditions towards non-Muslims in this document are foreign to the mentality of Caliph 'Umar and inconsistent with the consideration and extreme care he showed to *dhimmis*. The pact also suffers from an unreliable chain of narrators and some textual defects, both of which strongly suggest that 'Umar was not its originator. The emergence of this document in a later period seems to have been prompted by deterioration in political, economic and social conditions and a concomitant desire to exert greater control of *dhimmis*.

During the early period of Salah al-Din's rule in Egypt, the unstable political situation led him to apply harsh measures that deviated from the approved way of treating *dhimmis*. However, once the situation had settled, he returned to more appropriate policies. No religious link was proved between Salah al-Din's severe treatment of Christians in Egypt and his perception of the Crusader occupation of Jerusalem.

Both 'Umar and Salah al-Din placed great importance on Islamic Jerusalem. 'Umar tried to achieve the goal of the Prophet Muhammad and Caliph Abu Bakr to seize Aelia (Jerusalem and its environs) from the Byzantine empire. Salah al-Din similarly continued the efforts of his predecessor, Nur al-Din, to liberate this region from the Crusaders and spent more than twenty years preparing for the venture. Although a decisive battle took place before both the first and second Muslim conquests of Jerusalem – the battle of al-Yarmuk in 'Umar's campaign and Hittin in Salah al-Din's – the final victory over Jerusalem was achieved through peaceful surrender. The surrender terms were not harsh, and the Assurance of Safety granted by Caliph 'Umar to the People of Aelia was echoed and reimplemented by Salah al-Din 550 years later.

'Umar's Assurance is considered a turning point in Muslim treatment of non-Muslims. It reflected a spirit of tolerance towards non-Muslims in general, and to Christians in particular. The essence of this document is consistent across its several versions, and is in line with the tolerance of the pacts that Muslims issued to conquered peoples at that time. However, the late date of its appearance, its textual elaborations and other inaccuracies prevent me from stating with certainty that we have the original text issued in 16 AH/ 637 CE. It was also demonstrated that the ban on Jews from residing in Islamic Jerusalem resulted from the conflict between Christians and Jews, and was added later to the otherwise authoritative version of the document recorded by al-Tabari. The Greek Orthodox Church's version published in 1953 was shown to be an Ottoman-period forgery influenced by intra-Christian denominational conflict over the holy places.

'Umar's Assurance of Safety laid down basic principles for relations between Muslims and non-Muslims that are applicable in all times and places. Thus, Salah al-Din did not promulgate new edicts when he conquered Jerusalem. For him, 'Umar's Assurance represented the best practice. He refused to destroy the church of the Holy Sepulchre, and cited not only 'Umar's preservation of this church, but his delegation of control to the Christians themselves in return for payment of *jizyah* – examples that Salah al-Din followed.

Under 'Umar, the status of the Christians underwent a rapid change and rights were granted in their favour. One of his guarantees was that churches would not be destroyed and that Christian religious rights would be protected. For this reason he refused to pray in the Church of the Holy Sepulchre, in case

Muslims might later use this as an excuse to convert the building into a mosque to commemorate the first Islamic prayer in Aelia (Islamic Jerusalem). This event shows 'Umar's far-sighted tolerance towards the Christians and his application of the Qur'anic injunction, 'there is no compulsion in religion'. Christian confidence in Muslim tolerance was shown when Patriarch Sophronius handed over the keys to the Holy Sepulchre church to 'Umar, and later to a Muslim family. In this way, the patriarch guaranteed the church's safety as well as protecting it from future disputes between Christian denominations over who should control it.

The indigenous Christians of Islamic Jerusalem perceived both the first and second Muslim conquests as liberation from the domination of unsympathetic groups of their own co-religionists – the Byzantines and Latin Catholics respectively. In the first conquest, this was primarily related to the bitter theological disagreement between Jerusalem's Christians and the Byzantine emperor, and they looked to the Muslims to restore their religious privileges. They also had more social and cultural affinity with Arab culture than with Byzantine culture. In the second Muslim conquest the local Orthodox Christians sought freedom from the control of the Church of Rome, represented by the Crusaders. The local Christians were aware that in the days of Muslim rule, before the Crusaders, they had freedom to worship as they wished. Indeed, Salah al-Din restored the rights of all Christian denominations to worship freely.

Salah al-Din's magnanimity towards both the Crusaders in Islamic Jerusalem and the local Christians contrasts sharply with the violence of the Crusaders towards Muslims in 492 AH/1099 CE. His generous and fair-minded conduct was in accordance with Muslim teaching, which forbids the committing of such barbaric acts, and he was respected by the Muslim and Christian worlds alike.

Ostensibly, the Crusades were launched to rescue Christians in Islamic Jerusalem from Muslim persecution. But there is much evidence, discussed in this book, to show that Christians and

Muslims lived in peaceful coexistence in the city and that Christians were allowed to practice their religion freely.

The protracted negotiations between Salah al-Din and King Richard I at the end of the Third Crusade highlighted the crucial importance of Jerusalem to both sides. Initially, Richard claimed that not only Jerusalem, but the whole region, belonged to the Crusaders and that Muslims had no rights there. The king's demands dropped dramatically towards the end, to the point where he was willing to accept just a small village. Salah al-Din insisted that he would never give up Islamic Jerusalem or Muslim rights to it, but that he would also protect the rights of Christians in the city. In the Al-Ramla peace treaty, the sultan confirmed the right of indigenous Christians to live in Islamic Jerusalem, and of other Christians to visit the holy places.

'Umar and Salah al-Din are powerful examples of the teachings of Islam towards non-Muslims. I totally reject the arguments of some modern writers that the Muslim treatment of non-Muslims was oppressive or violent, and that Muslim teachings contain hatred and injustice toward non-Muslims. As shown in this book, Muslim policies in Islamic Jerusalem enabled Muslims to live in peaceful coexistence with Christians and Jews.

Peace, freedom and security in Jerusalem will never be restored until Islamic Jerusalem's vision is reimplemented. It is an inclusive vision that respects the holiness of the city and acknowledges its central position not only in Islam, but in the faiths of Christians and Jews. It has been shown in this book that the Christians tasted freedom of religion under Muslim rule. When they were under the rule of their fellow Christians they experienced oppression. An inclusive vision is, and always will be, the only safe haven for followers of other religions. The continuity of Arab Christians, their churches and holy places in Jerusalem up till today is evidence of the good treatment that non-Muslims received from Muslims.

NOTES

Introduction

1. AH stands for After Hijra, or after the migration. The term is from the Islamic calendar and signifies the date of Prophet Muhammad's migration from Makkah to Madinah in 622 CE. Its usage was introduced by the second Muslim caliph, 'Umar Ibn Al-Khattab, in 16 AH (637 CE). CE signifies Common Era, known in the Christian world as AD (Anno Domini).
2. El-Awaisi, Khalid. 2006. *'Mapping Islamicjerusalem: the Geographical extent of the Land of Bayt al-Maqdis, the Holy Land and the land of Barakah'*. (Unpublished Ph.D thesis). Dundee: Al-Maktoum Institute for Arabic and Islamic Studies, University of Aberdeen, pp. 328–9.
3. Professor Abd al-Fattah El-Awaisi. Principal and Vice-Chancellor of Al-Maktoum Institute for Arabic and Islamic Studies, in Scotland – UK, Chair in Islamicjerusalem Studies and Director of the Centre for Islamicjerusalem Studies.
4. Al-Ahlas, Aisha. 2004. *Islamic Research Academy (ISRA) 1994–2004: Background, Activities, and Achievements, with Special Reference to the New Field of Inquiry of Islamic Jerusalem Studies, 1994–2004*. Dundee: Islamic Research Academy (ISRA), pp. 7–9.
5. Ibid., pp. 9–11.
6. El-Awaisi, Abd al-Fattah. 2005. *Introducing Islamicjerusalem*. Dundee: Al-Maktoum Institute Academic Press, pp. 18–19.
7. Ibid., p. 14.
8. Abraham, A. J. and Haddad, G. 1989. *The Warriors of God: Jihad (Holy War) and the Fundamentalists of Islam*. Lima, OH: Wyndham Hall Press. p. 14.

9   The Sunnah contains the legal rules and forms of worship of the Prophet, and includes the Hadith: the sayings, deeds and traditions of the Prophet.

Chapter One

1. *Shari'ah* is found in the Qur'an and the various collections of Hadith. If the legislation of the Qur'an is somewhat unclear, that of Hadith is more so. Various Muslim scholars have attempted to synthesize this mass of legislation in the form of codes, some of which have become classics. The compilation of codes and the replies to particular questions (*fatwas*) were recognized as human efforts to understand or apply *shari'ah* and could not be directly identified with *shari'ah*. This human formulation of *shari'ah* is known as *fiqh*.
2. For example, al-Hakim was strict in his treatment with the Christians. He ordered them to wear clothes that distinguished from Muslims by a certain colour and to wear heavy wooden crosses around their necks, and prohibited them from celebrating some religious ceremonies. He also ordered the destruction of some churches in Egypt, the burning of some crosses, and that small mosques should be built on the roofs of churches. See Al-Maqrizi, Abu al-'Abbas Ahmad Ibn 'Ali. 1998. *Kitab al-Mawa'iz bi Dhikr al-Khitat wa al-Athar*. Beirut: Manshurat Muhammad 'Ali Baydun. Dar al-Kutub al-'Ilmiyyah. Vol. 4, p. 413.
3. Khallaf, 'Abd al-Wahab. 1986. *'Ilm Usul al-Fiqh*. Cairo: Dar al-Qalam, p. 36.
4. The consensus that is regarded as authoritative is not of Muslims as a whole, but of those who are learned and whose opinions are respected, that is, the *'ulama* or religious scholars. This group became a powerful force for conformity, gradually dominating Islamic jurisprudence among the Sunnis. Given that the community was the touchstone of Sunni Islam, it should be no surprise that 'community consensus' was invoked frequently in legal decisions where the Qur'an, the prophetic traditions, or analogy fell short.
5. The concept of analogy developed from the Qur'an and Sunnah, but was stricter. When a problem arose that neither the Qur'an nor the prophetic traditions could resolve, an attempt was made to find an analogous situation for which a clear determination had already been made.
6. Armstrong, Karen. 1996. *A History of Jerusalem One City, Three Faiths*. London: Harper Collins, p. 234.
7. Al-Qaradawi, Yusuf. 2000. 'al-Infitah 'Ala al-Gharb, Muqtadayatuhu wa Shrutuhu', in *Risalit al-Muslimin fi bilad al-Gharb*, ed. Abu-Shamalah, M.'A. Irbid, Jordan: Dar al-Amal, p. 17.

8 Al-Faruqi, Isma'il. 1998. *Islam and Other Faiths*. Leicester: The Islamic Foundation and the International Institute of Islamic Thought, pp. 211–36. See also Anees, Munawar Ahmad. 1991. 'The Dialogue of History', in *Christian-Muslim Relations, Yesterday, Today, Tomorrow*, ed. Davies, M. W. London: Grey Seal, pp. 7–33.
9 Qur'an, *al-'Ankabut*, v. 46.
10 Al-Qaradawi, 'al-Infitah', *op. cit.*, pp. 7–29.
11 Qur'an, *al-Ma'idah*, v. 5.
12 Hamidullah, Muhammad. 1997. *Introduction to Islam*. Cairo: El-Falah for Translation, Publication and Distribution, p. 304.
13 Qur'an, *al-Baqarah*, v. 187.
14 Qur'an, *ar-Rum*, v. 21.
15 'Ali, Muhammad Mohar. 1997. *Sirat al-Nabi and the Orientalists*. Madina: King Fahid Complex for the Printing of the Holy Qur'an and Centre for the Service of Sunnah and Sirah. Vol. IB, pp. 669–70.
16 Qur'an, *ar-Rum*, vv. 2–5.
17 Qur'an, *al-A'raf*, v. 189.
18 Qur'an, *al-Hujura*, v. 13.
19 Ibid.
20 Qur'an, *al-Baqarah*, v. 256.
21 Al-Wahidi, Abu al-Hasan 'Ali Ibn Ahmad. 1998. *Asbab al-Nuzul*. Cairo: Dar al-Hadith, p. 74.
22 Ibn Kathir's book is one of the better-known works on *tafsir*, perhaps second to al-Tabari, but with more emphasis on the soundness of reports, in particular a rejection of all foreign influences such as *isra'iliyat*. It discusses the *sanad* of various reports, often in detail, which makes it one of the more valuable books of *tafsir*. It makes much use of *tafsir al-Qur'an bi'l Qur'an*, referring readers to other relevant verses on the topic. See Denffer, Ahmad Von. 1994. *'Ulum Al-Qur'an, An Introduction to the Sciences of the Qur'an*. Leicester: The Islamic Foundation, p. 136.
23 Ibn Kathir, Abu al-Fida' Isma'il. 1994. *Tafsir al-Qur'an al-'Azim*. Riyadh: Maktabat Dar al-Salam. Vol. 1, p. 416.
24 This *tafsir* book of the well-known author Qutb has greatly influenced many Muslims, especially younger generations and particularly in the Middle East. Qutb wrote it mostly during his imprisonment (1954–64) and completed before he was executed by the Egyptian government because of his association with the Muslim Brothers. His aim in this Qur'anic commentary was to explain the true nature of Islam to contemporary Muslims, and to invite them at both the individual and the social level, to join the struggle for the establishment of Islam. He emphasized the differences that exist between Islam and non-Muslim

systems, as well as the need for Muslims to strive for the establishment of an Islamic movement. See Denffer, *'Ulum Al-Qur'an, op. cit.,* p. 139.

25 Qutb, Sayyid. 2001. *Fi Zilal al-Qur'an.* Beirut: Dar al-Shuruq. Vol. 1, p. 291. See also Qutb, Sayyid. 1999. *In the Shade of the Qur'an (Fi Zilal al-Qur'an),* trans. and ed. Salahi, M. A. and Shamis, A. A. Leicester: The Islamic Foundation. Vol. 1, p. 325.

26 Abu Zahra, Muhammad. 1979. 'International Relations in Islam', *al-Azhar Magazine,* 51(2): 59–101.

27 'Abdalati, Hammudah. 1975. *Islam in Focus.* Indianapolis: American Trust Publications, pp. 33–44.

28 Al-Mawdudi, Sayyid Abul A'la. 1988. *Towards Understanding the Qur'an.* English version of *Tafhim al-Qur'an,* trans. and ed. Ansari, Z. Leicester: The Islamic Foundation. Vol. 1, p. 199.

29 Al-Zuhaili, Wahba. 2001. *al-Tafsir al-Wasit.* Beirut and Damascus: Dar al-Fikr al-Mu'aser and Dar al-Fikr. Vol. 1, pp. 148–49.

30 Qur'an, *al-Baqarah,* v. 191.

31 Malekian, Farhad. 1994. *The Concept of Islamic International Criminal Law: A Comparative Study.* London: Graham & Trotman, p. 61.

32 Al-Baladhuri, Abu al-'Abbas Ahmad Ibn Yahya. 1987. *Futuh al-Buldan.* Beirut: Mu'assasat al-Ma'arif, pp. 171–72.

33 Qur'an, *An-Nahl,* v. 106.

34 Qur'an. *al-Mumtahana,* vv. 8–9.

35 Al-Tabari's book is among the most famous books of *tafsir* and is perhaps the most voluminous work we have on the subject. It belongs to the class of *tafsir bi'l-riwaya* and is based on the reports of the Prophet, his companions and the followers, giving the various chains of transmission and evaluating them. See Denffer, *'Ulum Al-Qur'an, op. cit.,* p.135.

36 Al-Tabari, Abu Ja'far Muhammad Ibn Jarir. 1999. *Tafsir al-Tabari, al-Musamma Jami' al-Bayan fi Ta'wil al-Qur'an.* Beirut: Manshurat Muhammad 'Ali Baydun, Dar al-Kutub al-'Ilmiyyah. Vol. 12, pp. 62–63.

37 This book was written by al-Qurtubi, a learned scholar of Andalusia (Spain), who was a follower of the Maliki School of *fiqh.* The aim of this *tafsir* is to deduce juristic injunctions and rulings from the Qur'an. Apart from focusing on juristic rulings, he has also provided an explanation of the verses, explaining difficult words and discussing style and composition. He provides several Hadiths and reports to support his arguments and explanations. Finally, this kind of *tafsir* is categorized under the *Tafsir al-Fuqaha',* the juristic exegeses. See Al-

Qattan, Manna'. 1986. *Mabahith fi 'Ulum al-Qur'an*. Beirut: Mu'assasat al-Risalah, pp. 380–81.

38 Al-Qurtubi, Abu 'Abdullah Muhammad. 1998. *al-Jami' li Ahkam al-Qur'an*. Beirut: Dar al-Fikr. Vol. 9, pp. 53–54.

39 This book was written by a well-known scholar of Andalusia, Ibn al-'Arabi, who was a follower of the Maliki school of *fiqh*. His aim in this *tafsir* was to deduce juristic injunctions and rulings from the Qur'an. This book is the most important juristic exegesis from the Maliki school. In it, Ibn al 'Arabi relied on Arabic grammar and lexicography as a way of deducing juristic injunctions. He paid much attention to *sanad* (the chain of transmitters). Finally, this kind of *tafsir* is categorized under the *'Tafsir al-Fuqaha'*, the juristic exegeses. See Al-Qattan, *Mabahith fi 'Ulum al-Qur'an, op. cit.*, p. 379.

40 Ibn al-'Arabi, Abu Bakr Muhammad, 1996. *Ahkam al-Qur'an*. Beirut: Manshurat Muhammad 'Ali Baydun, Dar al-Kutub al-'Ilmiyyah. Vol. 4, p. 228. See also Al-Qurtubi, *al-Jami', op. cit.*, Vol. 9, pp. 53–54.

41 Al-Zamakhshari's book is one of the well-known books of *tafsir* based on a *mu'tazila* approach and is considered the standard work of *mu'tazila tafsir*, with much emphasis on Arabic grammar and lexicography as a means of interpretation, with less attention given to *sanad* (chain of transmitters). See Denffer, *'Ulum Al-Qur'an, op. cit.*, p. 136.

42 Al-Zamakhshari, Abu al-Qasim Jarallah Mahmud. 1995. *Tafsir al-Kashshaf 'An Haqa'iq Ghawas al-Tanzil wa 'Uiwn al-Aqawil fi Wjuh al-Ta'wil*. Beirut: Manshurat Muhammad 'Ali Baydun. Dar al-Kutub al-'Ilmiyyah. Vol. 4, pp. 503–04.

43 Al-Razi's book is one of the most comprehensive works of *Tafsir bi'l-ra'y*, covering many areas often beyond the actual field of exegesis. See Denffer, *'Ulum Al-Qur'an, op. cit.*, p. 136.

44 Al-Razi, Fakhr al-Din Muhammad Ibn 'Umar. 1990. *al-Tafsir al-Kabir aw Mafatih al-Ghaib*. Beirut: Dar al-Kutub al-'Ilmiyyah. Vol. 15, p. 263.

45 Ibn Kathir, *Tafsir al-Qur'an al-'Azim, op. cit.*, Vol. 4, pp. 448–49. See also Ibn Kathir, Abu al-Fida' Isma'il. 2000. *Tafsir Ibn Kathir*. Abridged by group of scholars under the supervision of Shaykh Safiur-Rahman al-Mubarapuri. Houston, TX: Darussalam Publishers and Distributors. Vol. 9, pp. 595–98.

46 Qutb, *Fi Zilal al-Qur'an, op. cit*, Vol. 6, pp. 3544–45.

47 Mawlawi, Faisal. 2000. 'al-Mafahim al-Asasiyya lil Da'wah al-Islamiyyah fi Bilad al-Gharb', in *Risalit al-Muslimin fi bilad al-Gharb*, ed. Abu Shamalah, M. A. Irbid, Jordan: Dar al-Amal, p. 202.

48 Al-Bukhari, Abu 'Abd Allah Muhammad. n.d. *Sahih Al-Bukhari*. Riyadh: Dar Ishbilyya. Vol. 4, Part. 7, p. 71. See also Abu Dawud, Abu

Sulaiman Ibn al-Ash'ath. 1988. *Sunan Abi Dawud*. Beirut: Dar al-Jil. Vol. 2, p. 130, Hadith No. 1668.

49 Al-Qarafi, Abu al-'Abbas Ahmad Ibn Idris. 1998. *al-Furuq wa Anwar al-Buruq fi Anwa' al-Furuq*. Beirut: Manshurat Muhammad 'Ali Baydun, Dar al-Kutub al-'Ilmiyyah. Vol. 3, p. 31.
50 Qur'an, *al-Ma'idah*, v. 8.
51 Ibn al-'Arabi, *Ahkam al-Qur'an, op. cit.*, Vol. 2, p. 81. See also Al-Tabari, *Tafsir al-Tabari, op. cit.*, Vol. 4, p. 483.
52 Al-Zamakhshari, *Tafsir al-Kashshaf, op. cit.*, Vol. 1, p. 600.
53 Al-Qurtubi, *al-Jami', op. cit.*, Vol .3, p. 70–71.
54 Ibn Kathir, *Tafsir al-Qur'an al-'Azim, op. cit.*, Vol. 2, p. 44.
55 Abu Zahra, 'International Relations', *op. cit.*, pp. 59–101.
56 Qur'an *al-'Imran*, v. 28.
57 Qur'an *An-Nisa'*, vv. 138–39.
58 Al-Tabari, *Tafsir al-Tabari, op. cit.*, Vol. 3, pp. 227–29.
59 Qur'an, *al-Ma'idah*, v. 51.
60 Al-Qaradawi, Yusuf. 1997. *The Lawful and the Prohibited in Islam (al-Halal wal-Haram fil Islam)*. Cairo: El-Falah for Translation, Publishing and Distributing, p. 453.
61 Ibn Kathir, *Tafsir al-Qur'an-al-'Azim, op. cit.*, Vol. 2, p. 94.
62 Al-Zamakhshari, *Tafsir al-Kashshaf, op. cit.*, Vol. 1, p. 629.
63 Ibid., pp. 629–30. See also Ibn Kathir, *Tafsir al-Qur'an al-'Azim, op. cit.*, Vol. 2, pp. 95–96.
64 Al-Razi, *al-Tafsir al-Kabir, op. cit.*, Vol. 6, p. 15.
65 Al-Qurtubi, *al-Jami', op. cit.*, Vol. 3, pp. 157–58.
66 Ibn Kathir, *Tafsir al-Qur'an al-'Azim, op. cit.*, Vol. 2, pp. 95–96.
67 A well-known mountain in Madinah. One of the great battles of Muslim history, the battle of Uhud, took place at its foot.
68 Qur'an, *al-'Imran*, v. 28, *an-Nisa'*, v. 144, *al-Anfal*, v. 72–73, *al-Twbah*, vv. 23 and 71, and *al-Mumtahana*, v. 1.
69 An-Na'im, Abdullahi Ahmed. 1990. *Toward an Islamic Reformation: Civil Liberties, Human Rights and International Law*. New York: Syracuse University Press, pp. 144–45.
70 Qur'an. *al-Ma'idah*, v. 52.
71 Qur'an. *al-Mumtahana*, v. 7.
72 Ibn Manzur, Muhammad Ibn Makram. 1999. *Lisan al-'Arab*. Beirut: Dar Ihya' al-Turath al-'Arabi. Vol. 5, p. 59. See also Al-Fayruzabadi, Mujid al-Din Muhammad Ibn Ya'qubi. 1991. *al-Qamus al-Muhit*. Beirut: Dar Ihya' al-Turath al-'Arabi. Vol. 4, p. 162.
73 Al-Ghiryani, al-Sadiq. 2002. *Mudawanat al-Fiqh al-Maliki wa Adilatih*. Beirut: Mu'assasat al-Rayan. Vol. 2, p. 454.

74 Al-Buti, Muhammad Sa'id Ramadan. 1999. 'Mu'amalit al-Dawlah al-Islamiyyah Lighayr al-Muslimin: al-Quds Namudhajan', *Journal of Islamic Jerusalem Studies*, 3 (1): 8.
75 Al-Sarkhasi, Abu Bakr Muhammad Ibn Ahmad. 2001. *Kitab al-Mabsut*. Beirut: Manshurat Muhammad 'Ali Baydun. Dar al-Kutub al-'Ilmiyyah. Vol. 5, Part 10, p. 87; al-Kasani, 'Ala' al-Din Abi Bakr Ibn Mas'ud. 1997. *Bada'i' al-Sani' fi Tartib al-Shara'i'*. Beirut: Manshurat Muhammad 'Ali Baydun. Dar al-Kutub al-'Ilmiyyah. Vol. 9, p. 427.
76 'Oudah, 'Abd al-Qadir. n.d. *al-Tashri' al-Jina'i al-Islami Muqaranan Bilqanwn al-Wad'i*. Cairo: Maktabat Dar al-Turath. Vol.1, p. 338. See also Zaydan, 'Abd al-Karim. 1982. *Ahkam al-Dhimmiyyn wa al-Musta'minyn fi Dar al-Islam*. Baghdad: Maktabat al-Quds, pp. 63–64.
77 Prophet Muhummad says: 'whoever (referring to Muslims) dies without a pledge (*bay'ah*) dies as one belonging to the days of *jahiliyyah* (ignorance).'
78 Ibn Manzur, *Lisan al-'Arab*, op. cit., Vol. 2, p. 280. See also Al-Fairuzabadi, *al-Qamus al-Muhit*, op. cit., Vol. 4, p. 152; Ibn 'Abdin, Muhammad Amin. 1994. *Rad al-Muhtar 'Ala al-Dur al-Muktar Sharh Tanwir al-Absar*. Beirut: Manshurat Muhammad 'Ali Baydun, Dar al-Kutub al-'Ilmiyyah. Vol. 6, p. 317; Al-Jawhiri, Isma'il Ibn Hammad. n. d. *al-Sihah Taj al-Lughah wa Sihah al-'Arabiyyah*. Beirut: Dar al-'Ilm lil Malayin. Vol. 6, pp. 2302–03.
79 'Ali, 'Abduallah Yusuf. 1998. *The Holy Qur'an: Translation and Commentary*. Birmingham: IPCI: 'Islamic vision', p. 497.
80 Muslim, Abu al-Husain Ibn al-Hajjaj. 1996. *Sahih Muslim*, trans. Siddiqi, A. India: Adam Publishers. Vol. 3, p. 163.
81 For example, Al-Baladhuri says that one of the terms in the treaty between Maslamah Ibn 'Abd al-Malik (an army chief of al-Walid Ibn 'Abd al-Malik) and al-Jarajimah (a Christian tribe in al-Sham) was that al-Jarajimah would be exempted from paying the *jizyah* and would have to participate in the Muslim war. See Al-Baladhuri, *Futuh al-Buldan*, op. cit., p. 220. It is worth mentioning that Imam al-Shafi'i had permitted the participation of non-Muslims on the side of Muslims in their wars. He justified this by some examples in Muslim history, as when a number of the Jews of the Banu Qaynaqa' tribe had joined the Muslims in their war after Badr, and the participation of Safw'n (non-Muslim) on the Muslim side in the battle of Hunayn. However, Imam Abu Hanifah and Imam Malik disallowed the participation of non-Muslims on the side of Muslims; see Al-Mawardi, Abu al-Hasan 'Ali Ibn Muhammad. 1994. *Al-Hawi al-Kabir*. Beirut: Dar al-Fikr. Vol. 18, pp. 144–45.

82. Ibn al-Qayyim al-Jawziyya, Muhammad Abi Bakr. 1989. *Zad al-Ma'ad fi Hadi Khayr al-'Ibad*. Cairo: al-Maktabah al-Qayyimh. Vol. 3, p. 370.
83. Abu 'Ubayd, al-Qasim Ibn Sallam. 1986. *Kitab Al-Amwal*. Beirut: Dar al-Kutub al-'Ilmiyyah, p. 25.
84. Ibn Kathir, *Tafsir al-Qur'an al-'Azim*, *op. cit.*, Vol. 2, p. 456.
85. Qur'an. *Al-Tawba*, v. 29.
86. Al-Mawardi, A. 1996. *al-Ahkam as-Sultaniyyah: The Laws of Islamic Governance*, trans. Yate, A. London: Ta-Ha Publishers Ltd., pp. 209–10.
87. Ibn Juzay, Abu al-Qasim Muhammad Ibn Ahmad. n.d. *al-Qawanin al-Fiqhiyyah*. Beirut: Dar al-Fikr, pp.135–37.
88. Ibid.
89. Ibid., and Al-Mawardi, *al-Ahkam as-Sultaniyyah*, *op. cit.*, p. 210.
90. *Al-Wariq* means silver (*fiddah*); see Muhammad Ibn al-Jazriy. 1963. *al-Nihaya fi Gharib al-Hadith wa al-Athar*. Beirut: al-Maktabah 'Ilmiyyah. Vol. 5, p. 175.
91. Al-Asbahi, Malik Ibn Anas. n. d. *Al-Muwatta bi Riwayat Muhammad Ibn al-Hasan al-Shaibani*. Beirut: Dar al-Yarmuk, p. 112. Hadith No. 333; Ibn Juzay *al-Qawanin al-Fiqhiyyah*, *op. cit.*, pp. 135–37.
92. Abu Yusuf, Ya'qub Ibn Ibrahim. n.d. *Kitab ul-Kharaj*. Beirut: Dar al-Ma'rifa, pp. 122–26.
93. Ibid., pp 122–23; Al-Mawardi, *al-Ahkam as-Sultaniyyah*, *op. cit.*, p. 209; Al-Farra', Abi Ya'la Muhammad Ibn al-Husain. 1974. *al-Ahkam as-Sultaniyyah*. Beirut: Dar al-Fikr, p. 154.
94. Charity, purification, but commonly used in reference to the obligatory tax of about 2.5 per cent that affluent Muslims must pay to help the poor.
95. Al-Buti, Mu'amalit al-Dawlah al-Islamiyyah, *op. cit.*, pp. 8–9.
96. See chapter 2 of this book.
97. Al-Buti, Mu'amalit al-Dawlah al-Islamiyyah, *op. cit.*, p. 9.
98. Al-Zamakhshari, *Tafsir al-Kashshaf*, *op. cit.*, Vol. 2, p. 254.
99. Al-Razi, *al-Tafsir al-Kabir*, *op. cit.*, Vol. 8, p. 25.
100. Al-Qurtubi, *al-Jami'*, *op. cit.*, Vol. 4, p. 49.
101. Al-Tabari, *Tafsir al-Tabari*, *op. cit.*, Vol. 6, p. 349.
102. Ibn al-'Arabi, *Ahkam al-Qur'an*, *op. cit.*, Vol. 2, pp. 479–80.
103. Al-Zamakhshari, *Tafsir al-Kashshaf*, *op. cit.*, Vol. 2, p. 254. See also Al-Qurtubi, *al-Jami'*, *op. cit.*, Vol. 4, p. 49; Al-Tabari, *Tafsir al-Tabari*, *op. cit.*, Vol. 6, p. 349; Al-Razi, *al-Tafsir al-Kabir*, *op. cit.*, Vol. 8, p. 25 and Ibn Kathir, *Tafsir al-Qur'an al-'Azim*, *op. cit.*, Vol. 2, p. 458.
104. Al-Shafi'i, Abu 'Abd Allah Muhammad. 1993. *Kitab al-Umm*. Beirut: Dar al-Kutub al-'Ilmiyyah. Vol. 4, p. 249; Ibn al-Qayyim al-Jawziyya,

Muhammad Abi Bakr. 1995. *Ahkam Ahl al-Dhimma*. Beirut: Dar al-Kutub al-'Ilmiyyah. Vol. 1, p. 35.
105 Ibn Hazm, Abu Muhammad 'Ali Ibn Ahmad. 1984. *al-Muhalla bil Athar*. Beirut: Dar al-Kutub al-'Ilmiyyah. Vol. 5, p. 414.
106 Al-Nawawi, Abu Zakariyya Yahya. 1998. *Rawdat al-Talibin*. Beirut: Manshurat Muhammad 'Ali Baydun, Dar al-Kutub al-'Ilmiyyah. Vol. 7, pp. 503–04.
107 Ibn al-Qayyim, *Ahkam Ahl al-Dhimma*, *op. cit.*, Vol. 1, p. 35.
108 Abu Yusuf, *Kitab ul-Kharaj*, *op. cit.*, p. 123. See Abu Yusaf. 1979. *Kitab ul-Kharaj (Islamic Revenue Code)*, trans. 'Ali, A. Lahore: Islamic Book Centre, p. 248.
109 Al-Buti, Mu'amalit al-Dawlah al-Islamiyyah, *op. cit.*, p. 4.
110 Abu Yusaf, *Islamic Revenue Code*, *op. cit.*, pp. 246–47.
111 Abu Yusuf, *Kitab ul-Kharaj*, *op. cit.*, pp. 143–44.
112 A minority is a relatively small group of people who differ from others in the society of which they are a part, in race, religion, language, political persuasion, etc. Pearsall, J. and Trumble, B. 1996. *Oxford English Reference Dictionary*. Oxford: Oxford University Press, p. 921.
113 Al-Buti, Mu'amalit al-Dawlah al-Islamiyyah, *op. cit.*, p. 6.
114 Hamilton, Bernard. 2003. *The Christian World of the Middle Ages*. Stroud: Sutton Publishing, p. 216.
115 Abraham, A. J. and Haddad, G. 1989. *The Warriors of God: Jihad (Holy War) and the Fundamentalists of Islam*. Bristol, IN: Wyndham Hall Press, p. 14.
116 Ibid., p. 14.
117 Al-Mawardi, *al-Ahkam as-Sultaniyyah*, *op. cit.*, p. 10.
118 Al-Farra', *al-Ahkam as-Sultaniyyah*, *op. cit.*, p. 20. See also Al-Mawardi, *al-Ahkam as-Sultaniyyah*, *op. cit.*, p. 12.
119 Tritton, A. S. 1930. *The Caliphs and Their Non-Muslim Subjects: A Critical Study of the Covenant of 'Umar*. London: Oxford University Press, pp. 118–36.
120 Al-Farra', *al-Ahkam as-Sultaniyyah*, *op. cit.*, p. 32. See also Al-Mawardi, *al-Ahkam as-Sultaniyyah*, *op. cit.*, p. 44.
121 Al-Buti, Mu'amalit al-Dawlah al-Islamiyyah, *op. cit.*, p. 9.
122 Al-Sawa, 'Ali. 1994. 'Mawqif al-Islam min Ghayr al-Muslimin fi al-Mujtama' al-Islami' in *al-Mujaz fi Mu'amalit Ghayr al-Muslimin fi al-Islam*, ed. al-'Amad, I.S. Amman: al-Majma' al-Malaki li Buhuth al-Hadarah al-Islamiyyh. pp. 49-50.
123 Al-Mawardi, *al-Ahkam as-Sultaniyyah*, *op. cit.*, p. 208.
124 Abu Yusuf, *Kitab al-Kharaj*, *op. cit.*, pp. 124–25; Abu Yusaf, *Islamic Revenue Code*, *op. cit.*, p. 251.
125 Ibn Juzay, *al-Qawanin al-Fiqhiyyah*, *op. cit.*, pp. 136–37.

126 Al-Tabari, *Tarikh al-Umam, op. cit.,* Vol. 2, pp. 502–03.
127 Al-Qaradawi, Yusuf. 1983. *Ghayr al-Muslimin fi al-Mujtama' al-Islami.* Beirut: Mu'assasat al-Risalah. p.11.
128 Al-Qarafi, *al-Furuq, op. cit.,* Vol. 3, p. 29.
129 Ibn Taymiyyah, Ahmad. n. d. *Majmu' fatawa Shaikh al-Islam Ahmad Ibn Taymiyyah.* Saudi Arabia: al-Ri'asah al-'Ammah Lishu'un al-Haramayn al-Sharifayn. Vol. 28, p. 306.
130 Al-Mawardi, *al-Ahkam as-Sultaniyyah, op. cit.,* pp. 210–11.
131 Ibn Qudama, Muwafaq al-Din. 1996. *al-Mughni.* Cairo: Dar al-Hadith. Vol. 10, pp. 606–18.
132 Al-Farra', *al-Ahkam as-Sultaniyyah, op. cit.,* p.158.
133 Doi, 'Abdul Rahman. 1983. *Non-Muslims under Shari'ah: Islamic Law.* London: Ta-Ha Publishers, p. 60.
134 Al-Mubarakpuri, Safi-ur-Rahman. 1996. *Ar-Raheeq Al-Makhtum (The Sealed Nectar): Biography of the Noble Prophet.* Riyadh: Dar-us-Salam Publications, pp. 99–102.
135 Ibn Hisham, 'Abdul Malik. 1999. *al-Sira al-Nabawiyyah.* Egypt: Dar al-Taqwa. Vol. 1, p. 198.
136 Ibid., p.198.
137 For example, Qur'an, *al-'Ankabut,* v. 46.
138 Ibn Hisham, *al-Sira al-Nabawiyyah, op. cit.,* Vol. 2, pp. 108–10.
139 Al-Mubarakpuri, *Ar-Raheeq Al-Makhtum, op. cit.,* pp. 197–98.
140 Al-Buti, Mu'amalit al-Dawlah al-Islamiyyah, *op. cit.,* pp. 4–5.
141 Hamidullah, *Introduction to Islam, op. cit.,* p. 289.
142 El-Awaisi, Abd al-Fattah. 2005. *Introducing Islamicjerusalem.* Dundee: Al-Maktoum Institute Academic Press, p. 116.
143 Ibid., pp. 117–18.
144 Qur'an, *Saba',* v. 28.
145 Al-Mubarakpuri, *Ar-Raheeq Al-Makhtum, op. cit.,* pp. 350–63.
146 Ibid., pp. 355–56; Qur'an. *al-'Imran,* v. 64.
147 Al-Mubarakpuri, *Ar-Raheeq Al-Makhtum, op. cit.,* pp. 350–51.
148 Ibid., pp. 334–36.
149 Ibid., pp .336–39.
150 A village close to Ayla (*al-'aqabah*), according to *Yaquat al-Hamawi.*
151 Abu Yusuf, *Kitab al-Kharaj, op. cit.,* pp. 124–25; Abu Yusaf, *Islamic Revenue Code, op. cit.,* pp. 143–44; Abu 'Ubayd, *Kitab Al-Amwal, op. cit.,* pp. 201–02.
152 Abu 'Ubayd, *Kitab Al-Amwal, op. cit.,* pp. 212–13.
153 Ibid., p. 212.
154 Al-'Ajluni, Kashf al-Khafa', Vol. 1, p. 661 and Vol. 2, p. 303, Dar al-Turath, cited in Zaghlul, Abu Hajar Muhammad, n. d. *Mawsu'at Atraf al-Hadith al-Shrif.* Beirut: Dar al-Kutub al-'Ilmiyyah. Vol. 8, p. 5.

155 Al-Bukhari, *Sahih Al-Bukhari, op. cit.*, Vol 2, Part 4, p. 65; Al-Zubaidi, Ahmad Ibn 'Abdul-Latif, 1996. *Summarized Sahih al-Bukhari*, trans. Khan, M. M., Riyadh: Maktabat Dar-us-Salam, pp. 635–36. Hadith No. 1341; Abu Dawud, *Sunan Abi Dawud, op. cit.,* Vol. 3, p. 84. Hadith No. 2760; Al-Tabarani, Abu al-Qasim Sulaiman. 1999. *al-Mu'jam al-Awsat*. Amman: Dar al-Fikr. Vol. 6, pp. 64–65. Hadith No. 8011; Ibn Hajar, Ahmad Ibn 'Ali. 1997. *Bulugh al-Maram Min Adellat al-Ahkam*, Maktabat Dar al-Salam and Maktabat Dar al-Fayha' Riyadh and Damascus: Maktabat Dar al-Salam and Maktabat Dar al-Fayha', p. 396, Hadith No. 1314.

156 Abu Dawud, *Sunan Abi Dawud, op. cit.*, Vol. 3, p.38, Hadith No. 2614.

157 Al-Bukhari, *Sahih Al-Bukhari, op. cit.*, Vol. 2, part. 6, p. 195.

158 Abu Dawud, *Sunan Abi Dawud, op. cit.*, Vol. 3, p.168, Hadith No. 3052; Abu Yusuf, *Kitab al-Kharaj, op. cit.,* p. 125,

159 Ibn 'Abd al-Hakam, Abu al-Qasim 'Abd al-Rahman. 1996. *Futuh Misr wa Akhbaruha*. Beirut: Dar al-Fikr, pp. 49–50. See also Al-Baladhuri, *Futuh al-Buldan, op. cit.*, p. 307.

160 Among the vast literature is the latest book on *jihad* written by the Syrian jurist, Muhammad Khair Haikal. 1996. *al-Jihad wa al-Qital fi al-Siyasa al-Shar'iyyah*. Beirut: Dar al-Bairq, 3 vols.

161 Ibn Manzur, *Lisan al-'Arab, op. cit.,* Vol. 2, p. 397, see also Ibn 'Abdin, *Rad al-Muhtar, op. cit.,* Vol. 6, p. 197.

162 Qur'an. *al-Saff*, vv. 10–11.

163 Qur'an, *al-Baqarah*, v. 194.

164 Muslim, *Sahih Muslim, op. cit.*, Vol. 3, pp.162–63, Hadith No. 1731.

165 Qur'an, *al-Baqarah*, v. 190.

166 Al-Zubaidi, *Summarized Sahih al-Bukhari, op. cit.*, p. 613, Hadith No. 1293.

167 Al-Waqidi, Abu 'Abd Allah Muhammad Ibn 'Umar. n. d. *Futuh al-Sham*. Cairo: al-Maktaba al-Tawfiqiyya. Vol. 1, pp. 20–21.

Chapter Two

1 As-Suyuti, Jalal ad-Din. 1995. *The History of the Khalifahs Who Took the Right Way*. London: Ta-Ha Publishers, p. 110. See also Ibn al-Jawzi, Abu al-Faraj. 2001. *Sirat wa Manaqb Amir al-Mu'minin 'Umar Ibn al-Khattab*. Cairo: Dar al-Da'wah al-Islamiyyah, p. 9. The Prophet himself came from the Quraysh tribe.

2 Ibn al-Jawzi, *Sirat wa Manaqb, op. cit.,* pp. 51–55.

3 Ibid., p. 55.

4 Al-Qurashi, Ghalib. 1990. *Awlawiyat al-Faruq fi al-Idarah wa al-Qada'*. Sana'a: Maktabat al-Jil al-Jadid. Vol. 1, p 50.

5 Ibid., Vol. 1, pp. 97–100.

6 Rida, Muhammad. 1983. *Al-Faruq 'Umar Ibn al-Khattab*. Beirut: Dar al-'Ilmiyyah, p. 176.
7 As-Suyuti, *History of the Khalifahs, op. cit.,* p. 117. See also Ibn al-Jawzi, *Sirat wa Manaqb, op. cit.,* p. 20.
8 Rida, *Al-Faruq 'Umar Ibn al-Khattab, op. cit.,* p. 29. See also As-Suyuti, *The History of the Khalifahs, op. cit.,* p. 143.
9 Rida, *Al-Faruq 'Umar Ibn al-Khattab, op. cit.,* pp. 54–55.
10 Abu 'Ubayd, al-Qasim Ibn Sallam. 1986. *Kitab al-Amwal*. Beirut: Dar al-Kutub al-'Ilmiyyah, pp. 33–35. See also Al-Baladhuri, Abu al-'Abbas Ahmad Ibn Yahya. 1987. *Futuh al-Buldan*. Beirut: Mu'assasat al-Ma'arif, pp. 249–52, Abu Yusuf, Ya'qub Ibn Ibrahim. n.d. *Kitab ul-Kharaj*. Beirut: Dar al-Ma'rifa, pp. 120–21, Abu Yusaf. 1979. *Kitab ul-Kharaj (Islamic Revenue Code),* trans. 'Ali, A. Lahore: Islamic Book Centre, pp. 240–44, Ibn Adam, Yahya, n. d. *Kitab al-Kharaj*. Beirut: Dar al-Ma'rifa, pp .65–68.
11 Abu 'Ubayd, *Kitab al-Amwal. op. cit.,* pp. 33–35. See also Al-Baladhuri, *Futuh al-Buldan, op. cit.,* pp. 249–52; Abu Yusuf, *Kitab ul-Kharaj, op. cit.,* pp. 120–21; Abu Yusaf, *Islamic Revenue Code, op. cit.,* pp. 240–44; Ibn Adam, *Kitab al-Kharaj, op. cit.,* pp. 65–68.
12 Al-Tabari, Abu Ja'far Muhammad Ibn Jarir. 1997. *Tarikh al-Umam wa al-Muluk*. Beirut: Manshurat Muhammad 'Ali Baydun. Dar al-Kutub al-'Ilmiyyah. Vol. 2, p. 485; Ibn al-Athir, Abu al-Hasan 'Ali al-Shaibani. 1998. *al-Kamil fi al-Tarikh*. Beirut: Manshurat Muhammad 'Ali Baydun, Dar al-Kutub al-'Ilmiyyah.Vol. 2, pp. 377–78.
13 Al-Tabari, *Tarikh al-Umam, op. cit.,* Vol. 2, p. 485; Ibn al-Athir, *al-Kamil op. cit.,* Vol. 2 , p. 378.
14 Al-Tabari, *Tarikh al-Umam, op. cit.,* Vol. 2, p. 485, and Al-Tabari. 1989. *The History of al-Tabari,* trans. and annotated Juynboll, G. New York: State University of New York Press, Vol. XIII , p. 90; Ibn al-Athir, *al-Kamil, op. cit.,* Vol. 2, p. 378.
15 Al-Tabari, *Tarikh al-Umam, op. cit.,* Vol. 2, 485, see also Al-Mawardi, Abu al-Hasan 'Ali Ibn Muhammad. 1994. *Al-Hawi al-Kabir*. Beirut: Dar al-Fikr. Vol. 18, p. 399.
16 Al-Tabari, *Tarikh al-Umam, op. cit.,* Vol. 2, p. 485.
17 Ben Shemesh, A. 1958, *Taxation in Islam, the English Translation of Yahya Ibn Adams's Kitab al-Kharaj,* foreword by Goitein, S .D. Leiden: Brill. Vol. 1, p. 55.
18 Ibid., p. 195
19 'Azzam, 'Abd-al-Rahman. 1979. *The Eternal Message of Muhammad,* trans. Farah, C., London: Quartet Books, p. 55.
20 Ibn Sa'd. 1997. *Kitab al-Tabaqat al-Kubra*. Beirut: Manshurat Muhammad 'Ali Baydun, Dar al-Kutub al-'Ilmiyyah. Vol. 1, p. 239.

See also Ibn Saʿd. 1967. *Kitab al-Tabaqat al-Kabir*, trans. Haq, S. M. and Ghazanfar, H. K. Karachi: Pakistan Historical Society. Vol. 1, Part 2, p. 373.

21 Ibn Saʿd, *al-Tabaqat, op. cit.,* Vol. 1, pp. 222–70.
22 Al-Tabari, *Tarikh al-Umam, op. cit.,* Vol. 2, p. 485.
23 Ibid.
24 Nuʿmani, Shibli. 1957. *'Umar the Great (the second caliph of Islam).* Trans. Saleem, M. Lahore: Muhammad Ashraf Press. Vol. 2, p. 182.
25 Ibid., p.182.
26 Al-Tabari, *Tarikh al-Umam, op. cit.,* Vol. 2, p. 485.
27 Nuʿmani, *'Umar the Great, op. cit.,* Vol. 2, p. 183.
28 Caetani, Leone. 1910. *Annali Dell Islam.* Milan: Ulrico Hoeli. Vol. 2, p. 299.
29 Ben Shemesh, *Taxation in Islam, op. cit.,* Vol. 1, p. 56.
30 A percentage (one-tenth) to be taken from the trading between the *dhimmi* and the non-Muslims (*harbi*), who had no covenant with the Islamic state, when they pass through Islamic territory; or else one-tenth of the yield of land to be levied for public assistance.
31 Al-Shafiʿi, Abu ʿAbd Allah Muhammad. 1993. *Kitab al-Umm.* Beirut: Dar al-Kutub al-ʿIlmiyyah. Vol. 2, p. 364.
32 Ibn Adam, *Kitab al-Kharaj, op. cit.,* p. 62, Ben Shemesh, *Taxation in Islam, op. cit.,* Vol. 1, p. 55.
33 Al-Baladhuri, *Futuh al-Buldan, op. cit.,* pp. 251–52.
34 Known in Arabic as *al- Shurut al-'Umariyyah.*
35 Cohen, Mark.1999. 'What was the pact of 'Umar? A Literary-Historical Study', in *Jerusalem Studies in Arabic and Islam,* p. 100.
36 Al-Khallal, Abu Bakr Ahmad Ibn Muhammad. 1996. *Ahl al-Milah wa al-Ridah wa al-Zanadiqah wa Tarik al-Salah wa al-Fara'd Min Kitab al-Jameʿ.* Riyadh: Maktabet al-Maʿarif lil Nasher wa al-Tawziʿ. Vol. 2, pp. 431–34.
37 Ibn Hazm, Abu Muhammad ʿAli Ibn Ahmad. 1978. *Mratib al-Ijmaʿ fi al-ʿBadat wa al-Muʿamalat wa al-Muʿtaqadat.* Beirut: Dar al-Afaq al-Jadida, pp. 134–35. See also Ibn Hazm, *Al-Muhalla, op. cit.,* Vol. 3, p. 346.
38 Al-Tartushi, Abu Bakr Muhammad. 1990. *Siraj al-Muluk.* London: Riyad El-Rayyas Press, pp. 401–02.
39 Ibn Qudama, Muwafaq al-Din. 1996. *al-Mughni.* Cairo: Dar al-Hadith. Vol. 10, Vol. 12, pp 816–18. See also Ibn-Qudama al-Maqdisi. 1996. *al-Sharh al-Kabir.* Cairo: Dar al-Hadith. Vol. 12, pp. 806–09.
40 Ibn Taymiyyah, Ahmad. n. d. *Majmuʿ fatawa Shaikh al-Islam Ahmad Ibn Taymiyyah.* Saudi Arabia: al-Ri'asah al-ʿAmmah Lishu'un al-Haramayn al-Sharifayn. Vol. 28, pp. 651–53. See also Ibn Taymiyyah, Ahmad

'Abd al-Halim. 1996. *Eqtida' al-Sirat al-Mustaqim li mukhalfet Ashab al-Jahim.* Riyadh: Maktabat al-Rushed. Vol.1, pp. 225–26.

41 Ibn 'Asakir. 'Ali Ibn al-Hasan. 1995. *Tarikh Madinat Dimashq.* Lebanon: Dar al-fikr. Vol. 2, pp. 174–85.

42 Ibn al-Qayyim al-Jawziyya, Muhammad Abi Bakr. 1995. *Ahkam Ahl al-Dhimma.* Beirut: Dar al-Kutub al-'Ilmiyyah. Vol. 2, pp. 113–15. See also Ibn al-Qayyim. 1981. *Sharh al-Shurut al-'Umariyyah.* Beirut: Dar al-'Ilm li-lmalain, pp. 1–7.

43 Ibn Kathir, Abu al-Fida' Isma'il. 1994. *Tafsir al-Qur'an al-'Azim.* Riyadh: Maktabat Dar al-Salam. Vol. 2, pp. 458.

44 Al-Hindi, 'Ala' al-Din Ibn 'Ali al-Muttaqi. 1998. *Kanz al-'Umal fi Sunan al-Aqwal wa al-Af'al,* Beirut: Manshurat Muhammad 'Ali Baydun. Dar al-Kutub al-'Ilmiyyah. Vol. 4. Hadith No. 11489, pp. 215–16.

45 'Ajin, 'Ali. 1996. 'al-'Uhda al- 'Umariyyah, (Dirasa Naqdiyya)', *al-Hikma Journal,* No. 10. pp. 75–87.

46 Ibn al-Qayyim, *Sharh al-Shurut, op. cit.,* pp. 1–7.

47 Sa'id, Hammam. 1982. 'al-Wad' al-Qanwni li Ahl al-Dhimma', *Jordan University Journal,* 9 (1): 79.

48 Al-Quda, Zakariyya. 1987. 'Mu'ahadit fath Bayt al-Maqdis: al-'Uhda al-'Umariyyah', in *Bilad al-Sham fi Sader al-Islam,* ed. M. al-Bakhit and I. 'Abbas. Amman: University of Jordan and University of Yarmuk. Vol. 2, pp. 278–82.

49 Caetani, *Annali Dell Islam, op. cit.,* Vol. 3, pp. 957–59.

50 Tritton, A. S. 1930. *The Caliphs and Their Non-Muslim Subjects: A Critical Study of the Covenant of 'Umar.* London: Oxford University Press, pp. 5–17.

51 Cohen, 'What was the pact of 'Umar?', *op. cit.,* pp. 100–31.

52 Caetani, *Annali Dell Islam, op. cit.,* Vol. 3, p. 957 ; Arnold, T.W. 1913. *The Preaching of Islam: A History of the Propagation of the Muslim Faith.* London: Constable and Co., p. 59.

53 Al-Khallal, *Ahl al-Milah wa al-Ridah, op. cit.,* p. 94.

54 Ibn 'Asakir, *Tarikh Madinat Dimashq, op. cit.,* Vol. 2, p. 178–79.

55 Ibid., pp.174–81.

56 Ibn 'Asakir, *Tarikh Madinat Dimashq, op. cit.,* Vol. 2, pp. 174–80.

57 Al-Khatib al-Baghdadi, Abu Bakr Ahmad Ibn 'Ali. 1997. *Tarikh Baghdad aw Madinat al-Salam.* Beirut: Manshurat Muhammad 'Ali Baydun. Dar al-Kutub al-'Ilmiyyah. Vol. 14, pp. 117–18.

58 Al-Dhahabi, Muhammad Ibn Ahmad. 1995. *Mizan al-I'tidal Fi Naqd al-Rijal.* Beirut: Dar al-Kutub al-'Ilmiyyah. Vol. 4, p. 59. See also Al-Dhahabi. Muhammad Ibn Ahmad. 1997. *al-Mughni fi al-Du'afa'.* Beirut: Manshurat Muhammad 'Ali Baydun. Dar al-Kutub al-'Ilmiyyah. Vol. 2, p. 524.

59 'Ajin, 'al-'Uhda al-Umariyyah', *op. cit.*, p. 78.
60 Ibid., p 79.
61 Ibn al-Qayyim, *Ahkam Ahl al-Dhimma*, *op. cit.* Vol. 2, pp. 113–15
62 Ibid., p. 115.
63 'Ajin, 'al-'Uhda al-'Umariyyah', *op. cit.*, p. 79.
64 Sa'id, 'al-Wad' al-Qanuni', *op. cit.*, p.157.
65 'Ajin, 'al-'Uhda al-'Umariyyah', *op. cit.*, p. 83.
66 Ibid., p 83.
67 Al-Jazira is the name of the stretch of territory that lies between the Tigris and the Euphrates. It is bounded on the west by Asia Minor and Armenia, on the south by Syria, on the east by Iraq, and on the north by Armenia.
68 Ibn al-Qayyim, *Ahkam Ahl al-Dhimma*, *op. cit.*, Vol. 2, pp. 113–15. See also Ibn al-Qayyim, *Sharh al-Shurut*, *op. cit.*, pp. 1–7.
69 Qur'an, *At-tauubah*, v. 29.
70 'Ajin, 'al-'Uhda al-'Umariyyah', *op. cit.*, p. 84.
71 Ibn al-Qayyim, *Sharh al-Shurut*, *op. cit.*, from the Introduction.
72 Tritton, *The Caliphs*, *op. cit.*, pp. 6–15.
73 Ibn 'Asakir, *Tarikh Madinat Dimashq*, *op. cit.*, Vol. 2, pp. 120–21.
74 Ibid. The English translation of 'Umar's pact is quoted from Tritton, *The Caliphs*, *op. cit.*, pp. 6–8.
75 Ibn Taymiyyah, *Majmu' Fatawa Shaikh al-Islam*, *op. cit.*, Vol. 28, pp. 654.
76 Ibid., pp. 654–55.
77 Ibid., p. 654.
78 Ibn Taymiyyah, *Eqtida' al-Sirat al-Mustaqim*, *op. cit.*, Vol. 1, pp. 226–27.
79 Qur'an, *At-tawbah*, v. 29: 'Fight those who believe not in Allah nor the Last Day, Nor hold that forbidden which hath been forbidden by Allah and His Messenger, nor acknowledge the Religion of Truth, from among the People of the Book, until they pay the *jizyah* with willing submission, and feel themselves subdued.
80 Ibn Kathir, *Tafsir al-Qur'an al-'Azim*, *op. cit.*, Vol. 2, p. 458.
81 'Ajin, 'al-'Uhda al-'Umariyyah', *op. cit.*, p. 85.
82 Al-Albani, Muhammad Naser al-Din. 1985. *Irrwa' al-Ghalil fi Takhrij Ahadith Manar al-Sabil.* Beirut: al-Maktab al-Islami. Vol. 5, pp. 103–04
83 Caetani, *Annali Dell Islam*, *op. cit.*, Vol. 3, pp. 957–59.
84 Tritton, *The Caliphs*, *op. cit.*, p. 10.
85 Ibid., pp. 8–10.
86 Al-Shafi'i, *Kitab al-Umm*, *op. cit.*, Vol. 4, pp. 280–85. The English translation of this document is quoted, with some modifications, from Tritton, *The Caliphs*, *op. cit.*, pp. 12–16.
87 Tritton, *The Caliphs*, *op. cit.*, p. 12.
88 Al-Shafi'i, *Kitab al-Umm*, *op. cit.*, Vol. 4, p. 293.

89 Ibn al-Athir, *al-Kamil, op. cit.,* Vol. 2, p. 492.
90 Hamidullah, Muhammad. 1987. *Majmu'at al-Watha'iq al-Siyasiyya Lil'ahd al-Nabawi wa al-Khilafa al-Rashida.* Beirut: Dar al-Nafa's, pp. 756–57.
91 Ibid., p. 757.
92 Zaydan, 'Abd al-Karim. 1982. *Ahkam al-Dhimmiyyn wa al-Musta'minyn fi Dar al-Islam.* Baghdad: Maktabat al-Quds, pp. 6–640.
93 Al-Mutawakkil (d. 232 AH/786 CE) decreed that Christians and Jews should wear yellow garments, not white ones; that when riding they should use wooden stirrups; that their churches should be destroyed; that the *jizyah* should be doubled; that they should neither live in a Muslim quarter nor enter into Muslim employ. See Sell, E. 1901. *Essays on Islam.* Madras: SPCK Press, p. 187.
94 Safi, L., *Human Rights and Islamic Legal Reform.* http://home/att.net/louaysafi/articles/1999/human31/htmL. Seen on 4.4.2002.
95 Tritton, *The Caliphs, op. cit.,* pp. 22–25.
96 Qur'an, *al-Baqarah,* v. 256.
97 Abu 'Ubayd, *Kitab al-Amwal, op. cit.,* p. 39.
98 Qur'an, *al-Baqarah,* v. 256.
99 In addition, the conduct of Caliph 'Umar towards the Christians who were in the Muslim state clearly demonstrated full adherence to the concept of freedom of religion.
100 Al-Bukhari, Abu 'Abd Allah Muhammad. n.d. *Sahih Al-Bukhari.* Riyadh: Dar Ishbilyya. Vol. 2, Part 4, p. 6; Ibn Adam, *Kitab al-Kharaj, op. cit.,* p. 75; Abu Yusuf, *Kitab ul-Kharaj, op. cit.,* pp. 13–14; Al-Tabari, *Tarikh al-Umam op. cit.,* Vol. 2, p. 560; Ibn Hajar, Ahmad Ibn 'Ali. 1997. *Fath al-Bari Sharh Sahih al-Bukhari.* Riyadh and Damascus: Dar al-Salam and Dar al-Fayha', Vol. 6, p. 322, Hadith No. 3126.
101 Qur'an, *al-Tauba,* v. 60.
102 Abu Yusuf, *Kitab ul-Kharaj, op. cit.,* p. 126; Abu Yusaf, *Islamic Revenue Code, op. cit.,* p. 254.
103 Ibn al-Jawzi, *Sirat wa Manaqb Amir al-Mu'minin, op. cit.,* p. 89.
104 Ibid., p. 89.

Chapter Three

1 Donner, Fred McGraw. 1981. *The Early Islamic Conquest.* Princeton, NJ: Princeton University Press, p. 95.
2 Asaf, M. 1935. *The History of the Arab Rule in Palestine.* Tel-Aviv, Davar Press, cited in 'Athaminah, Khalil. 2000. *Filastin fi Khamsat Qurun Min al-Fath al-Islami Hatta al-Ghazw al-Faranji (634–1099) (Palestine in Five Centuries From the Islamic Conquest to the Frankish Invasion (634–1099).* Beirut: Mu'assasat al-Dirasat al-Filastiniyyah, p. 1.

3   Shahid, 'Irfan. 1984. *Byzantium and the Arabs in the Fourth Century.* Washington: Dumbarton Oaks, p. 339.
4   'Athaminah, *Filastin fi Khamsat, op. cit.,* pp. 6–9.
5   Abu 'layan, 'Azmi Muhammad. 1993. *al-Quds Bayn al-Ihtilal wa al-Tahrir 'Abr al-'Usur al-Qadimah wa al-Wsta wa al-Hadithah, (3000 BC–1967 CE).* Amman: Mu'assasat Bakir lil-Dirasat al-Thaqafiyyah, p. 134.
6   Ibid., pp. 127–33.
7   Hamilton, Bernard. 2003. *The Christian World of the Middle Ages.* Stroud, Gloucs: Sutton Publishing, p. 103.
8   Runciman, Steven.1987. *A History of the Crusades: The First Crusade and the Foundation of the Kingdom of Jerusalem.* Cambridge, UK: Cambridge University Press. Vol. 1, pp. 12–13.
9   Ibid., Vol.1, p. 12
10 Ibid., Vol. 1 p. 13.
11 Ibid., Vol. 1, p.6.
12 Al-Haytami, 'Ali Ibn Abi Bakr. *Manba' al-Fawa'id wa Majma' al-Zawa'id.* Vol. 9, p. 411, cited in al-Maqdisi, Muhammad Ibn 'Abd al-Wahid. 1988. *Fada'il Bayt al-Maqdis.* Beirut: Dar al-Fikr. p. 69.
13 Al-Bukhari, Abu 'Abd Allah Muhammad. n.d. *Sahih Al-Bukhari.* Riyadh: Dar Ishbilyya. Vol. 2, Part 4, p. 68; Ibn Hanbal, Ahmad Ibn Muhammad. 1995. *al-Musnad.* Cairo: Dar Al-Hadith. Vol. 17, p. 194, Hadith No. 23867.
14 Al-Bukhari, *Sahih al-Bukhari, op. cit.,* Vol.1, Part 2, p. 56; see also Muslim, Abu al-Husain Ibn al-Hajjaj. 1996. *Sahih Muslim,* trans. Siddiqi, A. Delhi: Adam Publishers. Vol. 2, p. 309, Hadith No. 827.
15 Ibn Hisham, 'Abdul Malik. 1999. *al-Sira al-Nabawiyyah.* Egypt: Dar al-Taqwa.Vol. 4, pp. 5–16.
16 Ibid., pp. 96–113.
17 Ibid., pp. 163, 196.
18 El-Awaisi, Abd al-Fattah. 1997. *Jerusalem in Islamic History and Spirituality: The Significance of Jerusalem in Islam, an Islamic Reference.* Dunblane: Islamic Research Academy, p. 24.
19 Ibn al-Murajja. Abu al-Ma'ali al-Musharraf. 1995. *Fada'il Bayt al-Maqdis wa-al-Khalil wa-Fada'il al-Sham,* ed. with an Introduction by Livne-Kafri, O. Shfaram: Aimashreq Ltd, p. 55.
20 El-Awaisi, Abd al-Fattah. 2005. *Introducing Islamicjerusalem.* Dundee: Al-Maktoum Institute Academic Press, p. 58.
21 Al-Tabari, Abu Ja'far Muhammad Ibn Jarir. 1997. *Tarikh al-Umam wa al-Muluk.* Beirut: Manshurat Muhammad 'Ali Baydun. Dar al-Kutub al-'Ilmiyyah.Vol. 2, p. 449; Al-Baladhuri, Abu al-'Abbas Ahmad Ibn Yahya. 1987. *Futuh al-Buldan.* Beirut: Mu'assasat al-Ma'arif, p. 189; Al-Waqidi, Abu 'Abd Allah Muhammad Ibn 'Umar. n. d. *Futuh al-Sham.*

Cairo: al-Maktaba al-Tawfiqiyya, pp. 326–28; Ibn al-Athir, Abu al-Hasan 'Ali al-Shaibani. 1998. *al-Kamil fi al-Tarikh*. Beirut: Manshurat Muhammad 'Ali Baydun, Dar al-Kutub al-'Ilmiyyah.Vol. 2, pp. 347–48; Ibn al-A'them, Abu Muhammad Ahmad. 1991. *Kitab al-Futuh*. Beirut: Dar al-Adwa'. Vol. 1, p. 224; Ibn al-Murajja, *Fada'il Bayt al-Maqdis, op. cit.*, p. 45.

22 Al-Tabari, *Tarikh al-Umam, op. cit.*, Vol. 2, p. 448; Ibn al-Jawzi, Abu al-Faraj 'Abd al-Rahman Ibn 'Ali. 1979. *Fada'il al-Quds*. Beirut: Dar al-Afaq al-Jadida. p. 12; Ibn al-Athir, *al-Kamil, op. cit.*, Vol. 2, p. 347; Ibn Kathir, Abu al-Fida' Isma'il. 1978. *al-Bidaya wa al-Nihaya*. Beirut: Dar al-Fikr. Vol. 4, Part 7, pp. 54–55.

23 Al-Baladhuri, *Futuh al-Buldan, op. cit.*, p. 54.

24 Gabrieli, Francesco. 1977. *Muhammad and the Conquest of Islam*, trans. from Italian by Luling, V. and Linell, R. Hampshire: World University Library, p. 150.

25 Al-Waqidi, *Futuh al-Sham, op. cit.*, Vol. 1, p. 322.

26 Ibid., pp. 325–26.

27 Ibid., p. 326.

28 Ibid., p. 323.

29 Ibn al-A'them, *Kitab al- Futuh, op. cit.*, Vol.1, p. 223.

30 Theophanes. 1997. *The Chronicle of Theophanes Confessor: Byzantine and Near Eastern History AD 284–813*, trans. with Introduction and Commentary by Mango, C. and Scott, R. Oxford: Clarendon Press, p. 471.

31 The Bible, Matthew 24:15. Cambridge, UK: Cambridge University Press.

32 Sahas, Daniel. 1994. 'Patriarch Sophronious, 'Umar Ibn al-Khattab and the Conquest of Jerusalem', in *Al-Sira' al-Islami al-Faranji 'ala Filastin fi al-Qurun al-Wasta* (The Frankish [Ifranji] Conflict over Palestine during the Middle Ages), ed. Hadia, Dajani-Shkeel and Burhan, Dajani. Beirut: The Institute for Palestine Studies, p. 65.

33 Al-Waqidi, *Futuh al-Sham, op. cit.*, Vol. 1, p. 333.

34 Al-Hanbali, Mujir al-Din. 1999. *al-Uns al-Jalil bi Tarikh al-Quds wa al-Khalil*. Hebron, Palestine: Maktabat Dandis. Vol. 1, p. 376.

35 Sahas, 'Patriarch Sophronious', *op. cit.*, p. 71.

36 Ibid., p. 54.

37 El-Awaisi, *Introducing Islamicjerusalem, op. cit.*, p. 103.

38 Al-Waqidi, *Futuh al-Sham, op. cit.*, Vol .1, p. 336.

39 Ibid., p. 336.

40 Al-Baladhuri, *Futuh al-Buldan, op. cit.*, pp. 188–89.

41 Ibid., p.189.

42 Ibid., p.189.

43 Ibn al-Athir, *al-Kamil, op. cit.,* Vol. 2, p. 348.
44 Al-Ya'qubi, Ahmad. 1999. *Tarikh al-Ya'qubi.* Beirut: Manshurat Muhammad 'Ali Baydun, Dar al-Kutub al-'Ilmiyyah. Vol. 2, p. 101.
45 Sa'id Ibn al-Batriq (Eutychius). 1905. *al-Tarikh al-Majmu' 'Ala al-Tahqiq wa al-Tasdiq.* Beirut: n. p. Vol. 2, p.16.
46 Al-Quda, Zakariyya. 1987. 'Mu'ahadit fath Bayt al-Maqdis: al-'Uhda al-'Umariyyah', in *Bilad al-Sham fi Sadr al-Islam,* ed. Muhammad al-Bakhit and Ihsan 'Abbas. Amman: University of Jordan and University of Yarmuk, 274. See also El-Awaisi, *Introducing Islamicjerusalem, op. cit.,* p. 70.
47 Ibn al-Jawzi, *Fada'il al-Quds, op. cit.,* pp. 123–24.
48 Al-Tabari, *Tarikh al-Umam, op. cit.,* Vol. 2, p. 449, See also Abu al-Fida', Isma'il Ibn 'Ali. 1997. *Tarikh Abi al-Fida' al-Musamma Al-Mukhtasar fi Akhbar al-Bashar.* Beirut: Manshurat Muhammad 'Ali Baydun, Dar al-Kutub al-'Ilmiyyah. Vol. 1, p. 200; Ibn al-Athir, *al-Kamil, op. cit.,* Vol. 2, p. 500; Ibn Kathir, *al-Bidaya op. cit.,* Vol.7, p. 55; and El-Awaisi, *Introducing Islamicjerusalem, op. cit.,* p. 70.
49 El-Awaisi, *Introducing Islamicjerusalem, op. cit.,* p. 71.
50 Al-Tabari, *Tarikh al-Umam, op. cit.,* Vol. 2, p. 449. English trans. taken from El-Awaisi, *Introducing Islamicjerusalem, op. cit.,* pp. 72–74.
51 'Ajin, 'al-'Uhda al-'Umariyyah', *op. cit.,* p.71.
52 Al-'Asfari, Khalifah Ibn Khayyat. 1993. *Tarikh Khalifah Ibn Khayyat,* Rewayet Baqi Ibn Khalid. Beirut: Dar al-Fikr. p. 265.
53 Ibid., p. 274.
54 El-Awaisi, *Introducing Islamicjerusalem, op. cit.,* pp. 71–72.
55 For example, the peace treaty given to the people of Damascus by Khalid Ibn al-Walid in the year 14 AH. See al-Baladhuri, *Futuh al-Buldan, op. cit.,* p. 166. Another example is the peace treaty given to the people of al-Jazirah by 'Ayyad Ibn Ghanam in 17 AH. See Abu 'Ubayd, al-Qasim Ibn Sallam. 1986. *Kitab al-Amwal.* Beirut: Dar al-Kutub al-'Ilmiyyah, p. 220.
56 El-Awaisi, *Introducing Islamicjerusalem, op. cit.,* pp. 66–67.
57 Al-Quda, 'Mu'ahadit fath Bayt al-Maqdis', *op. cit.,*p. 276.
58 Duri, 'Abd al-'Aziz.1990. 'Jerusalem in the Early Islamic Period: 7th–11th Centuries AD', in *Jerusalem in History,* ed. Asali, K. J. New York: Olive Branch Press, p. 107.
59 Al-Himyari, Muhammad. 1984. *al-Rawd al-Mi'tar Fi Khair al-Aqtar.* Beirut: Maktabat Lubnan, p. 69.
60 Ibn al-Jawzi, *Fada'il al-Quds, op. cit.,* pp. 123–24.
61 El-Awaisi, *Introducing Islamicjerusalem, op. cit.,* p.119.
62 Qur'an. *al-Mumtahana,* vv. 8–9.

'Allah forbids you not, with regard to those who fight you not for (your) faith nor drive you out of your homes, from dealing kindly and justly with them: For Allah loveth those who are just. Allah only forbids you, with regard to those who fight you for (your) faith, and drive you out of your homes, and support (others) in driving you out, from turning to them (for friendship and protection). It is such as turn to them (in these circumstances) that do wrong.'

63 Armstrong, Karen. 1997. 'Sacred Space: The Holiness of Islamic Jerusalem', in *Journal of Islamic Jerusalem Studies*, 1 (1): 14.
64 Wilkinson, J. 1990. 'Jerusalem under Rome and Byzantium 63 BC–637 AD', in *Jerusalem in History*, ed. Asali, K. J., p. 88; Al-'Arif, 'Arif. 1986. *al-Mufassal fi Tarikh al-Quds*. Jerusalem. Matba'it al-Ma'arif, p. 68; Abu 'Iyan, *al-Quds, op. cit.*, pp.132–33.
65 Al-'Arif, *al-Mufassal fi Tarikh al-Quds, op. cit.*, p. 68; Abu 'Iayan, *al-Quds, op. cit.*, pp.132–33.
66 Abu 'Iayan, *al-Quds, op. cit.*, pp. 136–37.
67 Al-Tabari, *Tarikh al-Umam, op. cit.*, Vol. 2, p. 418.
68 Sarkis, Khalil. 2001. *Tarikh al-Quds al-Ma'ruf bi Tarikh Urshalim*. Egypt: Maktabat al-Thaqafa al-Diniyyah. p. 101.
69 El-Awaisi, *Introducing Islamicjerusalem, op. cit.*, p. 85.
70 'Athaminah, *Filastin fi Khamsat, op. cit.*, p. 161.
71 Ibid., p.161.
72 El-Awaisi, *Introducing Islamicjerusalem, op. cit.*, p. 102.
73 Ibid., p. 87.
74 Ibid., pp. 77–78.
75 Al-'Affani, S. 2001. *Tadhkir al-Nafs bi Hadith al-Quds (wa Qudsah)*. Cairo: Maktabit Mu'ath Ibn Jabal. Vol. 1, p. 197.
76 '*Fulan*' is used in Arabic to refer to a person without specifying the name.
77 Al-Quda, 'Mu'ahadit fath Bayt al-Maqdis', *op. cit.*, p. 276.
78 El-Awaisi, *Introducing Islamicjerusalem, op. cit.*, p. 80.
79 It should be noted that the expression 'before the murder of Fulan' was absent from Mujir al-Din al-Hanbali's version of 'Umar's Assurance, which is very similar to al-Tabari's version.
80 Al-Tabari, *Tarikh al-Umam, op. cit.*, Vol. 2, p. 447.
81 El-Awaisi, *Introducing Islamicjerusalem, op. cit.*, p. 80.
82 Al-Tel, Othman. 2003. *The First Islamic Conquest of Aelia (Islamic Jerusalem) A Critical Analytical Study of the Early Islamic Historical Narratives and Sources*. Dundee: Al-Maktoum Institute Academic Press, pp. 109–20.
83 Ibn Kathir, *al-Bidaya, op. cit.*, Vol. 4, Part 7, pp.73–74
84 Al-Quda, 'Mu'ahadit fath Bayt al-Maqdis', *op. cit.*, p. 276.

85 Al-'Arif, *al-Mufassal fi Tarikh al-Quds, op. cit.*, p. 91. See also El-Awaisi, *Introducing Islamicjerusalem, op. cit.,* p. 92.
86 Al-'Arif, *al-Mufassal fi Tarikh al-Quds, op. cit.,* pp. 92–93.
87 Jasir, Shafiq. 1989. *Tarikh al-Quds wa al-'alaqa bayn al-Muslmin wa al-Masihiyyn hatta al-Hurub al-Salibiyya.* Amman: Matab'a al-Eman, p.116.
88 Sahas, 'Patriarch Sophronious', *op. cit.,* pp. 53–77.
89 This information was obtained from email communication with Dr Sahas on 23 May 2002 and 4 June 2002.
90 Al-'Arif, *al-Mufassal fi Tarikh al-Quds, op. cit.,* pp. 91–94.
91 El-Awaisi, *Introducing Islamicjerusalem, op. cit.,* pp. 95–96.
92 Al-'Arif, *al-Mufassafi fi Tarikh al-Quds, op. cit.,* p. 93.
93 El-Awaisi, *Introducing Islamicjerusalem, op. cit.,* pp. 97–98.
94 Ibid., pp. 99.
95 Asali, K. J. 1990. 'Jerusalem under the Ottomans (1515–1831 AD)', in *Jerusalem in History*, ed. Asali, K. J. New York: Olive Branch Press, p. 206.
96 Ibid., p. 206. In about the middle of the sixteenth century, dissension erupted between the Latin and the Greek Orthodox churches over their respective rights to the Christian holy places. Al-Dabbagh and al-'Arif pointed out that the quarrels between the Christian communities were sometimes so intense that they developed into bloody clashes, and this happened several times in the seventeenth century (e.g. 1666, 1669, 1674, 1756, 1808 and 1810, etc.). See Al-Dabbagh, Mustafa. 1988. *Biladuna Filastin.* Kufor Qar': Dar al-Shafaq. Vol. 10, pp. 147–49; al-'Arif, *al-Mufassal fi Tarikh al-Quds, op. cit.,* pp. 363–634.

In 1740 CE France succeeded in forcing on the Ottoman Caliphate a new version of the capitulations, in which France asserted rule as protector of the Roman Catholics and ensured the rights of the Franciscans in the Holy Sepulchre church and in other holy places in Islamicjerusalem. One result of the intervention of the European powers was an unprecedented increase in dissension between the Christian communities. The most violent of these clashes broke out in 1757 CE between the Latin and the Greek Orthodox communities inside the Holy Sepulchre. See Asali, 'Jerusalem under the Ottomans', *op. cit.,* p. 221.
97 Golubovich, G. 1906. *Biblioteca bio-bibliografica della Terra Santa e dell'Oriente Franciscano.* Firenze: Quarracchi, p. 163.
98 Asali, 'Jerusalem under the Ottomans', *op. cit.,* p. 210.
99 Golubovich, *Biblioteca bio-bibliografica, op. cit.,* p. 163.
100 Ibid., p. 163.
101 Al-Quda, 'Mu'ahadit fath Bayt al-Maqdis', *op. cit.,* p. 278.
102 El-Awaisi, *Introducing Islamicjerusalem, op. cit.,* p. 100.

103 Jasir, *Tarikh al-Quds, op. cit.,* p.117.
104 Ibid., p. 119.
105 Runciman, *History of the Crusades, op. cit.,* Vol.1, p. 20.
106 Ibid., Vol. 1, pp. 20–21.
107 Ibid.
108 Al-Azdi, Muhammad Ibn 'Abdullah. 1970. *Tarikh Futuh al-Sham.* Cairo: Mu'assasat Sijil al-'Arab, p. 111.
109 Caetani, *Annali Dell Islam, op. cit.,* Vol. 3, pp. 813–14.
110 Runciman, *History of the Crusades, op. cit.,* Vol. 1, p.6.
111 Armstrong, *History of Jerusalem, op. cit.,* p. 232.
112 Sahas, Patriarch Sophronious, *op. cit.,* p. 65.
113 Hitti, Philip. 1957. *Tarikh al-'Arab,* trans. Naf', M. M. Beirut: n. p. Vol. 2, p.143.
114 Butler, Alfred J. 1978. *The Arab Conquest of Egypt and the Last Thirty Years of the Roman Dominion.* Oxford: Clarendon Press, p. 158.
115 Ibid., pp. 158–59.
116 Runciman, *History of the Crusades, op. cit.,* Vol. 1, p. 21.
117 Armstrong, *History of Jerusalem, op. cit.,* p. 246.
118 Armstrong, 'Sacred Space', *op. cit.,* p. 19.
119 El-Awaisi, *Introducing Islamicjerusalem, op. cit.,* p. 105.
120 Tamimi, Azzam. 1999. 'Jerusalem under the Muslim Rule', *Al-Quds: Journal Concerned with the Issues on Jerusalem,* 1(2): 5.
121 Karlson, Anghmar. 1996. 'al-Fath al-Islami Harar al-Yahud min al-Itihad al-Masihi fi Ispanya', *Al-Quds al-'Arabi* newspaper, 7 (2097): 14.
122 Al-Hamarnah, Salih. 1999. 'Musahamat al-'Arab al-Masihiyyn fi al-Hadarah al-'Arabiyyah al-Islamiyyah, Nazrah 'Ala Bilad al-Sham', *Afaq al-Islam,* 3 (2): 77–78.
123 Hourani, Albert. 2002. *A History of the Arab Peoples.* London: Faber & Faber, pp. 23–24.
124 Shams al-Din, 'Muhammad Mahdi. 2001. 'al-Masihiyyah fi al-Mafhum al-Thqafi al-Islami al-Mu'aser', in *al-Nashrah,* al-Ma'had al-Malaki lil-Dirasat al-Diniyah, (Jordan), No. 18, p. 5. See also Fletcher, Richard. 2003. *The Cross and the Crescent: Christianity and Islam from Muhammad to the Reformation.* London: Penguin, p. 16; and Tamimi, 'Jerusalem', *op. cit.,* p. 7.
125 Tibawi, A. L. 1969. *Jerusalem, Its Place in Islam and Arab History.* Beirut: Institute for Palestine Studies, p. 11.
126 Al-Baladhuri, *Futuh al-Buldan, op. cit.,* p. 187.
127 Hamimi, Jamil, 'Islamic-Christian Relations in Palestine in a Civil Society: An Islamic Point of View', 1 March 2000. http://www.al-bushra.org/latpatra/hamami.htm.
Seen 14 September 2002.

128 El-Awaisi, *Introducing Islamicjerusalem, op. cit.,* p. 63.
129 Ibid., p. 106.
130 Hamimi, Islamic-Christian Relations, *op. cit.,* http://www.al bushra.org/latpatra/hamami.htm
131 Sa'id Ibn al-Batriq, *al-Tarikh al-Majmu', op. cit.,* Vol. 2, pp. 17–18.
132 Sahas, 'Patriarch Sophronious', *op. cit.,* p. 66.
133 Al-'Arif, *al-Mufassal fi Tarikh al-Quds, op. cit.,* pp. 96–98.
134 Al-Kilani, Ibrahim Zaid. 1999. 'Markaziyyat al-Quds wa Makanatuha fi Al-Islam', *Journal of Islamic Jerusalem Studies,* 2 (2): 49.
135 Runciman, *History of the Crusades, op. cit.,* Vol. 1, p. 3.
136 Yusuf, *Bayt al-Maqdis op. cit.,* p. 60.
137 Keyser, Jason. 'Muslims have kept watch over the doors of Christianity's holiest shrine for centuries', *Jordan Times,* 214 August 2002. http://www.icnacanada.org/modules.php?op=modload&name=News&file=article&sid=25
138 Al-'Arif, *al-Mufassal fi Tarikh al-Quds, op. cit.,* p. 521.
139 Ibid., p. 522.
140 Al-Dabbagh, *Biladuna Filastin, op. cit.,* Vol. 10, p. 145.
141 Abu 'Ubayd, *Kitab al-Amwal, op. cit.,* p. 168. See Also Al-Baladhuri, *Futuh al-Buldan, op. cit.,* p. 189.
142 Ibn al-Murajja, *Fada'il Bayt al-Maqdis, op. cit.,* p. 57.
143 Goitein, Shlomo. 1982. 'Jerusalem in the Arab period (638–1099)', in *The Jerusalem Cathedra. Studies in the History, Archaeology, Geography, and Ethnography of the land of Israel,* ed. Levine, L. I. Jerusalem: Yad Izhak Ben-Zvi Institute, p.174.
144 Ibid., p. 174.
145 Jasir, *Tarikh al-Quds, op. cit.,* pp. 59–62.
146 'Athaminah, *Filastin fi Khamsat, op .cit.,* p. 144.
147 Ibid., p.144.
148 Hamilton, *The Christian World, op. cit.,* p. 216.
149 Jasir, *Tarikh al-Quds, op. cit.,* p. 61.
150 Hamilton, *The Christian World, op. cit.,* p. 216.
151 Karlson, 'al-Fath al-Islami', *op. cit.,* p. 14.
152 Tibawi, *Jerusalem, op. cit.,* p. 11.
153 'Athaminah, *Filastin fi Khamsat, op. cit.,* p. 144.
154 Jasir, *Tarikh al-Quds, op. cit.,* p.184.
155 'Athaminah, *Filastin fi Khamsat, op. cit.,* pp. 144–45.
156 Jasir, *Tarikh al-Quds, op. cit.,* pp. 64–65.
157 Ibn al-Murajja, *Fada'il Bayt al-Maqdis, op. cit.,* pp. 55–57.
158 Al-'Arif, *al-Mufassal fi Tarikh al-Quds, op. cit.,* p. 94.

159 Ibn al-Murajja, *Fada'il Bayt al-Maqdis, op. cit.,* pp. 55–57; Al-'Arif, *al-Mufassal fi Tarikh al-Quds, op. cit.,* p .94.

Chapter Four

1. El-Awaisi, Abd al-Fattah. 2005. *Introducing Islamicjerusalem.* Dundee: Al-Maktoum Institute Academic Press, pp. 63–65.
2. Peters, Edward. 1998. *The First Crusade: The Chronicle of Fulcher of Chartres and Other Source Materials.* Philadelphia: University of Pennsylvania Press, p. 2.
3. Housley, Norman. 2002. *The Crusaders.* Stroud: Tempus Publishing, p. 13.
4. Peters, *The First Crusade, op. cit.,* pp. 24–37, 50–53. See also William of Tyre. 1976. *A History of Deeds Done Beyond the Sea,* trans. and annotated by Babcock, E. A. and Krey, A. C. New York: Octagon Books. Vol.1, pp. 89–91.
5. Peters, *The First Crusade, op. cit.,* p. 27.
6. Ibid., p. 27.
7. William of Tyre, *History of Deeds, op. cit.,* Vol.1, pp. 91.
8. Ibn al-Athir, Abu al-Hasan 'Ali al-Shaibani. 1998. *al-Kamil fi al-Tarikh.* Beirut: Manshurat Muhammad 'Ali Baydun, Dar al-Kutub al-'Ilmiyyah, Vol. 9, p. 19.
9. William of Tyre, *History of Deeds, op. cit.,* Vol.1, p. 372.
10. Ibid., Vol. 1, p. 82
11. Ibid., Vol. 1, pp. 82-93.
12. Ibid., Vol. pp. 89–91.
13. Runciman, *History of the Crusades, op. cit.,* Vol. 1, p. 108.
14. Ibid., Vol.1, p. 108.
15. Ibid., Vol. pp.108–09.
16. Fulcher of Chartres, 1967. *A History of the Expedition to Jerusalem* (1095–1127), trans. Fink, H. New York: University of Tennessee Press, p. 77.
17. Magdalino, Paul. 2002. 'The Medieval Empire (780–1204)', in *The Oxford History of Byzantine,* ed. Mango, C., Oxford: Oxford University Press, p. 190.
18. Anna Comnena: *The Alexiad, Book X: Second Battle with Heresy: The Cruman War: First Crusade (1094–1097),* p. 9. http://www.fordham.edu/halsall/basis/annacomnena-alexiad10.html. Seen 22 December 2002.
19. Magdalino, 'The Medieval Empire', *op. cit.,* p. 189.
20. Fletcher, *The Cross and the Crescent, op. cit.,* p. 77.
21. Peters, *The First Crusade, op. cit.,* p. 28.
22. William of Tyre, *History of Deeds, op. cit.,* Vol.1, pp. 89–93.

23 Yusuf, Hamad Ahmad 'Abd Allah. 1982. *Bayt al-Maqdis min al-'Ahd al-Rashidi wa Hata al-Dawla al-Ayyubiyya*. Jerusalem: Da'irat al-Awqaf wa al-Sh'un al-Islamiyyah, p. 146.
24 Ameer 'Ali, Syed. 1934. *A Short History of the Saracens*. London: Macmillan, p. 321.
25 Yusuf, *Bayt al-Maqdis, op. cit.,* p. 147.
26 Foss, Michael. 2000. *People of the First Crusade*. London: Caxton, p. 29.
27 Ameer 'Ali, *Short History, op. cit.,* p. 321.
28 Al-Maqdisi, Abu 'Abd Allah Muhammad. 1909. *Ahsan al-Taqasim Fi Ma'rift al-Aqalim*. Leiden: Matba'at Brill. p.167. See also Al-Muqaddasi, Abu 'Abd Allah Muhammad. 2001. *The Best Divisions for Knowledge of the Regions*. English trans. Collins, B. of *Ahsan al-Taqasim Fi Ma'rift al-Aqalim*. Reading: Garnet, p. 141.
29 Khusraw, Nasir-i. 1983. *Safarnama*, trans. from Persian into Arabic by al-Khashab, Y. Beirut: Dar al-Kitab al-Jadid, p. 69.
30 Al-'Arif, 'Arif. 1986. *al-Mufassal fi Tarikh al-Quds*. Jerusalem. Matba'it al-Ma'arif, p. 148.
31 Hamilton, Bernard. 2003. *The Christian World of the Middle Ages*. Stroud: Sutton Publishing Ltd., p. 217.
32 Courbage, Youssef and Fargues, Philippe. 1997. *Christians and Jews under Islam*, trans. Mabro, J. London: I. B. Tauris, p. 45.
33 Hiyari, Mustafa A. 1990. 'Crusader Jerusalem (1099-1187 AD)', in *Jerusalem in History*. ed. Asali, K. J. New York: Olive Branch Press, pp. 137–40.
34 William of Tyre, *History of Deeds, op. cit.,* Vol. 1, p. 372.
35 Anonymous. 1962. *Gesta Francroum et aliorum hierosolimitanroum. The Deeds of the Franks and the Other Pilgrims to Jerusalem*, ed. Hill, R. London: Thos. Nelson & Sons, pp. 91–93.
36 Fletcher, *The Cross and the Crescent, op. cit.,* p. 123.
37 D'Aguilers, Raymond. 1968. *Historia Francorum Qui Ceperunt Iherusalem*, trans. with introduction and notes by Hill, J. and Hill, L. Philadelphia: American Philosophical Society, pp. 127–28.
38 Ibn al-Athir, *al-Kamil, op. cit.,* Vol. 9, p.19.
39 Ibn al-'Ibri, Grigurius al-Malti. 1992. *Tarikh Mukhtasar al-Duwal*. Beirut: Dar al-Mashreq, p. 197.
40 Ibn al-Jawzi, Abu al-Faraj. 1995. *al-Muntazam fi Tarikh al-Muluk wa al-Umam*. Beirut: Dar al-Kutub al-'Ilmiyyah.Vol. 17, p. 47.
41 Ibn al-Qalanisi, Abu Ya'la Hamza Ibn Asad. 1932. *The Damascus Chronicle of the Crusades*, extracted and trans. Gibb, H. A. R. from *The Chronicle of Ibn al-Qalanisi*, London: Luzac & Co., p. 48.
42 Hiyari, 'Crusader Jerusalem', *op. cit.,* pp. 140–41.

43 Ibn Shaddad, Baha' al-Din. 2000. *al-Nawadir al-Sultaniyya wa'al-Mahasin al-Yusufiyya*. Cairo: Dar al-Manar, p. 4. See also Ibn al-Athir, *al-Kamil, op. cit.*, Vol. 10, p. 16.
44 Abu Shama, 'Abd al-Rahman Ibn Isma'il. 1997. *Kitab al-Rawdatayn fi Akhbar al-Dawlatayn al-Nuriyya wal al-Salahiyya*. Beirut: Mu'assasat al-Risalah. Vol. 1, p, 403; Ibn Khalikan, Shams al-Din Ahmad Ibn Muhammad. n. d. *Wafiyat al-A'yan wa Anba' Abna' al-Zaman,*. Beirut: Dar Sader. Vol. 7, p. 139; Ibn Taghribardi, Jamal-al-Din Yusuf. 1992. *al-Nujum al-Zahira fi Muluk Misr wa al-Qahira*, Beirut: Dar al-Kutub al-'Ilmiyyah. Vol. 6, p. 3; Al-Maqrizi, Abu al-'Abbas Ahmad Ibn 'Ali. 1998. *Kitab al-Mawa'iz bi Dhikr al-Khitat wa al-Athar*, Beirut: Manshurat Muhammad 'Ali Baydun, Dar al-Kutub al-'Ilmiyyah. Vol. 3, p. 405.
45 Al-Hamawi, Yaqut. n. d. *Mu'jam al-Buldan*. Beirut: Dar al-Kutub al-'Ilmiyyah. Vol. 2, p. 558.
46 Ibn al-Athir, *al-Kamil, op. cit.*, Vol. 10, p.16. See also Ibn Taghribardi, *al-Nujum al-Zahira, op. cit.*, Vol .6, p. 3; Ibn Khalikan, *Wafiyat al-A'yan, op. cit.*, Vol. 7, p. 139; Al-Maqrizi, *Kitab al-Mawa'z, op. cit.*, Vol. 3, p. 405; Abu Shama, *Kitab al-Rawdatayn, op. cit.*, Vol. 1, p. 403.
47 Ibn Taghribardi, *al-Nujum al-Zahira, op. cit.*, Vol. 6, p. 4.
48 Ibid.
49 Ibn Khalikan, Shams al-Din Ahmad Ibn Muhammad. 1998. *Wafiyat al-A'yan wa Anba' Abna' al-Zaman*. Beirut: Manshurat Muhammad 'Ali Baydun, Dar al-Kutub al-'Ilmiyyah. Vol.1, p. 254.
50 Ibn Kathir, *al-Bidaya, op. cit.*, Vol. 12, p. 271.
51 Abu Shama, *Kitab al-Rawdatayn, op. cit.*, Vol. 1, p. 404, Ibn Taghribardi, *al-Nujum al-Zahira, op. cit.*, Vol. 6, p. 4. See also Ibn Khalikan, *Wafiyat al-A'yan, op. cit.*, Vol. 7, p. 142.
52 Abu Shama, *Kitab al-Rawdatayn, op. cit.*, Vol. 1, p. 404.
53 Ibn Kathir, *al-Bidaya, op. cit.*, Vol. 12, p. 271
54 Abu Shama, *Kitab al-Rawdatayn, op. cit.*, Vol.1, p. 404; Ibn Khalikan, *Wafiyat al-A'yan, op. cit.*, Vol. 7, p.143.
55 Ibn Khalikan, *Wafiyat al-A'yan, op. cit.*, Vol. 1, p. 254. See also Ibn Kathir, al-*Bidaya, op. cit.*, Vol. 12, p. 272, and Abu Shama, *Kitab al-Rawdatayn, op. cit.*, Vol.1, p. 404.
56 Ibn al-'Imad, Shihab al-Din Abi al-Falah. 1991. *Shadharat al-Dhahab fi Akhbar Man Dhahab*. Damascus: Dar Ibn Kathir. Vol. 6, p. 375.
57 Ibn Kathir, *al-Bidaya, op. cit.*, Vol. 12, p. 272. See also Ibn Khalikan, *Wafiyat al-A'yan, op. cit.*, Vol. 7, p. 145.
58 Ibn al-'Imad, *Shadharat al-Dhahb, op. cit.*, Vol. 6, p. 375; Abu Shama, *Kitab al-Rawdatayn, op. cit.*, Vol.1, p. 405.
59 Regan, Geoffrey. 1987. *Saladin and the Fall of Jerusalem*. London: Croom Helm, p. 17.

60 Ibn Shaddad, *al-Nawadir, op. cit.,* pp. 23–26; See also Richards, D. S. 2001. *The Rare and Excellent History of Saladin or al-Nawadir al-Sultaniyya wa'l Mahasin al-Yusufiyya.* English trans. of Ibn Shaddad, Al-Nawadir al-Sultaniyya wa'l Mahasin al-Yusufiyya. Hampshire: Ashgate, pp. 41–45.
61 Ibn Shaddad, *al-Nawadir, op. cit.,* pp. 26–28.
62 Ibid., p. 31; Richards, *The Rare and Excellent, op. cit,* p. 51.
63 Regan, *Saladin, op. cit.,* p. 36.
64 Lane-Poole, Stanley. 1985. *Saladin and the Fall of the Kingdom of Jerusalem.* London: Darf Publishers, pp. 368–69.
65 Sawirus Ibn al-Muqaffa'. 1959. *Tarikh Batarikat al-Kanisah al-Misriyya, al-Ma'ruf bi siyar al-Bai'a al-*Muqaddasa, ed. 'Abd al-Masih, Y. and Suriyal, 'A. Cairo: n. p. Vol. 3, Part 2, p. 97.
66 Ibid.
67 Ibid.
68 Salam, Salam Shafi'i. 1982. *Ahl al-Dhimma fi Misr fi al-'Asr al-Fatimi al-Thani Wa al-'Asr al-Ayyubi* (467–648 AH/ 1074–1250 CE). Egypt: Dar al-Ma'arif, pp. 228-229.
69 Al-Armani, Abu Salih. 1895. *The Churches and Monasteries of Egypt and Some Neighbouring Countries,* ed. and trans. into English by Evetts, B. Oxford: Oxford University Press, p. 4.
70 Al-Armani, *The Churches and Monasteries, op. cit.,* p. 4.
71 Ibid., p. 5.
72 Sawirus, *Tarikh Batarikat al-Kanisah, op. cit.,* Vol. 3, Part. 2, p. 98.
73 Ibid., Vol. 3, Part 2, pp. 97–98.
74 Salam, *Ahl al-Dhimma fi Misr, op. cit.,* p. 244.
75 Sawirus, *Tarikh Batarikat al-Kanisah, op. cit.,* Vol. 3, Part. 2, pp. 97–98.
76 Al-Armani, *The Churches and Monasteries, op. cit.,* pp. 8–9. See also Al-Nuwairi, Shihabab al-Din Ahmad Ibn 'Abd Al-Wahab. 1940. *Nihayat al-Irab fi Funun al-Adab.* Cairo: n. p. Vol. 17, p. 10.
77 Sawirus, *Tarikh Batarikat al-Kanisah, op. cit.,* Vol. 3, Part 2, p. 96.
78 Ibid., Vol. 3, Part.1, p. 1.
79 Al-Maqrizi, *Kitab al-Mawa'iz, op. cit.,* Vol. 4, p. 415. See also Sawirus, *Tarikh Batarikat al-Kanisah, op. cit.,* Vol. 2, Part 2, p. 199.
80 Salam, *Ahl al-Dhimma fi Misr, op. cit.,* p. 230.
81 Hillenbrand, Carol. 1999. *The Crusades: Islamic Perspective.* Edinburgh: Edinburgh University Press, p. 414.
82 Ibn Jubayr, Abu al-Hussain Muhammad Ibn Ahmad. n. d. *Rihlat Ibn Jubayr.* Beirut: Dar Sader, p. 36.
83 Salam, *Ahl al-Dhimma fi Misr, op. cit.,* p. 246.
84 Ibn Taghribardi, *al-Nujum al-Zahira, op. cit.,* Vol. 6, pp. 6–7.
85 Ibn Wasil, Jamal al-Din. 1960. *Mufarij al-Kurub fi Akhbar Bani Ayyu*b. Cairo: n. p. Vol. 3, p. 292.

86 Al-Maqrizi, *Kitab al-Mawa'iz,* op. cit., Vol. 3, p. 4.
87 Ibid., Vol. 3, p. 5.
88 Lyons, M. and Jackson, D. 1982. *Saladin: The Politics of the Holy War.* Cambridge, UK: Cambridge University Press, p. 34.
89 Al-Hamawi, Yaqut. 1999. *Mu'jam al-Udaba' : Irshad al-Arib Ila Ma'rifat al-Adib.* Beirut: Mu'assasat al-Ma'arif. Vol. 2, pp. 403–04.
90 Abu Shama, *Kitab al-Rawdatayn,* op. cit., Vol. 2, pp. 130–31; Ibn Wasil, *Mufarij al-Kurub,* op. cit., Vol. 2, p. 479.
91 Salam, *Ahl al-Dhimma fi Misr,* op. cit., pp. 228–29.
92 Al-Maqrizi, *Kitab al-Mawa'iz,* op. cit., Vol. 3, p. 4; Lyons, M and Jackson, D. *Saladin,* op. cit., p. 34.
93 Majed, 'Abd al-Mun'im. 1968. *Zuhur Khilaphat al-Fatimiyyn wa Suqutuhm fi Misr.* Alexandria: n. p., pp. 487–88.
94 Sawirus, *Tarikh Batarikat al-Kanisah,* op. cit., Vol. 2, part. 2, p. 249.
95 Glubb, Faris. 1999. 'Jerusalem: the central point in Saladin's life', *Journal of Islamic Jerusalem Studies,* 2(2): 49–69.
96 'Imad al-Din al-Asfahani, Abu 'Abd Allah Muhammad. n. d. *Kitab al-Fath al-Qussi fi al-Fath al-Qudsi.* n. p., p. 39.
97 Ibn Shaddad, *al-Nawadir,* op. cit., p. 26.
98 Dajani-Shikail, Hadia. 1993. *Al-Qadi al-Fadil 'Abd al-Rahman al-Bisani al-'Asqalani, (526–596 AH /1131–1199 CE) Dawruhu al-Takhtiti fi Dawlet Salah al-Din wa Futuhateh.* Beirut: Mu'assasat al-Dirasat al-Filastiniyyah, pp. 180–83.
99 Ibn Shaddad, *al-Nawadir,* op. cit., pp. 49–51.
100 Glubb, *Jerusalem,* op. cit., pp. 64. For more information about the sermons selected and preached, see 'Imad al–Din al-Asfahani, *Kitab al-Fath al-Qussi,* op. cit., pp. 48–50. See also Abu Shama, *Kitab al-Rawdatayn,* op. cit., Vol. 3, p. 379; al-Hanbali, Mujir al-Din. 1999. *al-Uns al-Jalil bi Tarikh al-Quds wa al-Khalil.* Hebron-Palestine: Maktabat Dandis. Vol. 1, pp. 477–83.

Chapter Five

1 Hittin is a village between Arsuf and Qisariya which contains the tomb of the Prophet Shu'ib. Al-Hamawi, Yaqut. 1995. *Mu'jam al-Buldan.* Beirut: Dar Sader Publishers. Vol. 2, p. 315.
2 Ibn Shaddad, Baha' al-Din. 2000. *al-Nawadir al-Sultaniyya wa'al-Mahasin al-Yusufiyya.* Cairo: Dar al-Manar, pp. 49–50; 'Imad al-Din al-Asfahani, Abu 'Abd Allah Muhammad. n.d. *Kitab al-Fath al-Qussi fi al-Fath al-Qudsi.* n. p., pp. 18–19; Abu Shama, 'Abd al-Rahman Ibn Isma'il. 1997. *Kitab al-Rawdatayn fi Akhbar al-Dawlatayn al-Nuriyya wal al-Salahiyya.* Beirut: Mu'assasat al-Risalah. Vol. 3, pp. 275–88; Abu al-Fida', Isma'il

Ibn 'Ali. 1997. *Tarikh Abi al-Fida' al-Musamma al-Mukhtasar fi Akhbar al-Bashar.* Beirut: Manshurat Muhammad 'Ali Baydun, Dar al-Kutub al-'Ilmiyyah. Vol. 2, p. 155; Ibn al-Athir, Abu al-Hasan 'Ali al-Shaibani. 1998. *al-Kamil fi al-Tarikh.* Beirut: Manshurat Muhammad 'Ali Baydun, Dar al-Kutub al-'Ilmiyya. Vol. 10, pp. 146–48; al-Hanbali, Mujir al-Din. 1999. *al-Uns al-Jalil bi Tarikh al-Quds wa al-Khalil.* Hebron: Maktabat Dandis. Vol. 1, pp. 463–64; Runciman, Steven. 1952. *A History of the Crusades: The Kingdom of Jerusalem and the Frankish East (1100–1187).* Cambridge, UK: Cambridge University Press, Vol. 2, pp. 457–58; 'Ashur, Sa'id 'Abd al-Fattah. 1986. *al-Haraka al-Salibiyya, Safha Musharifa fi Tarikh al-Jihad al-Islami fi al-'Usur al-Wsta.* Cairo: Maktabt al-Anjlu al-Masriyyah. Vol. 2, .pp .633–36; Lane-Poole, Stanley. 1985. *Saladin and the Fall of the Kingdom of Jerusalem.* London: Darf Publishers, pp. 206–14.
3   Morgan, M. R. 1973. *The Chronicle of Ernoul and the Continuations of William of Tyre.* London: Oxford University Press, pp. 41–44.
4   Ibn Shaddad, *al-Nawadir, op. cit.,* p. 51.
5   'Imad al-Din al-Asfahani, *Kitab al-Fath al-Qussi, op. cit.,* pp. 19–20.
6   Abu Shama, *Kitab al-Rawdatayn, op. cit.,* Vol. 3, pp. 288–89.
7   Ibn al-'Adim, Kamal al-Din Abi al-Qasim. 1996. *Zubdat al-Halab min Tarikh Halab.* Beirut: Dar al-Kutub al-'Ilmiyya, pp. 408–09.
8   Abu al Fida', *al-Mukhtasar, op. cit.* Vol. 2, p. 155.
9   Al-Hanbali, *al-Uns al-Jalil, op. cit.,* Vol. 1, pp. 464–65.
10 Runciman, *History of the Crusades, op. cit.,* Vol. 2, pp. 459–60.
11 Ibn Shaddad, *al-Nawadir, op. cit.,* p. 51. See also Ibn al-'Adim, *Zubdat al-Halab, op. cit.,* pp. 409–10; Al-Dhahabi, Shams al-Din Abi 'Abd Allah. 1999. *Duwal al-Islam.* Beirut: Dar Sader. Vol. 2, p. 96; Ibn al-Athir, *al-Kamil, op. cit.,* Vol. 10, p. 142.
12 These cities included al-Karak and al-Shawbak, as well as some fortresses in the north, such as Tiberius, Acre, Kawkab, Nablus, Haifa, Caesarea, Saffuriya, Nazareth and Safad.
13 Ibn Shaddad, *al-Nawadir, op. cit,* pp. 51–52, See also Ibn al-Athir, *al-Kamil, op. cit.,* Vol. 10, pp. 145–54.
14 Ibn Shaddad, *al-Nawadir, op. cit,* pp. 52–53; 'Imad al-Din al-Asfahani, *Kitab al-Fath al-Qussi, op. cit.,* p. 35.
15 Abu Shama, *Kitab al-Rawdatayn, op. cit.,* Vol. 3, p. 336.
16 'Imad al-Din al-Asfahani, *Kitab al-Fath al-Qussi, op. cit.,* p. 40.
17 Ibid., p. 40.
18 Ashkelon or 'Asqalan, a city on the coast of the Mediterranean between Gaza and Bayt Jibrin.
19 Ibn Shaddad, *al-Nawadir, op. cit.,* p. 53.
20 Lane-Poole, *Saladin, op. cit.,* p. 226.

21 A military machine for hurling stones, etc.
22 Runciman, *History of the Crusades, op. cit.,* Vol. 2, p. 464.
23 Ibn Shaddad, *al-Nawadir, op. cit.,* p. 53.
24 Ibn al-Athir, *al-Kamil, op. cit.,* Vol. 10, p. 155
25 A person who digs a tunnel or trench to conceal assailants' approach to a fortified place, Oxford English Dictionary, p. 1283.
26 Ibn al-Athir, *al-Kamil, op. cit.,* Vol. 10, pp. 155–56; Abu Shama, *Kitab al-Rawdatayn, op. cit.,* Vol. 3, p. 331.
27 Runciman, *History of the Crusades, op. cit.,* Vol. 2, p. 464.
28 Abu Shama, *Kitab al-Rawdatayn, op. cit.,* Vol. 3, p. 329.
29 Ibid.
30 Lane-Poole, *Saladin, op. cit.,* pp. 223–25.
31 'Imad al-Din al-Asfahani, *Kitab al-Fath al-Qussi, op. cit.,* p. 35.
32 Runciman, *History of the Crusades, op. cit.,* Vol. 2, p. 463.
33 Ibid., Vol. 2, p. 464.
34 Runciman, *History of the Crusades, op. cit.,* Vol. 2, p. 463.
35 Ibid., Vol. 2, p. 463.
36 'Imad al-Din al-Asfahani, *Kitab al-Fath al-Qussi, op. cit.,* p. 42. See also Ibn al-Athir, *al-Kamil, op. cit.,* Vol. 10, p. 156; Abu Shama, *Kitab al-Rawdatayn, op. cit.,* Vol. 3, p. 340; Ibn Kathir. *Al-Bidaya, op. cit.,* Vol.12, p. 323; Ibn al-'Ibri, Grigurius al-Malti. 1992. *Tarikh Mukhtasar al-Duwal.* Beirut: Dar al-Mashreq, p. 221; Abu al-Fida', *al-Mukhtasar, op. cit.,* Vol. 2, pp. 156–57; al-Hanbali, *al-Uns al-Jalil, op. cit.,* Vol. 1, p. 473.
37 Regan, Geoffrey. 1987. *Saladin and the Fall of Jerusalem.* London: Croom Helm, pp.150–51.
38 Ibid., p.151.
39 Ibn al-Athir, *al-Kamil, op. cit.,* Vol. 10, p. 156.
40 'Imad al-Din al-Asfahani, *Kitab al-Fath al-Qussi, op. cit.,* p. 43; Ibn al-Athir, *al-Kamil op. cit.,* Vol 10, p. 156; Ibn Shaddad, *al-Nawadir, op. cit.,* p. 53; Ibn Kathir, *al-Bidaya op. cit.,* Vol. 12, p. 323; Ibn al-'Adim, *Zubdat al-Halab, op. cit.,* p. 411; Abu al-Fida', *al-Mukhtasar, op. cit.,* Vol .2, p. 157; Ibn al-'Ibri, *Tarikh Mukhtasar al-Duwal, op. cit.,* p. 221.
41 'Imad al-Din al-Asfahani, *Kitab al-Fath al-Qussi, op. cit.,* p. 43. See also Ibn al-Athir, *al-Kamil, op. cit.,* Vol. 10, p. 156; al-Hanbali, *al-Uns al-Jalil, op. cit.,* Vol.1, p. 473.
42 Ibn al-Athir, *al-Kamil, op. cit.,* Vol. 10, p. 158.
43 'Imad al-Din al-Asfahani, *Kitab al-Fath al-Qussi, op. cit.,* p. 43; Ibn al-'Adim, *Zubdat al-Halab, op. cit.,* pp. 411–12.
44 'Imad al-Din al-Asfahani, *Kitab al-Fath al-Qussi, op. cit.,* p. 43.
45 Qur'an. *al-Isra',* v. 1.
46 Ibn Shaddad, *al-Nawadir, op. cit.,* pp. 52–54.
47 Ibid.

48 'Imad al-Din al-Asfahani, *Kitab al-Fath al-Qussi, op. cit.,* p. 47.
49 Runciman, *History of the Crusades, op. cit.,* Vol. 2, p. 466; Lane-Poole, *Saladin, op. cit.,* pp. 231–32.
50 Lane-Poole, *Saladin, op. cit.,* p. 232.
51 'Imad al-Din al-Asfahani, *Kitab al-Fath al-Qussi, op cit.,* p. 43; Abu Shama, *Kitab al-Rawdatayn, op. cit.,* Vol. 3, p. 343; Ibn al-Athir, *al-Kamil, op. cit.,* Vol. 10, p. 157; al-Hanbali, *al-Uns al-Jalil, op. cit.,* Vol. 1, p. 474.
52 'Imad al-Din al-Asfahani, *Kitab al-Fath al-Qussi, op cit.,* p. 43; Abu Shama, *Kitab al-Rawdatayn, op. cit.,* Vol. 3, p. 343; Ibn al-Athir, *al-Kamil, op. cit.,* Vol. 10, p. 157; al-Hanbali, *al-Uns al-Jalil, op. cit.,* Vol. 1, p. 474.
53 'Imad al-Din al-Asfahani, *Kitab al-Fath al-Qussi, op. cit.,* p. 44. See also Lyons, M. and Jackson, D. 1982. *Saladin, the Politics of the Holy War.* Cambridge, UK: Cambridge University Press, p. 257.
54 Runciman, *History of the Crusades, op. cit.,* Vol. 2, p. 466.
55 'Imad al-Din al-Asfahani, *Kitab al-Fath al-Qussi, op. cit.,* p. 43. See also al-Hanbali, *al-Uns al-Jalil, op. cit.,* Vol. 1, p. 473.
56 'Imad al-Din al-Asfahani, *Kitab al-Fath al-Qussi, op. cit.,* p. 44.
57 Runciman, *History of the Crusades, op. cit.,* Vol. 2, p. 466.
58 Ibn Shaddad *al-Nawadir op. cit.,* p. 53. See also Regan, *Saladin, op. cit.,* p. 153.
59 Regan, *Saladin, op. cit.,* p. 153.
60 'Imad al-Din al-Asfahani, *Kitab al-Fath al-Qussi, op. cit.,* p. 47. See also Ibn al-Athir, *al-Kamil, op. cit.,* Vol. 10, p.157; Abu Shama, *Kitab al-Rawdatayn, op. cit.,* Vol. 3, p. 401.
61 Esposito, John. L. 1998. *Islam: The Straight Path.* Oxford: Oxford University Press, p. 59.
62 Hillenbrand, Carol. 1999. *The Crusades: Islamic Perspective.* Edinburgh: Edinburgh University Press, p. 316.
63 Qur'an. *al-Mumtahana,* v. 8.
64 'Imad al-Din al-Asfahani, *Kitab al-Fath al-Qussi, op. cit.,* p. 35; Abu Shama, *Kitab al-Rawdatayn op. cit.,* Vol. 3, p. 402. See also Runciman, *History of the Crusades, op. cit.,* Vol. 2, p. 468.
65 Al-'Arif, *al-Mufassal fi Tarikh al-Quds, op. cit.,* p. 176.
66 'Imad al-Din al-Asfahani, *Kitab al-Fath al-Qussi, op. cit.,* pp. 53–54.
67 Ibid., p. 54; Abu Shama, *Kitab al-Rawdatayn, op. cit.,* Vol. 3, p. 402; Ibn Kathir, *al-Bidaya, op. cit.,* Vol. 12, p. 327; al-Hanbali, *al-Uns al-Jalil, op. cit.,* Vol. 1, p. 485.
68 Al-Maqrizi, Abu al-'Abbas Ahmad Ibn 'Ali. 1997. *al-Suluk Li Ma'rifat Diwal al-Muluk.* Beirut: Manshurat Muhammad 'Ali Baydun, Dar al-Kutub al-'Ilmiyyah. Vol. 1, pp. 210–11.
69 Ibn Shaddad, *al-Nawadir, op. cit.,* p. 53.
70 Abu Shama, *Kitab al-Rawdatayn, op. cit.,* Vol. 3, p. 377.

71 Ibid., Vol. 3, p. 377.
72 Abu Shama, *Kitab al-Rawdatayn, op. cit.,* Vol. 3, pp. 392–93, 'Imad al-Din al-Asfahani, *Kitab al-Fath al-Qussi, op. cit.,* p. 48; al-Hanbali, *al-Uns al-Jalil, op. cit.,* Vol. 1, pp. 475–76.
73 According to the Ayyubid historian, Abu al-Fida' (d. 732 AH/ 1332 CE), St Anne was a church before the advent of Islam and became a school during the Islamic period, before 1099 CE. *al-Mukhtasar, op. cit.,* Vol. 2, pp. 169–70.
74 'Imad al-Din al-Asfahani, *Kitab al-Fath al-Qussi, op. cit.,* p. 53; al-Hanbali, *al-Uns al-Jalil op. cit.,* Vol. 1, p. 485.
75 'Imad al-Din al-Asfahani, *Kitab al-Fath al-Qussi, op. cit.,* p. 318; al-Hanbali, *al-Uns al-Jalil, op. cit.,* Vol. 1, p. 537.
76 'Imad al-Din al-Asfahani, *Kitab al-Fath al-Qussi, op. cit.,* pp. 47–48; Abu Shama, *Kitab al-Rawdatayn, op. cit.,* Vol. 3. p.158; Ibn al-Athir, *al-Kamil, op. cit.,* Vol. 10, p. 158; Runciman, *History of the Crusades, op. cit.,* Vol. 2, p. 467.
77 'Imad al-Din al-Asfahani, *Kitab al-Fath al-Qussi, op. cit.,* p. 48.
78 Arnold, T. W. 1986. *The Preaching of Islam: A History of the Propagation of the Muslim Faith.* London: Constable & Co., p. 91.
79 Runciman, *History of the Crusades, op. cit.,* Vol. 2, pp. 467–68.
80 Regan, *Saladin, op. cit.,* p. 155.
81 'Ashur, *al-Haraka al-Salibiyya, op. cit.,* Vol. 2, p. 649.
82 Ibid., Vol. 2, p. 645.
83 Regan, *Saladin, op. cit.,* p. 142.
84 Runciman, *History of the Crusades, op. cit.,* Vol. 2, pp. 464–65.
85 Ibid
86 Arnold, *The Preaching of Islam, op. cit.,* p. 96.
87 Sawirus Ibn al-Muqaffa'. 1959. *Tarikh Batarikat al-Kanisah al-Misriyya, al-Ma'ruf bi siyar al-Bai'a al-Muqaddasa,* ed. 'Abd al-Masih, Y. and Suriyal, 'A, Cairo: n. p. Vol. 2, Part. 2, p. 249.
88 Khuri, Shuhadh and Niqula. 1925. *Khulaset Tarikh Kanisat Urshalim al-Orthuthiksiyyah.* Jerusalem: Matba'at Bayt al-Maqdis, pp. 78–80.
89 'Ashur, Sa'id 'Abd al-Fattah. 1968. 'Ba'd Adwa' Jadida 'la al-'laqat Bayn Misr wa al-Habasha fi al-'Usur al-Wsta', *al-Majala al-Misriyya al-Tarikhiyya.* Vol. 14, p. 22.
90 Ibid.
91 There is no mention here of the Second Crusade (1147–49 CE), because Salah al-Din played no role in it due to his extreme youth – he was born in 532 AH /1137 CE. The Crusade came to a disastrous end because of lack of leadership and failed to take even Damascus.
92 'Imad al-Din al-Asfahani, *Kitab al-Fath al-Qussi, op. cit.,* p. 192; Abu Shama, *Kitab al-Rawdatayn, op. cit.,* Vol. 4, pp.129–30; Ibn al-'Adim,

Zubdat al-Halab, op. cit., p. 421; al-Hanbali, *al-Uns al-Jalil, op. cit.,* Vol. 1, pp. 510–11.

93 Stubbs, William. 2000. *Itinerarum Peregrinorum et gesta Regis Ricardi,* trans. into Arabic as *al-Harb al-Salibiyya al-Thalitha (Salah al-Din and Richard)*, by Habashi, Hasan. Egypt: al-Hay'a al-Misriyya al-'Ama lil Kitab. Vol. 1, pp. 57–63.

94 Ibn Shaddad, *al-Nawadir, op. cit.,* p. 122–24. See also Richards, D. S., 2001. *The Rare and Excellent History of Saladin or al-Nawadir al-Sultaniyya wa'l Mahasin al-Yusufiyya.* English trans. of Ibn Shaddad, Al-Nawadir al-Sultaniyya wa'l Mahasin al-Yusufiyya. Hampshire: Ashgate, pp. 152–53. 'Imad al-Din al-Asfahani, *Kitab al-Fath al-Qussi, op. cit.,* p. 253.

95 Ibn Shaddad, *al-Nawadir, op. cit.,* pp. 125–26. See also Richards, *The Rare and Excellent op. cit.,* p. 155; 'Imad al-Din al-Asfahani, *Kitab al-Fath al-Qussi, op. cit.,* p. 253.

96 Ibn Shaddad, *al-Nawadir, op. cit.,* pp. 128–29. See also Richards, *The Rare and Excellent, op. cit.,* pp. 158–60; 'Imad al-Din al-Asfahani, *Kitab al-Fath al-Qussi, op. cit.,* p. 259.

97 Ibn Shaddad, *al-Nawadir, op. cit.* p. 131. See also Richards, *The Rare and Excellent, op. cit,* p.161; 'Imad al-Din al-Asfahani, *Kitab al-Fath al-Qussi, op. cit.,* p. 259.

98 Ibn Shaddad, *al-Nawadir, op. cit.* p. 134; Richards, *The Rare and Excellent, op. cit.,* p.164; 'Imad al-Din al-Asfahani, *Kitab al-Fath al-Qussi, op. cit.,* pp. 268–69.

99 'Imad al-Din al-Asfahani, *Kitab al-Fath al-Qussi, op. cit.,* p. 269. See also Al-Dhahabi, Muhammad Ibn Ahmad. 1999. *Duwal al-Islam.* Beirut: Dar Sader. Vol. 2, pp. 95–96; Abu al-Fida', *al-Mukhtasar, op. cit.,* Vol. 2, p. 165; al-Hanbali, *al-Uns al-Jalil, op. cit.,* Vol. 1, p. 524.

100 Ibn al-'Adim, *Zubdat al-Halab, op. cit.,* p. 425.

101 Hallam, Elizabeth. 1989. *Chronicles of the Crusades: Eye Witness Accounts of the Wars Between Christianity and Islam.* London: Guild Publishing, p.153.

102 Lane-Poole, *Saladin, op. cit.,* p. 306.

103 Ibid., p. 306.

104 Ibn Shaddad, *al-Nawadir, op. cit.,* pp. 141–42, See also Richards, *The Rare and Excellent, op. cit.,* p. 174.

105 Ibn Shaddad, *al-Nawadir, op. cit.,* p. 151–52. See also Richards, *The Rare and Excellent, op. cit.,* pp. 185–86; and Abu Shama, *Kitab al-Rawdatayn, op. cit.,* Vol. 4, pp. 285–86.

106 Ibn Shaddad, *al-Nawadir, op. cit.,* p. 152. See also Richards, *The Rare and Excellent, op. cit.,* p. 186; and Abu Shama, *Kitab al-Rawdatayn, op. cit.,* Vol. 4, p. 286.

107 Ibn Shaddad, *al-Nawadir, op. cit.,* pp. 153–54, See also Richards, *The Rare and Excellent op. cit.,* pp. 187–88; 'Imad al-Din al-Asfahani, *Kitab al-*

Fath al-Qussi, op. cit., pp. 284–85; and Abu Shama, *Kitab al-Rawdatayn, op. cit.,* Vol. 4, pp. 283–84.

108 Ibn Shaddad, *al-Nawadir, op. cit.,* pp. 153–54; Richards, *The Rare and Excellent, op. cit.,* pp. 187–88; 'Imad al-Din al-Asfahani, *Kitab al-Fath al-Qussi, op. cit.,* pp. 284–85; Abu Shama, *Kitab al-Rawdatayn, op. cit.,* Vol. 4, p. 284.

109 Geofffrey de Vinsauf. 1948. *Itinerary of Richard I and others to the Holy Land,* trans. as *'Conjoin labour of a Classical Scholar and a Gentlemen well read in Medieval History'.* London: Henry G. Bohm, p. 301.

110 Abu Shama, *Kitab al-Rawdatayn, op. cit.,* Vol. 4, p. 310.

111 Ibn Shaddad, *al-Nawadir, op. cit.,* p. 174; Abu Shama, *Kitab al-Rawdatayn, op. cit.,* Vol. 4, p. 310.

112 Ibn Shaddad, *al-Nawadir, op. cit.,* pp. 168–75; Richards, *The Rare and Excellent, op. cit.,* pp. 209–12; Abu Shama, *Kitab al-Rawdatayn, op. cit.,* Vol. 4, p. 306.

113 Ibn Shaddad, *al-Nawadir, op. cit.,* p. 175; Abu Shama, *Kitab al-Rawdatayn, op. cit.,* Vol. 4, p. 311.

114 Ibn Shaddad, *al-Nawadir, op. cit.,* p. 176; Richards, *The Rare and Excellent, op. cit.,* pp. 213–14.

115 Ibid., Ibn Shaddad; Richards, *The Rare and Excellent, op. cit.,* p. 214.

116 Ibn Shaddad, *al-Nawadir, op. cit.,* p.177.

117 Ibid., p. 177.

118 Ibid., pp. 184–85.

119 Ibn Shaddad, *al-Nawadir, op. cit.,* p. 188.

120 Lane-Poole, *Saladin, op. cit.,* p. 357.

121 Ibn Shaddad, *al-Nawadir, op. cit.,* p. 188; Richards, *The Rare and Excellent, op. cit.,* pp. 227–28.

122 Ibn Shaddad, *al-Nawadir, op. cit.,* p. 189.

123 Ibid., p.192.

124 Ibn al-Athir, *al-Kamil, op. cit.,* Vol.10, p. 218; Ibn Shaddad, *Al-Nawadir, op. cit.,* p.191.

125 Ibn al-Athir, *al-Kamil, op. cit.,* Vol.10, p. 218.

126 Ibn al-'Adim, *Zubdat al-Halab, op. cit.,* p. 426.

127 Abu al-Fida', *al-Mukhtasar, op. cit.,* Vol. 2, p. 169; Al-Maqrizi, Abu al-'Abbas Ahmad Ibn 'Ali. 1998. *Kitab al-Mawa'iz bi Dhikr al-Khitat wa al-Athar.* Beirut: Manshurat Muhammad 'Ali Baydun, Dar al-Kutub al-'Ilmiyya. Vol. 3, p. 409.

128 Al-Qalqashandi, Ahmad Ibn 'Ali. n. d. *Subh al-A'sha fi Sina'at al-Insa.* Beirut: Manshurat Muhammad 'Ali Baydun. Dar al-Kutub al-'Ilmiyyah. Vol. 4, pp. 183-84; Ibn Kathir, *al-Bidaya, op. cit.,* Vol. 12, p. 350.

Notes

129 Ibn Shaddad, *al-Nawadir, op. cit.,* p.192; Richards, *The Rare and Excellent, op. cit.,* p. 231; al-Hanbali, *al-Uns al-Jalil, op. cit.,* Vol. 1, p. 536.
130 Ibn Shaddad, *al-Nawadir, op. cit.,* p.193; Richards, *The Rare and Excellent, op. cit.,* p. 232.
131 Ibn Shaddad, *al-Nawadir, op. cit.,* p.193; 'Imad al-Din al-Asfahani, *Kitab al-Fath al-Qussi, op. cit.,* p. 317; Abu Shama, *Kitab al-Rawdatayn, op. cit.,* Vol. 4, p. 330; al-Hanbali, *al-Uns al-Jalil, op. cit.,* Vol. 1, p. 537.
132 Abu Shama, *Kitab al-Rawdatayn, op. cit.,* Vol. 4, pp. 330–31.
133 Stubbs, *Itinerarum Peregrinorum, op. cit.,* Vol.1, pp. 274–77.
134 Richards, *The Rare and Excellent, op. cit.,* p. 150.
135 Ibn Shaddad, *al-Nawadir, op. cit.,* p.196. See also 'Imad al-Din al-Asfahani, *Kitab al-Fath al-Qussi, op. cit.,* p. 317.
136 Ibn Shaddad, *al-Nawadir, op. cit.,* p. 196; 'Imad al-Din al-Asfahani, *Kitab al-Fath al-Qussi, op. cit.,* p. 317; al-Hanbali, *al-Uns al-Jalil, op. cit.,* Vol. 1, p. 537.
137 Ibn Shaddad, *al-Nawadir, op., cit.,* p. 196.
138 Ibid.
139 Ibn Shaddad, *al-Nawadir, op. cit.,* pp.197–203. See also 'Imad al-Din al-Asfahani, *Kitab al-Fath al-Qussi, op. cit.,* pp. 325–27; al-Hanbali, *al-Uns al-Jalil, op. cit.,* pp. 538–39.
140 Lane-Poole, *Saladin, op. cit.,* p. 367.
141 Ibn Shaddad, *al-Nawadir, op. cit.,* pp. 118–19. See also Richards, *The Rare and Excellent, op. cit.,* pp.147–48; Ibn Taghribardi, *al-Nujum al-Zahira, op. cit.,* Vol. 6, p. 10; al-Hanbali, *al-Uns al-Jalil, op. cit.,* Vol. 1, p. 518.

BIBLIOGRAPHY

Primary Sources

The Holy Qur'an. Trans. Mushaf al-Madinah An-Nabawiyyah. Revised and ed. Ifta, Call and Guidance. Saudi Arabia

'Imad al-Din al-Asfahani, Abu 'Abd Allah Muhammad. n. d. *Kitab al-Fath al-Qussi fi al-Fath al-Qudsi.* n. p.

Abu 'Ubayd, al-Qasim Ibn Sallam. 1986. *Kitab al-Amwal.* Beirut: Dar al-Kutub al-'Ilmiyyah

Abu al-Fida', Isma'il Ibn 'Ali. 1997. *Tarikh Abi al-Fida' al-Musamma al-Mukhtasar fi Akhbar al-Bashar.* Beirut: Manshurat Muhammad 'Ali Baydun, Dar al-Kutub al-'Ilmiyyah

Abu Dawud, Abu Sulaiman Ibn al-Ash'ath. 1988. *Sunan Abi Dawud.* Beirut: Dar al-Jil

Abu Shama, 'Abd al-Rahman Ibn Isma'il. 1997. *Kitab al-Rawdatayn fi Akhbar al-Dawlatayn al-Nuriyya wal al-Salahiyya.* Beirut: Mu'assasat al-Risalah

Abu Yusaf, Ya'qub Ibn Ibrahim. 1979. *Kitab ul-Kharaj* (Islamic Revenue Code). Trans. 'Ali, A. and ed. Siddiqi, 'A. Lahore: Islamic Book Centre

Abu Yusuf, Ya'qub Ibn Ibrahim. n. d. *Kitab ul-Kharaj.* Beirut: Dar al-Ma'rifa

Anonymous. 1962. *Gesta Francroum et aliorum hierosolimitanroum, The Deeds of the Farnks and the other Pilgrims to Jerusalem.* Ed. Hill, R. London: Thos. Nelson & Sons

Al-Armani, Abu Salih. 1895. *The Churches and Monasteries of Egypt and some Neighbouring Countries.* Ed. and trans. into English by Evetts. B. Oxford: Oxford University Press

Al-Asbahi, Malik Ibn Anas. n.d. *al-Muwatta' bi riwayat Muhammad Ibn al-Hasan al-Shaibani.* Beirut: Dar al-Yarmuk

Al-Asfari, Khalifah Ibn Khayyat. 1993. *Tarikh Khalifah Ibn Khayyat.* Rewayet Baqi Ibn Khalid. Beirut: Dar al-Fikr

As-Suyuti, Jalal ad-Din. 1995. *The History of the Khalifahs Who Took the Right Way.* London: Ta-Ha Publishers

Al-Azdi, Muhammad Ibn 'Abdullah. 1970. *Tarikh Futuh al-Sham.* Cairo: Mu'assasat Sijil al-'Arab

Al-Baladhuri, Abu al-'Abbas Ahmad Ibn Yahya. 1987. *Futuh al-Buldan.* Beirut: Mu'assasat al- Ma'arif

Al-Bukhari, Abu Abd Allah Muhammad. n.d. *Sahih Al-Bukhari.* Riyadh: Dar Ishbilyya

D'Aguilers, Raymond. 1968. *Historia Francorum Qui Ceperunt Iherusalem.* Trans. with Introd. and notes by Hill, J. H. and Hill, L. L. Philadelphia: The American Philosophical Society

Al-Dhahabi, Muhammad Ibn Ahmad. 1995. *Mizan al-I'tidal Fi Naqd al-Rijal.* Beirut: Dar al-Kutub al-'Ilmiyyah

———. 1997. *al-Mughni fi al-Du'afa'.* Beirut: Manshurat Muhammad 'Ali Baydun, Dar al-Kutub al-'Ilmiyyah

———. 1999. *Duwal al-Islam.* Beirut: Dar Sader

Al-Farra', Abi Ya'la Muhammad Ibn al-Husain. 1974. *al-Ahkam as-Sultaniyyah.* Beirut: Dar al-Fikr

Al-Fayruzabadi, Mujid al-Din Muhammad Ibn Ya'qubi. 1991. *al-Qamus al-Muhit.* Beirut: Dar Ihya' al-Turath al-'Arabi

Fulcher of Chartres. 1967. *A History of the Expedition to Jerusalem* (1095–1127), Trans. Fink, H. New York: University of Tennessee Press

Geofffrey de Vinsauf. 1948. *Itinerary of Richard I and others to the Holy Land,* trans. as *'Conjoint labour of a Classical Scholar and a Gentlemen well read in Medieval History'.* London: Henry G. Bohm

Al-Hamawi, Yaqut. 1995. *Mu'jam al-Buldan*. Beirut: Dar Sader

———. 1999. *Mu'jam al-Udaba': Irshad al-Arib Ila Ma'rifat al-Adib*. Beirut: Mu'assasat al-Ma'arif

Al-Hanbali, Mujir al-Din. 1999. *al-Uns al-Jalil bi Tarikh al-Quds wa al-Khalil*. Hebron: Maktabat Dandis

Al-Himyari, Muhammad. 1984. *al-Rawd al-Mi'tar Fi Khair al-Aqtar*. Beirut: Maktabat Lubnan

Al-Hindi, 'Ala' al-Din Ibn 'Ali al-Muttaqi. 1998. *Kanz al-'Umal fi Sunan al-Aqwal wa al-Af'al*. Beirut: Manshurat Muhammad 'Ali Baydun, Dar al-Kutub al-'Ilmiyyah

Ibn 'Abd al-Hakam, Abu al-Qasim 'Abd al-Rahman.1996. *Futuh Misr wa Akhbaruha*. Beirut: Dar al-Fikr

Ibn 'Abdin, Muhammad Amin. 1994. *Rad al-Muhtar 'Ala al-Dur al-Muktar Sharh Tanwir al-Absar*. Beirut: Manshurat Muhammad 'Ali Baydun, Dar al-Kutub al-'Ilmiyyah

Ibn 'Asakir. 'Ali Ibn al-Hasan. 1995. *Tarikh Madinat Dimashq*. Beirut: Dar al-fikr

Ibn Adam, Yahya. n.d. *Kitab al-Kharaj*. Beirut: Dar al-Ma'rifa

Ibn al-'Adim, Kamal al-Din Abi al-Qasem. 1996. *Zubdat al-Halab min Tarikh Halab*. Beirut: Dar al-Kutub al-'Ilmiyyah

Ibn al-'Arabi, Abu Bakr Muhammad. 1996. *Ahkam al-Qur'an*. Beirut: Manshurat Muhammad 'Ali Baydun, Dar al-Kutub al-'Ilmiyyah

Ibn al-'Ibri, Grigurius al-Malti. 1992. *Tarikh Mukhtasar al-Duwal*. Beirut: Dar al-Mashreq

Ibn al-'Imad, Shihab al-Din Abi al-Falah. 1991. *Shadharat al-Dhahab fi Akhbar Man Dhahab*. Damascus: Dar Ibn Kathir

Ibn al-A'them, Abu Muhammad Ahmad. 1991. *Kitab al-Futuh*. Beirut: Dar al-Adwa'

Ibn al-Athir, Abu al-Hasan 'Ali al-Shaibani. 1998. *al-Kamil fi al-Tarikh*. Beirut: Manshurat Muhammad 'Ali Baydun, Dar al-Kutub al-'Ilmiyyah

Ibn al-Athir, Muhammad Ibn al-Jazriy. 1963. *al-Nihaya fi Gharib al-Hadith wa al-Athar.* Beirut: al-Maktabah al-'Ilmiyyah

Ibn al-Jawzi, Abu al-Faraj 'Abd al-Rahman Ibn 'Ali. 1979. *Fada'il al-Quds.* Beirut: Dar al-Afaq al-Jadida

———. 2001. *Sirat wa Manaqb Amir al-Mu'minin 'Umar Ibn al-Khattab.* Cairo: Dar al-Da'wah al-Islamiyyah

———. 1995. *al-Muntazam fi Tarikh al-Muluk wa al-Umam.* Beirut: Dar al-Kutub al-'Ilmiyyah

Ibn al-Murajja, Abu al-Ma'ali al-Musharraf. 1995. *Fada'il Bayt al-Maqdis wa-al-Khalil wa-Fada'il al-Sham.* Ed. with Introd. by Livne-Kafri, O. Shfaram: Aimashreq

Ibn al-Qalanisi, Abu Ya'la Hamza Ibn Asad. 1932. *The Damascus Chronicle of the Crusades*, extracted and trans. from *The Chronicle of Ibn al-Qalanisi*, by Gibb, H. A. R. London: Luzac & Co.

Ibn al-Qayyim al-Jawziyya, Muhammad Abi Bakr. 1981. *Sharh al-Shurut al-'Umariyyah.* Beirut: Dar al-'lm li-lmalain

———. 1995. *Ahkam Ahl al-Dhimma.* Beirut: Dar al-Kutub al-'Ilmiyyah

———. 1989. *Zad al-Ma'ad fi Hadi Khair al-'ibad.* Cairo: al-Maktabah al-Qayyimh

Ibn Hajar, Ahmad Ibn 'Ali. 1997. *Bulugh al-Maram Min Adillat al-Ahkam.* Riyadh and Damascus: Maktabat Dar al-Salam and Maktabat Dar al-Fayha'

———. 1997. *Fath al-Bari Sharh Sahih al-Bukhari.* Riyadh and Damascus: Maktabat Dar al-Salam and Maktabat Dar al-Fayha'

Ibn Hanbal, Ahmad Ibn Muhammad. 1995. *al-Musnad.* Cairo: Dar Al-Hadith

Ibn Hazm, Abu Muhammad 'Ali Ibn Ahmad. 1978. *Mratib al-Ijma' fi al-'Badat wa al-Mu'amalat wa al-Mu'taqadat.* Beirut: Dar al-Afaq al-Jadida.

———. 1984. *al-Muhalla bil Athar.* Beirut: Dar Al-Kutub al-'Ilmiyyah

Ibn Hisham, 'Abdul Malik. 1999. *al-Sira al-Nabawiyyah.* Egypt: Dar al-Taqwa

Ibn Jubayr, Abu al-Husain Muhammad Ibn Ahmad, n.d. *Rihlat Ibn Jubayr.* Beirut: Dar Sader

Ibn Juzay, Abu al-Qasim Muhammad Ibn Ahmad. n.d. *al-Qawanin al-Fiqhiyyah.* Beirut: Dar Fikr

Ibn Kathir, Abu al-Fida' Isma'il. 1994. *Tafsir al-Qur'an al-'Azim.* Riyadh: Maktabat Dar al-Salam

———. 1978. *al-Bidaya wa al-Nihaya.* Beirut: Dar al-Fikr

———. 2000. *Tafsir Ibn Kathir.* Abridgement supervised by Shaykh Safiur-Rahman al-Mubarapuri. Houston, TX: Darussalam Publishers

Ibn Khalikan, Shams al-Din Ahmad Ibn Muhammad. 1998. *Wafiyat al-A'yan wa Anba' Abna' al-Zaman.* Beirut: Manshurat Muhammad 'Ali Baydun. Dar al-Kutub al-'Ilmiyyah

———. n. d. *Wafiyat al-A'yan wa Anba' Abna' al-Zaman.* Beirut: Dar Sader

Ibn Manzur, Muhammad Ibn Makram. 1984. *Mukhtasar Tarikh Dimashq Li Ibn 'Asakir.* Damascus: Dar al-fikr

———. 1999. *Lisan al-'Arab.* Beirut: Dar Ihya' al-Turath al-'Arabi

Ibn Qudama al-Maqdisi. 1996. *al-Sharh al-Kabir.* Cairo: Dar al-Hadith

Ibn Qudama, Muwafaq al-Din. 1996. *al-Mughni.* Cairo: Dar al-Hadith

Ibn Sa'd. 1997. *Kitab al-Tabaqat al-Kubra.* Beirut: Manshurat Muhammad 'Ali Baydun, Dar al-Kutub al-'Ilmiyyah

———. 1967. *Kitab al-Tabaqat al-Kabir.* Trans. Haq, S. M. and Ghazanfar, H. K. Karachi: Pakistan Historical Society

Ibn Shaddad, Baha' al-Din. 2000. *al-Nawadir al-Sultaniyya wa'al-Mahasin al-Yusufiyya.* Cairo: Dar al-Manar

Ibn Taghribardi, Jamal al-Din Yusuf. 1992. *al-Nujum al-Zahira fi Muluk Misr wa al-Qahira.* Beirut: Dar al-Kutub al-'Ilmiyyah

Ibn Taymiyyah, Ahmad 'Abd al-Halim. 1996. *Eqtida' al-Sirat al-Mustaqim li mukhalfet Ashab al-Jahim.* Riyadh: Maktabat al-Rushed

———. n.d. *Majmu' fatawa Shaikh al-Islam Ahmad Ibn Taymiyyah*. Riyadh: al-Ri'asah al-'Ammah Lishu'un al-Haramayn al-Sharifayn

Ibn Wasil, Jamal al-Din. 1960. *Mufarij al-Kurub fi Akhbar Bani Ayyub*. Cairo: n. p.

Al-Jawhiri, Isma'il Ibn Hamad. n.d. *al-Sihah Taj al-Lughah wa Sihah al-'Arabiyyah*. Bierut: Dar al-'Ilm lil Malayn.

Al-Kasani, 'Ala' al-Din Abi Bakr Ibn Mas'ud. 1997. *Bada'i' al-Sani' fi Tartib al-Shara'i'*. Beirut: Manshurat Muhammad 'Ali Baydun, Dar al-Kutub al-'Ilmiyyah

Al-Khallal, Abu Bakr Ahmad Ibn Muhammad. 1996. *Ahl al-Milah wa al-Ridah wa al-Zanadiqah wa Tarik al-Salah wa al-Fara'd Min Kitab al-Jame'*, Riyadh: Maktabet al-Ma'arif lil Nasher wa al-Tawzi'

Al-Khatib al-Baghdadi, Abu Bakr Ahmad Ibn 'Ali. 1997. *Tarikh Baghdad aw Madinat al-Salam*. Beirut: Manshurat Muhammad 'Ali Baydun, Dar al-Kutub al-'Ilmiyyah

Khusraw, Nasir-i. 1983. *Safarnama*, Trans. from Persian into Arabic by al-Khashab, Y. Beirut: Dar al-Kitab al-Jadid

Al-Maqdisi, Abu 'Abd Allah Muhammad. 1909. *Ahsan al-Taqasim Fi Ma'rift al-Aqalim*. Leiden: Matba't Brill

Al-Maqdisi, Muhammad Ibn 'Abd al-Wahid. 1988. *Fada'il Bayt al-Maqdis*. Beirut: Dar al-Fikr

Al-Maqrizi, Abu al-'Abbas Ahmad Ibn 'Ali. 1997. *al-Suluk Li Ma'rifat Diwal al-Muluk*. Beirut: Manshurat Muhammad 'Ali Baydun, Dar al-Kutub al-'Ilmiyyah

———. 1998. *Kitab al-Mawa'iz bi Dhikr al-Khitat wa al-Athar*, Beirut: Manshurat Muhammad 'Ali Baydun, Dar al-Kutub al-'Ilmiyyah

Al-Mawardi, Abu al-Hasan 'Ali Ibn Muhammad. 1994. *Al-Hawi al-Kabir*. Beirut: Dar al-Fikr

———. 1996. *Al-Ahkam as-Sultaniyyah: the laws of Islamic governance*. Trans. Yate, A. London: Ta-Ha Publishers

Al-Muqaddasi, Abu 'Abd Allah Muhammad. 2001. *The Best Divisions for Knowledge of the Regions*. Eng. trans. by Collins, B. of *Ahsan al-Taqasim Fi Ma'rift al-Aqalim*. Reading: Garnet Publishers

Muslim, Abu al-Husain Ibn al-Hajjaj. 1996. *Sahih Muslim*. Trans. Siddiqi, A. Delhi: Adam Publishers

Al-Nawawi, Abu Zakariya Yahya. 1998. *Rawdat al-Talibin*. Beirut: Manshurat Muhammad 'Ali Baydun, Dar al-Kutub al-'Ilmiyyah

Al-Nuwairi, Shihab al-Din Ahmad Ibn 'Abd al-Wahab. 1940. *Nihayat al-Irab fi Funun al-Adab*. Cairo: n. p.

Al-Qalqashandi, Ahmad Ibn 'Ali. n. d. *Subh al-A'sha fi Sina'at al-Insa*. Beirut: Manshurat Muhammad 'Ali Baydun, Dar al-Kutub al-'Ilmiyyah

Al-Qarafi, Abu al-'Abbas Ahmad Ibn Idris. 1998. *al-Furuq wa Anwar al-Buruq fi Anwa' al-Furuq*. Beirut: Manshurat Muhammad 'Ali Baydun, Dar al-Kutub al-'Ilmiyyah

Al-Qurtubi, Abu 'Abdullah Muhammad. 1998. *al-Jami' li Ahkam al-Qur'an*. Beirut: Dar al-Fikr

Al-Razi, Fakhr al-Din Muhammad Ibn 'Umar. 1990. *al-Tafsir al-Kabir aw Mafatih al-Ghaib*. Beirut: Dar al-Kutub al-'Ilmiyyah

Richards, D.S., 2001. *The Rare and Excellent History of Saladin or Al-Nawadir al-Sultaniyya wa'l Mahasin al-Yusufiyya*. Eng. trans. of Ibn Shaddad, al-Nawadir al-Sultaniyya wa'l Mahasin al-Yusufiyya. Hampshire: Ashgate

Sa'id Ibn al-Batriq (Eutychius). 1905. *al-Tarikh al-Majmu' 'Ala al-Tahqiq wa al-Tasdiq*. Beirut: n. p.

Al-Sarkhasi, Abu Bakr Muhammad Ibn Ahmed. 2001. *Kitab al-Mabsut*. Beirut: Manshurat Muhammad 'Ali Baydun, Dar al-Kutub al-'Ilmiyyah

Sawirus Ibn al-Muqaffa'. 1959. *Tarikh Batarikat al-Kanisah al-Misriyya, al-Ma'ruf bi siyar al-Bai'a al-Muqaddasa*. Ed. 'Abd al-Masih, Y. and Suriyal, 'A, Cairo: n. p.

Al-Shafi'i, Abu 'Abd Allah Muhammad. 1993. *Kitab al-Umm*. Beirut: Dar al-Kutub al-'Ilmiyyah

Stubbs, Willaim. 2000. *Itinerarum Peregrinorum et gesta Regis Ricardi*, Trans. into Arabic as *al-Harb al-Salibiyya al-Thalitha (Salah al-Din and Richard)*, by Habashi, H. Egypt: al-Hay'a al-Misriyya al-'Ama lil Kitab

Al-Tabarani, Abu al-Qasim Sulaiman. 1999. *al-Mu'jam al-Awsat*. Amman: Dar al-Fikr

Al-Tabari, Abu Ja'far Muhammad Ibn Jarir. 1989. *The History of al-Tabari*. Trans. and annotated Juynboll, G. New York: State University of New York Press

———. 1999. *Tafsir al-Tabari, al-Musamma Jami' al-Bayan fi Ta'wil al-Qur'an*. Beirut: Manshurat Muhammad 'Ali Baydun, Dar al-Kutub al-'Ilmiyyah

———. 1997. *Tarikh al-Umam wa al-Muluk*. Beirut: Manshurat Muhammad 'Ali Baydun, Dar al-Kutub al-'Ilmiyyah

The Holy Bible. Cambridge, UK: Cambridge University Press.

Theophanes. 1997. *The Chronicle of Theophanes Confessor: Byzantine and Near Eastern History AD 284–813*. Trans. with Introd. and commentary by Mango, C. and Scott, R. Oxford: Clarendon Press

Al-Turtushi, Abu Bakr Muhammad. 1990. *Siraj al-Muluk*. London: Riyad El-Rayyas Press

Al-Wahidi, Abu al-Hasan 'Ali Ibn Ahmad. 1998. *Asbab al-Nuzul*. Cairo: Dar al-Hadith

Al-Waqidi, Abu 'Abd Allah Muhammad Ibn 'Umar. n.d. *Futuh al-Sham*. Cairo: al-Maktaba al-Tawfiqiyya

William of Tyre. 1976. *A History of Deeds Done Beyond The Sea*. Trans. and annotated by Babcock, E. A. and Krey, A. C. New York: Octagon Books

Al-Ya'qubi, Ahmad. 1999. *Tarikh al-Ya'qubi*. Beirut: Manshurat Muhammad 'Ali Baydun, Dar al-Kutub al-'Ilmiyyah

Al-Zamakhshari, Abu al-Qasim Jarallah Mahmud. 1995. *Tafsir al-Kashshaf 'An Haqa'iq Ghawas al-Tanzil wa 'Uiwn al-Aqawil fi Wjuh al-Ta'wil,* Beirut: Manshurat Muhammad 'Ali Baydun, Dar al-Kutub al-'Ilmiyyah

Al-Zubaidi, Ahmad Ibn Abdul-Latif. 1996. *Summarized Sahih al-Bukhari.* Trans. Khan, M. M. Riyadh: Maktabat Dar-us-Salam

Secondary Sources

'Abdalati, Hammudah. 1975. *Islam in focus.* Indianapolis: American Trust Publications

'Ali, 'Abduallah Yusuf. 1998. *The Holy Qur'an: Translation and Commentary.* Birmingham: IPCI: Islamic Vision

'Ali, Muhammad Mohar. 1997. *Sirat al-Nabi and the Orientalists.* Madina: King Fahid Complex for the Printing of the Holy Qur'an and Centre for the Service of Sunnah and Sirah

Al-'Arif, 'Arif. 1986. *al-Mufassal fi Tarikh al-Quds.* Jerusalem. Matba'it al-Ma'arif

'Ashur, Sa'id 'Abd al-Fattah, 1986. *al-Haraka al-Salibiyya, Safha Musharifa fi Tarikh al-Jihad al-Islami fi al-'Usur al-Wsta.*Cairo: Maktabt al-Anjlu al-Masriyyah

'Athaminah, Khalil. 2000. *Filastin fi Khamsat Qurun:Min al-Fath al-Islami Hatta al-Ghazw al-Faranji (634–1099) (Palestine in Five Centuries From the Islamic Conquest to the Frankish Invasion (634–1099):* Beirut: Mu'assasat al-Dirasat al-Filastiniyyah

'Azzam, 'Abd al-Rahman. 1979. *The Eternal Message of Muhammad.* Trans. Farah, C. London: Quartet Books

'Oudah, 'Abd al-Qadir. n. d. *al-Tashri' al-Jina'i al-Islami Muqaranan Bilqanwn al-Wad'i.* Cairo: Maktabat Dar al-Turath

Abraham, A.J and Haddad, G. 1989. *The Warriors of God: Jihad (Holy War) and the Fundamentalists of Islam.* Lima, OH: Wyndham Hall Press

Abu 'layan, 'Azmi Muhammad. 1993. *al-Quds Bayn al-Ihtilal wa al-Tahrir 'Abr al-'Usur al-Qadimah wa al-Wsta wa al-Hadithah, (3000 B.C–1967* Amman: Mu'assasat Bakir lil-Dirasat al-Thaqafiyya

Al-Affani, S. 2001. *Tadhkir al-Nafs bi Hadith al-Quds (wa Qudsah).* Cairo: Maktabit Mu'ath Ibn Jabal

Al-Ahlas, Aisha. 2004. *Islamic Research Academy (ISRA) 1994–2004: Background, activities, and achievements, with special reference to the New Field of inquiry of Islamic Jerusalem Studies.* Dundee: Islamic Research Academy (ISRA)

Al-Albani, Muhammad Nasser al-Din. 1985. *Irrwa' al-Ghalil fi Takhrij Ahadith Manar al-Sabil.* Under the Supervision of al-Shawish M. Beirut: al-Maktab al-Islami

Ameer 'Ali, Syed. 1934. *A Short History of the Saracens.* London: Macmillan & Co.

An-Na'im, Abdullahi Ahmed. 1990. *Toward an Islamic Reformation: Civil Liberties, Human Rights and International Law.* New York: Syracuse University Press

Armstrong, Karen. 1996. *A History of Jerusalem: One City, Three Faiths.* London: Harper Collins

Arnold T. W. 1913 and 1986 editions. *The Preaching of Islam: A History of the Propagation of the Muslim Faith.* London: Constable & Co.

El-Awaisi, Abd al-Fattah. 2005. *Introducing Islamicjerusalem.* Dundee: Al-Maktoum Institute Academic Press

———. 1997. *Jerusalem in Islamic History and Spirituality: The Significance of Jerusalem in Islam, an Islamic Reference.* Dunblane: Islamic Research Academy

El-Awaisi, Khalid. 2006. '*Mapping Islamicjerusalem: the Geographical extent of the Land of Bayt al-Maqdis, the Holy Land and the land of Barakah*'. (Unpublished Ph.D thesis). Dundee: Al-Maktoum Institute for Arabic and Islamic Studies, University of Aberdeen

Ben Shemesh, A. 1958. *Taxation in Islam, the English Translation of Yahya Ibn Adams's Kitab al-Kharaj,* Foreword by Goitein, S. Leiden: Brill

Butler, Alfred J. 1978. *The Arab Conquest of Egypt and the last Thirty Years of the Roman Dominion.* Oxford: Clarendon Press

Caetani, Leone. 1910. *Annali Dell Islam.* Milan: Ulrico Hoeli

Courbage, Youssef and Fargues, Philippe. 1997. *Christians and Jews under Islam*. Trans. Mabro, J. London: I. B. Tauris

Al-Dabbagh, Mustafa. 1988. *Biladuna Filastin*. Kufor Qar': Dar al-Shafaq

Dajani-Shikail, Hadia. 1993. *Al-Qadi al-Fadil 'Abd al-Rahman al-Bisani al-'Asqalani, (526–596 AH / 1131–1199 AD) Dawruhu al-Takhtiti fi Dawlet Salah al-Din wa Futuhateh*. Beirut: Mu'assasat al-Dirasat al-Filastiniyyah

Denffer, Ahmad Von. 1994. *'Ulum Al-Qur'an, An Introduction to the Sciences of the Qur'an*. Leicester: The Islamic Foundation

Doi, 'Abdul Rahman. 1983. *Non-Muslims under Shari'ah: Islamic Law*. London: Ta-Ha Publishers

Donner, Fred McGraw. 1981. *The Early Islamic Conquest*. Princeton, NJ Jersey: Princeton University Press

Esposito, John. L. 1998. *Islam: The Straight Path*. Oxford: Oxford University Press

Al-Faruqi, Isma'il. 1998. *Islam and other Faiths*. Leicester: The Islamic Foundation and the International Institute of Islamic Thought

Fletcher, Richard. 2003. *The Cross and the Crescent, Christianity and Islam from Muhammad to the Reformation*. London: Penguin Books

Foss, Michael. 2000. *People of the First Crusade*. London: Caxton

Gabrieli, Francesco. 1977. *Muhammad and the Conquest of Islam*. Trans. from Italian by Luling, V. and Linell, R. Hampshire: World University Library

Golubovich, G. 1906. *Biblioteca bio-biblio grafica della Terra Santa e dell'Oriente Franciscano*. Florence: Quarracchi

Hallam, Elizabeth. 1989. *Chronicles of the Crusades: Eyewitness Accounts of the Wars between Christianity and Islam*. London: Guild Publishing

Hamidullah, Muhammad. 1997. *Introduction to Islam*. Cairo: El-Falah for Translation, Publication and Distribution

———. 1987. *Majmu'at al-Watha'iq al-Siyasiyya Lil'ahd al-Nabawi wa al-Khilafa al-Rashida.* Beirut: Dar al-Nafa's

Hamilton, Bernard. 2003. *The Christian World of the Middle Ages.* Stroud, Gloucs: Sutton Publishing

Hillenbrand, Carol. 1999. *The Crusades: Islamic Perspective.* Edinburgh: Edinburgh University Press

Hitti, Phillip. 1957. *Tarikh al-'Arab.* Trans. Naf', M. M. Beirut: n. p.

Hourani, Albert. 2002. *A History of the Arab Peoples.* London: Faber & Faber

Housley, Norman. 2002. *The Crusaders.* Stroud: Tempus Publishing

Jasir, Shafiq, 1989. *Tarikh al-Quds wa al-'alaqa Bayn al-Muslmin wa al-Masihiyyn hatta al-Hurub al-Salibiyya.* Amman: Matabi' al-Iman

Khallaf, 'Abd al-Wahab. 1986. *'Ilm Usul al-Fiqh.* Cairo: Dar al-Qalam

Khuri, Shuhadh and Niqula. 1925. *Khulaset Tarikh Kanisat Urshalim al-Orthuthiksiyya.* Jerusalem: Matba'at Bayt al-Maqdis

Lane-Poole, Stanley. 1985. *Saladin and the Fall of the Kingdom of Jerusalem.* London: Darf Publishers

Lyons, M and Jackson D. 1982. *Saladin, the Politics of the Holy War.* Cambridge, UK: Cambridge University Press

Majed, 'Abd al-Mun'im. 1968. *Zuhur Khilaphat al-Fatimiyyn wa Suqutuhm fi Misr.* Alexandria: n. p.

Malekian, Farhad. 1994. *The Concept of Islamic International Criminal Law: A Comparative Study.* London: Graham & Trotman

Al-Mawdudi, Sayyid abul A'la. 1988. *Towards Understanding the Qur'an.* English version of *Tafhim al-Qur'an.* Trans. and ed Ansari, Z. Leicester: The Islamic Foundation

Morgan, M. R. 1973. *The Chronicle of Ernoul and the Continuations of William of Tyre.* London: Oxford University Press

Al-Mubarakpuri, Safi-ur-Rahman. 1996. *Ar-Raheeq Al-Makhum (The Sealed Nectar) Biography of the Noble Prophet.* Riyadh: Dar-us-Salam Publications

Nu'mani, Shibli. 1957. *'Umar the Great (the second caliph of Islam.* Trans. Saleem, M. Lahore: Muhammad Ashraf Press

Pearsall, J. and Trumble, B. 1996. *The Oxford English Reference Dictionary.* Oxford: Oxford University Press

Peters, Edward. 1998. *The First Crusade: The Chronicle of Fulcher of Charters and Other Source Materials.* Philadelphia, PA: University of Pennsylvania Press

Al-Qaradawi, Yusuf. 1983. *Ghayr al-Muslimin fi al-Mujtama' al-Islami.* Beirut: Mu'assasat al-Risala

——. 1997. *The Lawful and the Prohibited in Islam (al-Halal wal-Haram fil Islam).* Cairo: El-Falah for Translation, Publication and Distribution

Al-Qattan, Manna'. 1986. *Mabahith fi 'Ulum al-Qur'an.* Beirut: Mu'assasat al-Risalah

Al-Qurashi, Ghalib. 1990. *Awlawiyat al-Faruq fi al-Idarah wa al-Qada'.* Sana'a: Maktabat al-Jil al-Jadid

Qutb, Sayyid. 1999. *In The Shade of the Qur'an (Fi Zilal al-Qur'an).* Trans. and ed. Salahi, M. A. and Shamis, A. A. Leicester: The Islamic Foundation

——. 2001. *Fi Zilal al-Qur'an.* Beirut: Dar al-Shuruq

Regan, Geoffrey. 1987. *Saladin and the Fall of Jerusalem.* London: Croom Helm.

Rida, Muhammad. 1983. *Al-Faruq 'Umar Ibn al-Khattab.* Beirut: Dar al-'Ilmiyyah

Runciman, Steven. 1987. *A History of the Crusades: The First Crusade and the Foundation of the Kingdom of Jerusalem.* Cambridge, UK: Cambridge University Press

——. 1952. *A History of the Crusades: The Kingdom of Jerusalem and the Frankish East (1100–1187).* Cambridge, UK: Cambridge University Press

Salam, Salam Shafiʻi. 1982. *Ahl al-Dhimma fi Misr fi al-'Asr al-Fatimi al-Thani Wa al-'Asr al-Ayyubi* (467–648 AH /1074–1250 CE). Egypt: Dar al-Maʻarif

Sarkis, Khalil. 2001.*Tarikh al-Quds al-Maʻruf bi Tarikh Urshalim*. Egypt: Maktabat al-Thaqafa al-Diniyyah

Sell, E. 1901. *Essays on Islam*. Madras: SPCK Press

Shahid, 'Irfan. 1984. *Byzantium and the Arabs in the Fourth Century*. Washington: Dumbarton Oaks

Al-Tel, Othman. 2003. *The First Islamic Conquest of Aelia (Islamic Jerusalem) A Critical Analytical Study of the Early Islamic Historical Narratives and Sources*. Dundee: Al-Maktoum Institute Academic Press

Tibawi, A. L. 1969. *Jerusalem: Its Place in Islam and Arab History*. Beirut: Institute for Palestine Studies

Tritton, A. S. 1930. *The Caliphs and Their Non-Muslim Subjects: A Critical Study of the Covenant of 'Umar*. London: Oxford University Press

Yusuf, Hamad Ahmad 'Abd Allah. 1982. *Bayt al-Maqdis min al-'Ahd al-Rashidi wa Hata al-Dawla al-Ayyubiyya*. Jerusalem: Da'irat al-Awqaf Wa al-Sh'wn al-Islamiyyah

Zaghlul, Abu Hajar Muhammad. n.d. *Mawsu'at Atraf al-Hadith al-Shrif*. Beirut: Dar al-Kutub al-'Ilmiyyah

Zaydan, 'Abd al-Karim. 1982. *Ahkam al-Dhimmiyyn wa al-Musta'minyn fi Dar al-Islam*. Baghdad: Maktabat al-Quds

Al-Zuhaili, Wahba. 2001. *al-Tafsir al-Wasit*. Beirut and Damascus: Dar al-Fikr al-Muʻaser and Dar al-Fikr

Articles

'Ajin, 'Ali. 1996. 'Al-'Uhda al-Umariyyah, (Dirasa Naqdiyya)', *al-Hikma Journal*.

Abu Zahra, Muhammad. 1979. 'International Relations in Islam', *al-Azhar Magazine*

Anees, Munawar Ahmad. 1991. 'The Dialogue of History', in *Christian-Muslim Relations, Yesterday, Today, Tomorrow*, ed. Davies, M. W. London: Grey Seal

Armstrong, Karen. 1997. 'Sacred Space: The Holiness of Islamic Jerusalem', *Journal of Islamic Jerusalem Studies*

Asali, K. J. 1990. 'Jerusalem under the Ottomans (1515–1831 AD)', *Jerusalem in History*, ed. Asali, K. J. New York: Olive Branch Press

Ashur, Sa'id 'Abd al-Fattah. 1968. 'Ba'd Adwa' Jadida 'la al-'laqat Bayn Misr wa al-Habasha fi al-'Usur al-Wsta', *al-Majala al-Misriyya al-Tarikhiyya*.

Al-Buti, Muhammad Sa'id Ramadan. 1999. 'Mu'amalit al-Dawlah al-Islamiyya Lighayr al-Muslimin: al-Quds Namudhajan', *Journal of Islamic Jerusalem Studies*

Cohen, Mark. 1999. 'What was the pact of 'Umar? A Literary-Historical Study', *Jerusalem Studies in Arabic and Islam*

Duri, 'Abd al-'Aziz.1990. 'Jerusalem in the early Islamic period: 7th –11th centuries AD', in *Jerusalem in History*, ed. Asali, K. J. New York: Olive Branch Press

Glubb, Faris. 1999. 'Jerusalem: the central point in Saladin's life', *Journal of Islamic Jerusalem Studies*

Goitein, Shlomo. 1982. 'Jerusalem in the Arab period (638–1099)', *The Jerusalem Cathedra (Studies in the History, Archaeology, Geography, and Ethnography of the land of Israel*, ed. Levine, Lee I. Jerusalem: Yad Itzhak Ben-Zvi Institute

Al-Hamarnah, Salih, 1999. 'Musahamat al-'Arab al-Masihiyyn fi al-Hadarah al-'Arabiyyah al-Islamiyyah, Nazrah 'Ala Bilad al-Sham', *Afaq al-Islam*

Hiyari, Mustafa A. 1990. 'Crusader Jerusalem (1099-1187 AD)', in *Jerusalem in History*, ed. Asali, K. J. New York: Olive Branch Press

Karlson, Anghmar. 1996. 'al-Fath al-Islami Harar al-Yahud min al-Itihad al-Masihi fi Ispanya', *Al-Quds al-'Arabi newspaper*

Al-Kilani, Ibrahim Zaid. 1999. 'Markaziyt Al-Quds wa Makanatuha fi Al-Islam', *Journal of Islamic Jerusalem Studies*

Magdalino, Paul. 2002. 'The Medieval Empire (780–1204)', in *The Oxford History of Byzantine*, ed. Mango, C. Oxford: Oxford University Press

Mawlawi, Faisal. 2000. 'al-Mafahim al-Asasiyya lil Da'wah al-Islamiyyah fi Bilad al-Gharb', in *Risalit al -Muslimin fi bilad al-Gharb*, ed. Abu Shamalah, M. 'A, Irbid, Jordan: Dar al-Amal

Al-Qaradawi, Yusuf. 2000. 'al-Infitah 'Ala al-Gharb, Muqtadayatuhu wa Shrutuhu', in *Risalit al-Muslimin fi bilad al-Gharb*, ed. Abu Shamalah, M.'A. Irbid, Jordan: Dar al-Amal

Al-Quda, Zakariyya. 1987. 'Mu'ahadit fath Bayt al-Maqdis: al-'Uhda al-'Umariyyah', in *Bilad al-Sham fi Sadr al-Islam*, ed. Muhammad al-Bakhit and Ihsan 'Abbas. Amman: University of Jordan and University of Yarmuk

Sa'id, Hammam. 1982. 'Al-Wad' al-Qanwni li Ahl al-Dhimma', *Jordan University Journal*

Sahas, Daniel. 1994. 'Patriarch Sophronious, 'Umar Ibn al-Khattab and the Conquest of Jerusalem', in *Al-Sira' al-Islami al-Faranji 'ala Filastin fi al-Qurun al-Wasta'* (The Frankish (Ifranji) conflict over Palestine during the Middle Ages, ed. Dajani-Shkeel, H. and Dajani, B. Beirut: Institute for Palestine Studies

Al-Sawa, 'Ali. 1994. 'Mawqif al-Islam min Ghayr al-Muslimin fi al-Mujtama' al-Islami' in *al-Mujaz fi Mu'amalit Ghayr al-Muslimin fi al-Islam*, ed. al-'Amad, I.S. Amman: al-Majma' al-Malaki li Buhuth al-Hadarah al-Islamiyyh

Shams al-Din, Muhammad Mahdi. 2001. 'al-Masihiyyah fi al-Mafhum al-Thqafi al-Islami al-Mu'aser', *al-Nashrah*, al-Ma'had al-Malaki lil-Dirasat al-Dinyah (Jordan)

Tamimi, Azzam. 1999. 'Jerusalem under the Muslim Rule', *Al-Quds: Journal Concerned with the Issues on Jerusalem*

Electronic Publications

Anna Comnena: *The Alexiad*, Book X: Second Battle with Heresy: The Cruman War: First Crusade (1094–1097), p. 9. http://www.fordham.edu/halsall/basis/annacomnena-alexiad10.html,

Hamami, Jamil, 'Islamic-Christian Relations in Palestine in a Civil Society: 'An Islamic Point of View'. 1 March 2000. http://www.albushra.org/latpatra/hamami.htm,

Keyser, Jason, 'Muslims have kept watch over the doors of Christianity's holiest shrine for centuries', *Jordan Times*, 14 August 2002.

http://www.icnacanada.org/modules.php?op=modload&name=News&file=article&sid=25.

Safi, Louay, 'Human Rights and Islamic Legal Reform'. http://home/att.net/louaysafi/articles/1999/human31/htmL

Şiddiqi, Muzammil H, Spirit of Tolerance in Islam. http://www.messageonline.org/2002aprilmay/cover5.htm

GLOSSARY

'Afu	Pardon
Abu/Abi	Father of
Ahl al-kitab	Jews and Christians
Al-'adl	Justice
Al-ansar	The helpers; Muslim supporters from Madinah
Al-muhajirun	Muslim migrants from Makkah to Madinah
Al-tadafu'	Counterbalance
Aman	Safety
Bay'ah	Pledge of allegiance
Bayt al-mal	The treasury in a Muslim state
Banu	Children of
Caliph	The head of a Muslim state
Caliphate	A Muslim state

Dhimmi	A non-Muslim with citizenship status who lives under the protection of the Muslim state
Din	Religion
Dinar	An ancient gold coin
Faqih	An expert in Muslim jurisprudence (*fiqh* = law)
Fatwa	Legal opinion or edict concerning Muslim law
Fiqh	Muslim jurisprudence, the understanding and application of *shari'ah*. It has two sections: *'ibadat*, worship, where only what is prescribed is permitted; and *mu'amalat*, social affairs, where everything is permitted except what is explicitly prohibited
Hadith	The sayings, deeds and traditions of the Prophet Muhammad
Harbi	A non-Muslim who has no *dhimmi* pact or political treaty with Muslims
Hijrah	The migration of the Prophet and other Muslims to Madinah
Hilm	Forbearance
Hukm	A judgement or legal decision
Ibn	Son of
Imam	The person who leads others in prayer, or is the leader of a Muslim state. Also a title for a famous scholar

Jihad	Striving, personal effort in the advancement of a sacred cause; struggle against the forces of evil; a military campaign
Kitab	Book
Safh	Forgiveness
Sahih	Authentic, with reference to Hadith
Sunnah	The legal rules, orders, acts of worship and statements of Prophet Muhammad that have become models for Muslims to follow.
Tafsir	Interpretation of verses of the Qur'an
Ummah	The community of Muslims throughout the world. It is based not on language, race or colour, but includes all who believe in God and his Messenger.
Wazir	Minister of the state
Zakah	Charity, purification; commonly used in reference to the obligatory tax of about 2.5 per cent that affluent Muslims must pay to help the poor.

INDEX

A

'Abdelati, Hammudah 14
al-'Adid 133, 138, 177
al-'Affani, S 98
'Ahd 'Umar 62
'Ajin, 'Ali 63, 68–71, 93
'Amilah tribe 82
al-'Arif, 'Arif 102, 111–12, 116, 127
'Asqalan 145–6, 148, 167, 169
'Athaminah, Khalil 82, 97, 114–15
al-'Uhda al-'Umariyyah 81, 88
'Umar's Assurance 4, 6, 81, 88–9, 91–3, 95, 99, 101, 104, 109, 113–14, 116, 126, 159, 179
Abbasid 29, 77, 97, 133
Abraham and Haddad 5, 31
Abu al-Fida' 89, 144, 149, 169
Abu Bakr 19, 30, 47, 51, 56, 59, 66–7, 84, 168-9, 178
Abu Yusuf 27, 29, 33, 46, 57, 78
Abu 'Ubayd, al-Qasim 26, 57, 70, 78, 112–13
Abu 'Ubaydah 70, 75, 85–6, 89–90, 99, 106
Abu Hanifah 26
Abu Shama 132, 139, 144, 147, 149, 152, 156
Abu Zahra, Muhammad 14, 21
Abyssinia 37–8, 44–5, 159
Adhruh 46
Aelia Capitolina 2
Aleppo 75, 132, 134
Analogy (*qiyas*) 8
Antioch 82, 105, 120
al-Aqsa mosque 83, 130, 141, 145, 150, 156
Arab peninsula 57, 61, 81

al-Armani, Abu Salih 136
Armenians 82, 100, 102, 115, 138, 152
Arnold, T.W. 157–8
Arsuf 163
Asali, Kamil 103
Ascent (*mi'raj*) 88, 117, 151
al-Asfahani, 'Imad al-Din 140–1, 144–5, 148, 151–2, 155, 157
El-Awaisi, Abd al-Fattah 2–3, 43, 84, 88, 93–8, 102, 104, 107, 109
El-Awaisi, Khalid 6
Ayla 46–7
Ayyubid 135
al-Azdi, Muhammad 75, 106, 112

B

al-Baghdadi, al-Khatib 68
Bahrain 44–5
al-Baladhuri, Abu al-'Abbas 46, 57, 75, 89–90, 99, 108–9
Baldwin I 158
Balian of Ibelin 144, 147–51, 158
Banu 'Adi 56
Banu Taghlib 4, 27, 55, 57–62, 80, 178
Barbarossa, Frederick 159–60

Batit, Yusuf 158
Bay'ah 25
Bayt al-mal 60, 79
Bayt al-Maqdis 1, 3, 83–4, 91
Bayt Nuba 165–6
Bethlehem 100, 171
al-Bimaristan al-salahi 156
al-Birr 18–19, 22, 176
al-Bukhari, Muhammad 19
al-Buti, Muhammad 25, 27–9, 31, 42
Butler, Alfred 106–7
Byzantine 1, 11–12, 44, 56–8, 82, 84–5, 87, 92–3, 96–9, 104–9, 114–16, 120, 123–4, 152, 157, 178, 180

C

Caesar 44
Caetani, Leone 61, 63, 71, 106
Caliphate 56, 77, 102–3, 107, 133, 135, 138–9, 177
Chalcedonian 82, 106, 114
Chosroes 44
Church of Rome 158, 180
Citizenship 25, 31, 53
Clermont 120–1
Cohen, Mark 63
Comnena, Alexius 124
Comnena, Anna 124
Consensus (*ijma'*) 8, 35, 99

Constitution of Madinah
37, 39, 42, 176
Copts 49, 79, 100, 102–3,
136–7, 139, 159
Counterbalance 43
Crusades 119–21, 124–6,
156, 158, 180

D
Dayr al-Sultan 159
Damascus 15, 44, 70, 132–
3, 140–1, 143–4, 146, 171
Damascus Gate 146
Dar al-Islam 33, 76
Deus lo volt 123
al-Dhahabi, Muhammad 68
Dhimma 6, 8, 25–6, 31–3,
35, 48, 65, 71, 77, 176–7
Dhimmi, Dhimmis 4–5, 25,
27–9, 31, 33–7, 48, 51–3,
60, 62, 75, 77–9, 89, 96,
100, 107, 109, 135–9, 142,
157, 176–8
Dinar 27, 73, 136, 151–2,
154, 161
Dirham 26–7, 101, 131
Dome of the Rock 130,
150, 152, 156

E
Eastern Orthodox 1, 156-7
Egypt 44–5, 49, 56, 77, 79,
119, 121, 126, 133–40,
142, 145, 151, 171, 178

Ernoul 147–8
Eutychius (Ibn al-Batiiq)
89, 91, 110

F
Fada'il al-Quds 95
Fahl 106
al-Fahmi, Khalid Ibn Thabit
90, 112
al-Farra', Abi Ya'la 32, 36
Fatamids 133, 138–9
Fatwas 7–8
Fiqh 4, 49, 71, 133, 156
First Crusade 119–20, 153
Frankish 124, 148, 161–2,
170
Franks 100, 102, 129–31,
161, 163, 166, 168
Freedom of belief 13–14,
109
Fulan 93, 98
Fulcher of Chartres 129

G
Gabrieli, Francesco, 85
Goitein, S. D. 101, 113–14
Golubovich, G. 103
Greek Orthodox 99, 102–
5, 110, 156–8, 179
Gregory 103
Guy of Lusignon 143–5,
148, 152

H

Hadith 49–50, 65, 68, 71
al-Hakim 126
Hammam Sa'id 63
Hamami 109
al-Hamarnah, Salih 108
Hamidullah 42, 76
Hamilton 114, 127
Hanafi 5, 26, 28, 35
Hanbali 5, 26, 28, 32, 36
al-Hanbali, Mujir al-Din 89, 91, 116
Hashemite 104
Hattin 143
Helpers (*al-ansar*) 39
Henry IV 125
Heraclius 44–5, 82, 107, 149, 152
Hillenbrand, Carol 137, 154
Hims (Homs) 75
al-Himyari, Muhammad 89, 95
al-Hindi, 'Ala' al-Din 63
Hindus 11
al-Hira 30
Hitti, Phillip 106
Holy Land 121, 123–5, 160
Holy Sepulchre 100–1, 103–4, 109–11, 114, 117, 124, 127, 129, 152, 155–6, 159, 167, 171, 179–80
Hospitallers 143, 153, 165
Hourani, Albert 108
Housley, Norman 120
Human Brotherhood 5, 8, 12–13, 52

I

Ibn 'Abd al-Hakam 49
Ibn 'Abdin 35
Ibn 'Abdul 'Aziz, 'Umar 70, 77
Ibn 'Asakir, 'Ali Ibn al-Hasan 63, 65–70
Ibn 'Uqbah, al-Walid 57–8
Ibn al-A'them 75, 112
Ibn Abi Talib, 'Ali 62, 91–2
Ibn Adam, Yahya 57–8, 61
Ibn al-'Arabi, Abu Bakr 17, 28
Ibn al-'As, 'Amr 79, 85, 91, 93, 98–9
Ibn al-'Ibri, Grigurius 106, 130, 149
Ibn al-Athir 75, 89–90, 120, 130, 146–7, 149, 152, 154
Ibn al-Jawzi 89, 91, 95, 130
Ibn al-Muqaffa', Sawirus 135, 137
Ibn al-Murajja 84, 113, 116
Ibn al-Nu'man, 'Ubada 58
Ibn al-Qalanisi 131
Ibn al-Qayyim 26, 29, 63, 68–9, 71, 77
Ibn al-Walid, Khalid 30, 84, 86, 93

Ibn Buraid, Sulaiman 50
Ibn Ghanam, 'Abd al-Rahman 63, 67, 69–70
Ibn Hazm 29, 35, 63
Ibn Hudayr, Ziyad 61
Ibn Jubayr 138
Ibn Juzay 34
Ibn Kathir 14, 17, 21–3, 26, 63, 71, 76, 132
Ibn Khalikan 132
Ibn Nusaibah, 'Abd Allah 112
Ibn Qudama 36, 63
Ibn Qunbur, Marcus 136–7
Ibn Sa'd 59–60
Ibn Sawa, Mundhir 44
Ibn Shaddad 140–1, 144–7, 149, 151–2, 160–2, 166–8, 171–2
Ibn Shammer, Harith 44
Ibn Taymiyyah 35, 63, 70–1
Ibn Zayd, Osama 84
Immigrants (*al-muhajirun*) 39
Islamicjerusalem 2–3, 6
Islamization 117
Isnad 65, 76, 93
Israeli 2, 101

J

Jabiyah (the Golan Heights) 85, 90
Jacobites 100, 102, 115–16, 157
Jaffa (Yafa) 2, 146, 163
Jaifer 44
Jarash 46
al-Jarbah 46
Jasir, Shafiq 101, 105, 113, 115
al-Jazira 69
Jenin 2
Jericho 2
Jews 1, 9–10, 13, 20, 22–3, 25, 35, 39–44, 78–9, 88, 92, 94–7, 104, 107, 120, 126–7, 131, 139, 173, 175–6, 179, 181
Jihad 5, 8, 49–51, 60, 133, 177
Jizyah 4–5, 8, 25–30, 32–3, 36, 46–8, 50, 52–3, 57–8, 60, 62, 69, 72–5, 79, 85, 89–90, 92, 97–8, 100, 102–5, 107, 109, 112, 115, 138, 157, 177–9
John the Baptist Church 136
John V 114
Jordan 2, 47, 56, 81, 104, 106, 163
Judaism 7, 9
Judham 82
Justice (*'adl*) 16–8, 20–1, 34, 38, 41–4, 46, 52, 56–7, 79, 130, 137, 171, 175–6,

K

Karak 2
Karlson, Anghmar 108, 115
al-Khallal, Abu Bakr 63
al-Khanqah al-salahiyya 156
al-Kharaj (land tax) 58, 90
Khusraw, Nasir-i- 126
al-Kilani, Ibrahim 111

L

Lakhm 82
Lane-Poole, Stanley 134, 146–7, 152, 162, 171
Latin 1, 103, 105, 123, 127, 139, 143, 157–9, 170–1, 180
Latin kingdom of Jerusalem 139, 143, 158–159
Le Strange, Guy 127
Lebanon 56, 81
Levites 120, 122
Loyalty (*al-Muwalah*) 21

M

Madinah 8, 13, 20, 26, 34, 37, 39, 41–4, 57, 83–4, 86, 88, 90, 92, 117, 135, 176–7
al-Madrasa al-salahiyya 156
Magdalino, Paul 123
Magians (*Majus*) 10
Makkah 8, 11, 39, 56, 73, 74, 83, 88, 151, 171
Malekian, Farhad 15
Malikanis 115
al-Maqdisi, Muhammad 126
Maqna 46
Maronites 100, 102
al-Marwadi, Abu al-Hasan 32, 33, 35
Massacres 87, 121, 127, 129–30, 142, 149–50, 156, 162
Mawlawi, Faisal 18
Michael of Syria 95
Minbar (carved pulpit) 56
Monophysites 82, 106, 108, 114–15
Mu'ta 84, 105
al-Mubarakpuri, Safi-ur-Rahman 41
al-Mukhallisi, Yusuf al-Shammas 115
Muslim state 1, 7–9, 12, 20, 22, 25–7, 29, 31–5, 37, 39, 42–4, 48, 53, 56, 62–3, 76, 84–6, 96, 109, 114, 125, 135, 176–7
al-Mutawakkil, Ja'far 70, 77, 126

N

Nablus 148, 152
Najm al-Din Ayyub 131–2
Najran 46
al-Nawawi, Abu Zakariya 29

Negus 38, 44–45
Nestorians 100, 102, 106
Night Journey (*isra'*) 88, 117, 151, 164
Nu'mani Shibli 61
Nur al-Din 133–4, 140–1, 156, 178

O

Obligations (*wajibat*) 35
Oman 44, 46
Orientalist 2, 57, 61, 63, 77
Orthodox patriarchate of Jerusalem 89, 99
Ottoman 102–3

P

Pact of 'Umar 4, 55, 62–3, 68, 70–1, 75–7, 79–80, 93, 116, 139, 178
Pagans 11, 129–30
Palestine 2, 56, 77, 81–2, 90–1, 98, 145, 158
People of the Book 9–11, 13, 23, 25–6, 32–3, 37–8, 43–6, 48–9, 71, 79, 97, 117, 175
Persia 11, 44–5, 56
Persian empire 11
Peter, the Hermit 121
Philip II 159
Pierucci, Armando 111
Pope Gregory VII 125
Pope Honorius I 82
Pope Urban II 119, 121, 123, 142
Prophet Muhammad 8–9, 18, 26, 33, 37–9, 42, 46–9, 56, 60, 80, 83–4, 88, 117, 151, 178

Q

al-Qaradawi, Yusuf 10, 22, 35
al-Qarafi, Abu al-'Abbas 19, 35
Qiblah 88
al-Quda, Zakariyya 63, 95, 98, 104
al-Quds al-Sharif 100, 102
al-Qurtubi, Abu 'Abdullah 17, 20, 23
Qutb, Sayyid 14, 17–8

R

al-Ramla 160, 166, 169, 171, 179
al-Rashid, Harun 29, 33, 70, 77
Rawadiyya Kurds 131
Raymond D'Aguilers 130
al-Razi, Fakhr al-Din 17, 23, 28
Regan, Geoffrey 150, 153, 157–8
Reynald of Chatillon 144–5
Ribat 156

Richard I ('the Lion-heart') 143, 159–71, 181
Rights (*huquq*) 33
Roman Catholic 103–4, 114, 125, 157, 170
Roman empire 11, 96
Rome 11, 44, 82, 126, 158, 180
Retaliation (*qisas*) 46, 79
al-Ruha (Urfa) 120, 152
Runciman, Steven 82, 105–7, 111, 123, 144, 147–9, 153, 157–8

S
al-Sa'ati, Ra'if Mikha'il 125
Sabians 10
Sadaqa 27–8, 59–60, 79, 178
Safi, L. 77
Sahas Daniel 88, 101, 106, 110
Sahih 25
Sarkis, Khalil 96
Seljuks 123
al-Shafi'i, Muhammad Ibn Idris 26–7, 29, 62, 71, 75
Shahid, Irfan 81
al-Sham 47, 51, 56, 63, 69–70, 75, 81–6, 89–90, 94–7, 103, 105–6, 108–9, 115, 119, 120, 133–5, 139, 141

Shams al-Din, Muhammad 108
Shari'ah 8, 31, 61, 77
Shirkuh, Asad al-Din 131–3, 138–9
al-Shurut al 'Umariyyah 55
Siddiqi, A. 25
Simeon 121
Sophronious 81, 85, 88, 95, 100, 110–11, 113, 126, 180
St Helena 115
Subdued (*saghirun*) 26, 28–9, 69, 71
Sultan Murad IV 103
Sunnah 5, 7–8, 37, 63, 71, 176–7
Sur (Tyre) 145
Syria 35, 47, 56, 70, 77, 81, 89, 95, 141, 151, 170

T
al-Tabari, Abu Ja'far 16–7, 22, 28, 57–8, 60–1, 75, 89, 91–5, 97–9, 104, 112, 179
Tabuk 84
Takrit 131–2
Tamimi, Azzam 107
Taqwa 13
al-Tartushi, Abu Bakr 63
Templars 148, 153, 165
Theophanes 87

Third Crusade 159–60, 171, 181
Tritton, A. 32, 63, 69, 71, 75
Tuqsitu 17
al-Tusi, Shihab al-Din 136

U
Ummah (nation) 71

W
Walter, Hubert 170
al-Waqidi, Abu 'Abd Allah 75, 89, 112
Wazir 133, 135–6, 138, 140
William of Tyre 121, 125, 127

Y
al-Ya'qubi, Ahmad 75, 89, 91, 112
Yamamah 44
Yemen 46–7, 81, 134

Z
Zakah 27, 33, 177
al-Zamakhshari, Abu al-Qasim 17, 20, 22–3, 28
Zanki, 'Imad al-Din 132–3
Ziyadah, Niqula 115
Zoar 2
Zoroastrians 11, 25, 107
al-Zuhaili, Wahba 14
Zunar 64, 69

www.ingramcontent.com/pod-product-compliance
Lightning Source LLC
Chambersburg PA
CBHW061439300426
44114CB00014B/1752